FOOD ADDICTS
in Recovery Anonymous

FOOD ADDICTS
in Recovery Anonymous

Food Addicts in Recovery Anonymous, Inc.
Woburn, Massachusetts
www.foodaddicts.org

FOOD ADDICTS IN RECOVERY ANONYMOUS

Published by Food Addicts in Recovery Anonymous, Inc.
400 West Cummings Park, Suite 1700
Woburn, MA 01801
www.foodaddicts.org

The stories related in this work have been provided by members of Food Addicts in Recovery Anonymous (FA), who have each represented that his or her story is accurate and based on personal experience. The FA members have further represented that they have properly assigned the copyright for their stories to FA, which has not attempted to verify accuracy of the stories.

This is FA World Service Conference–approved literature.

Revisions to the fifth printing reflect the decision of the 2017 FA World Service Conference to capitalize the words God, Higher Power, and any other words referring to God or Higher Power.

Library of Congress Control Number 2013934614

ISBN 978-1-932021-80-6

Printed in the United States of America

First Edition, Fifth Printing 2017

10 9 8 7 6 5

FOOD ADDICTS
in recovery anonymous

Contents

✧ ✧ ✧

Despite All Circumstances

They Finally Had to Admit Defeat

Through Life's Transitions

The Twelve Steps

Appendices

Preface

✧ ✧ ✧

THIS BOOK DESCRIBES the illness of food addiction and the possibility of recovery offered by Food Addicts in Recovery Anonymous (FA), a program based on the Twelve Steps pioneered by Alcoholics Anonymous. We've written it both for people who are struggling and for those who have already found recovery in FA.

We hope our book will also be useful to anyone who is worried about the weight or eating habits of a family member or friend, and that it will attract the attention of professionals who work with those suffering from food addiction: doctors and nurses, psychotherapists, social workers, physical therapists, dentists, and businesspeople.

The book is divided into three sections. The first section, chapters 1–6, is an introduction to FA for those who wonder if they might be food addicts, as well as those who've never thought of addiction in relationship to eating. The second section contains the stories of thirty FA members—personal accounts that will help read-ers better understand food addiction and FA recovery. The final section, chapters 7–12, offers a brief discussion of the Twelve Steps, the means by which we obtain and sustain freedom from addiction.

The opinions expressed in the personal stories are solely those of each storyteller. FA has no position or opinion on medical, religious, or any other non-FA matters, including the use or discontinuance of prescription medications. We urge our members to consult their physicians regarding all medical questions and, when they are guiding newer members in FA, to suggest that they do the same.

Like all addictions, food addiction affects every aspect of a sufferer's life. We wish to be of help in any way we can. Please do not hesitate to contact us. For details and more information about FA, see our website: www. foodaddicts.ORG. (Please note that www.foodaddicts.COM is the website of an organization separate from and unrelated to FA.)

An Introduction to FA

✧ ✧ ✧

Chapter 1

Perhaps You're a Food Addict?

You wonder. *What's a food addict?! How can anyone be addicted to food? We all have to eat.* Perhaps the term sounds extreme. *No,* you think, *even if I lose control sometimes, I'm no addict.* Yet there's something to the two words *food* and *addict* that has made you pause.

We wrote this book for you.

You may be like us. You've battled with your weight. You've tried diets from books, magazines, nutritionists, and neighbors. Grapefruit diets. Cleansing diets. All-you-can-eat low-carbohydrate diets. You've spent hundreds of dollars on commercial weight loss programs. Perhaps you've found recovery in other twelve-step programs, yet you are still unable to control your eating. You dread weddings and other social occasions because you're ashamed of how you look and are afraid you won't be able to find anything to wear. You may have already developed diabetes, or your doctor might have told you that you're a candidate for a heart attack or stroke. You can't button your suit jacket and have to buy your clothes through specialty stores. You've quit all the sports you love because it's hard to bend over or run.

Maybe you've been more successful at the weight loss game. You look normal, or even thin. You've won this at a high cost. Perhaps your obsession with food and weight tortures you. Your mind no longer feels like it's your own. You might have lost and gained the same 10 or 20 pounds repeatedly for years. Always on a diet or trying to start one, you constantly feel deprived. Or perhaps, according to your family, friends, and even your doctor, you are alarmingly thin. You eat everything you crave, but then you make yourself run fifteen miles or find a bathroom where you can throw up.

There is an answer. We've found a way to be free from food obsession and cravings and yet achieve a healthy, slender, stable weight. Who are we? We are people who have tried all the approaches we've described and more—hypnosis, therapy, acupuncture, medications, laxatives, amphetamines, positive thought, fasting, prayer, exercise programs, and regular meetings with nutritionists, doctors, healers, and personal trainers. A few of us have had gastric bypass or lap-band surgery, as well. Nothing worked long term. Our misery became unbearable.

One of our members—we'll call her Mary—describes this experience well:

> I used to sit down every night with a one-pound bag of pretzels. Each time, I would say to myself, *I'm just going to have a few.* Then I'd think, *Just two more. Just one more. Just a little more.* After I'd finished them all, I'd look at the empty bag and wonder, *Where did all the pretzels go?*

I also bought baguettes at the supermarket—the long, thin French breads. They came in three-loaf packages. I figured I'd buy extra for the kids, who'd be bringing their friends home. Of course, my children never got the baguettes, because I ate them all. After a while, I started buying two packages of baguettes—six loaves of bread.

Despite all I knew, I couldn't stop eating. I'm trained as a nurse, and I understood metabolic rates and heart disease. I stood up in front of students as an instructor in a university's nursing school and taught nutrition classes, yet, at five feet, three inches tall, I ended up weighing 218 pounds.

I wanted to go to a doctor, but what could I say? "I'm dying. I can't stop eating." I knew the doctor would just tell me to stop. That was the solution, of course, but I couldn't do it. The more I ate, the more I craved and my failure created a terrible loneliness. I was in a prison of my own making, and I didn't know how to get out.

Whether you are too fat, too thin, or of normal weight, you may identify with Mary's description of her experiences with food. Clearly, this is not the story of a woman who simply had a weight problem. Her misery was too extreme. A successful adult and medical professional, she lost the battle with herself. She was driven to eat what she knew she shouldn't eat. Even more demoralizing, her troubles with food got worse instead of better. She didn't begin her life at 218 pounds. She watched herself gain that weight, pound by pound, during all the years she struggled against it. She was defeated.

We in FA are just like Mary, whether we wanted to admit it initially or not. When we were honest with ourselves, we had to allow that our reactions to food or weight were not normal. We ate foods we swore we would not eat. We hid our eating. We lied. We stole food. We starved ourselves. We ate to celebrate. We ate to escape. We ate for no reason we could discern. Sometimes, though thin as a bone, we thought we were fat. Whatever our size, we found that one mouthful of food beyond the restrictions of our diet inevitably led us to a binge.

Isn't this kind of irrationality and dependency a hallmark of addiction? We believe so, and more and more doctors and researchers are beginning to agree. Dr. Carl Lowe, Jr., is a bariatric surgeon practicing in Charlotte, North Carolina. A fellow of the American College of Surgeons, he offers some observations we think are helpful. Whether we were physically huge, slightly overweight, or too thin, we have struggled with the same lack of control that Dr. Lowe sees in his patients. He writes,

> I've been doing bariatric surgery since 2004, so I've had eight years of meeting with hundreds and hundreds of people who have struggled with their weight. In my view, undeniably, food addiction is real. I see it every day.
>
> Food addiction is not simply a physical problem. My patients know that they should not eat the foods they eat. They know their eating is taking them down a destructive road of weight gain and the medical problems associated with it—diabetes, high blood pressure, high cholesterol—but they can't help themselves. They

have to eat as powerfully as other people have to have a cigarette.

You might be thinking my patients don't know any better, that education is the solution, but ignorance is not the problem. Most of the people I see are more educated than I am about nutrition and dieting and low-calorie foods. Our nutritionist talks with them. We tell them what we want them to eat. We give them lists of the healthy foods, but they still can't stop themselves from eating high-carbohydrate, high-fat, or calorically dense foods—flour and sugar foods, as FA would put it. People in FA are familiar with this experience.

My patients come to me because they want a solution, and they haven't ever been able to find one. They've tried exercise. They've tried commercial weight loss programs. They've had personal trainers and tried every diet known to man—diets from books, green tea diets, cabbage soup diets.

Unfortunately, looking at the scientific data, we see that there's no easy solution when people can't control how much and what they eat. The medical literature tells us that if someone weighs 100 or 150 pounds too much, that person has just a 1–2 percent chance of losing that weight and keeping it off over a sustained period of time.

In a gold standard study done in Sweden, researchers tracked about sixteen hundred people who were classified as morbidly obese.[1] One group of about

1. Lars Sjöström et al., "Lifestyle, Diabetes, and Cardiovascular Risk Factors 10 Years after Bariatric Surgery," *New England Journal of Medicine* 351 (December 2004): 2683–93.

eight hundred people were to lose weight under a doctor's supervision, with a nutrition program, any medications that seemed helpful at the time, and advice regarding exercise and calories. After ten years, they were heavier than when they started. None of them had access to anything like FA during that time.

A second group of eight hundred had bariatric surgery. That group did much better, but the Swedish study and others indicate that surgery can be only one small part of a solution. It can potentially help people with medically diagnosed morbid obesity get down to obesity and then to a place where they're merely overweight, but it's highly unusual for anyone to reach what is medically considered a healthy body weight after bariatric surgery. Typically, a year and a half after the operation, people reach their lowest weight— about 50 percent of what they need to lose—and then, over the next ten years, they slowly regain some of what they've lost, until they reach a plateau.

I tell my patients all the time that they have to change their perception of food and how they relate to it or they will regain their weight. "We can plan surgery for your stomach so that you can't eat large volumes of food," I say, "but I can't do anything to make you wisely select the kinds of food you put into your stomach."

Dr. Lowe's account matches our own experiences. Not all of us were morbidly obese, but like his patients, we needed more than just a medical or nutritional solution. If we were normal, we food addicts could and would have listened to the sound advice we heard for years. Self-control and rational good sense would have saved us, and we would have avoided the foods we knew we shouldn't eat.

Instead, as is typical of addicts, we've experienced a disconcerting problem with our minds. In a masterful description of alcoholic drinking that applies just as accurately to our eating, *Alcoholics Anonymous* alludes to a "strange mental blank spot"—a complete failure of rational thought. How many times did Mary tell herself that she could have just a few pretzels? Despite a 100 percent record of failure and the resulting terrible consequences, she repeatedly forgot and tried eating them again. Just like an alcoholic taking a first drink, she was unable to remember who she was: a person who could never stop at just one mouthful.

As food addicts, we also now know that there is another level to our illness. True, we have sometimes forgotten who we are. Other times, though, we remembered and didn't care. We've been unable to harness an inner will to take care of ourselves. People who merely have a problem with food can ultimately change course when necessary. Food addicts cannot. We are unable or unwilling to value ourselves and to protect our own health and lives.

Chapter 2

About FA

You may still resist the notion of food addiction. Perhaps you think that a person addicted to food would have to stop eating in order to refrain from addiction. We agree that that's impossible. Yet, though we are as bound to food as alcoholics are bound to alcohol, there is a solution for us.

By trial and error, we in FA have discovered that we can't safely eat foods containing flour or sugar. We have also realized that without help, we are unable to sanely control the quantities of the foods we eat. Our bodies and minds are different from those of other people. When we have just one mouthful of the wrong foods or attempt to live without clear boundaries regarding food quantities, we lose our freedom. Either we can't stop ourselves from eating more or we're possessed by an unremitting obsession with food and weight.

The obvious solution is to refrain from the behaviors and choices that make us lose control. Alcoholics can stop drinking. Drug addicts can stop using drugs. People with our problem can abstain from eating flour, sugar, and unlimited quantities of food. We can plan our meals ahead of time, using measurements to limit the amounts we eat.

We see the beginnings of a solution in this way of thinking, which is the basis of abstinence in FA—the equivalent of sobriety in AA. FA defines abstinence as simple, weighed and measured meals, with nothing eaten between mealtimes. In abstinence, we avoid foods made with or dusted in sugar or flour of any kind. We exclude sweeteners like maple syrup, honey, and corn syrup, which affect us as powerfully as sugar. Alcohol is also not included in our food plans because of its high sugar content and the danger it poses to anyone who is already an addict.

Abstinence probably looks as impossible to you as it did to us. We were horrified by the suggestion that we give up desserts, pastas, and breads, yet when we joined FA, we discovered that the FA program made abstinence comfortably possible. FA provides all that we need to obtain and sustain our recovery without struggling with obsession or food cravings. It offers a total solution to a problem that is physical, mental, and spiritual.

Dr. Lowe, the surgeon quoted previously, has seen how well FA works for his patients who wholeheartedly try it.[2] We think you will find his description of our program useful:

---

2. Dr. Lowe has no financial or professional affiliation with FA.

I was first exposed to FA about three or four years ago. I met some members and took a few brochures from them, but I didn't know much about the organization. I remembered it a few years later, after a conversation I had with one of my patients. She'd successfully kept her weight off, didn't snack, didn't eat a lot of carbohydrates, exercised, and ate small portions. "What is the secret, so I can tell other people?" I asked. "You know, Dr. Lowe," she said, "you operated on my stomach, but until something clicked in my heart and mind, nothing was going to change."

I knew she was right. Hearing her, and looking for more ways to help my patients alter their thinking about food and their relationship to it, I called one of the members of FA and asked if I could sit in on a meeting. She was very welcoming, and when I went, I was stunned by what I heard. I stayed for a good while after the meeting ended, because I couldn't pull myself away. I saw the changes FA was making in people's lives, and I thought, *This is exactly what my patients need.*

Most bariatric surgeons hold support groups at least monthly, but a meeting once a month or even once a week is not enough to help a person deal with the day-to-day yearnings and cravings to eat certain foods. I loved FA. Each of the members had a sponsor, someone he or she could talk with daily. The people there were the warmest you could ever meet, and the results were amazing. I saw people who had lost 60 pounds and 100 pounds. I even met a woman who had lost 200 pounds.

FA seemed to me to be a perfect solution. It offered wonderful support, frequent meetings, and a human being who could talk with a struggling person every single day until he or she got strong. We in the medical community can't give enough of the intense interaction that's needed by a person trying to overcome addiction. You can't put a child on a bike and expect him or her to ride right away. Addicts need someone to talk with several times a day.

The clincher for me is the spiritual nature of the program. We are all humans. We all have frailties. We don't have the strength and the power to do many of the things in life that we think we can do. When you are in a situation of addiction and you start believing that you can pull yourself up by your bootstraps and solve the problem yourself, you are destined for failure. Clearly, the addiction has the upper hand. That's what makes it an addiction—it's something that you cannot control.

In addiction, you are facing a spiritual battle, a psychological and physical battle. You have to have a partner right with you. You cannot do it by yourself. You need other people and you need a Higher Power. Until and unless you acknowledge that fact and allow a Higher Power to come into your life, you are doomed. Twelve-step programs like Food Addicts in Recovery Anonymous and Alcoholics Anonymous, which are based on spiritual recovery, have long track records of success. Why fight what works so well?

Regardless of their situations, I refer all of my patients to FA. I sit down with them and have a conversation.

This takes time. A lot of doctors don't have that time, and they are not comfortable bringing up spirituality with their patients. They don't want to talk about a Higher Power. It's easier to tell someone, "Cut your calories to under 1,500 and exercise five times a week," but time in conversation is time well spent. If I just handed my patients an FA brochure and said, "Try this out," none of them would go to a meeting. People need to understand FA and how it can help them.

When I meet someone for the first time, I start with questions about their eating. I ask, "Do you ever eat out of stress? Do you eat when you are nervous? Do you eat when you are happy? Do you eat to celebrate or reward yourself? If you've had a good day or have done something especially well, do you tell yourself, 'Hey! I deserve a treat.' Do you sneak food? Do you ever feel like you want to eat something and know you shouldn't, but you eat it anyway because you just can't help yourself?" I use the twenty questions that are in the FA brochures.

I don't bring up the term *food addict*. Usually, as the patients answer my questions, they realize they have a problem and convict themselves. Then it's easier for me to introduce them to Food Addicts in Recovery Anonymous. I tell them, "There's a great program, and it's free." Patients' ears perk up when I say "free," because they're so used to having to pay money to lose weight. Everywhere they've been, they've had to pay money—to get B-12 shots or see a therapist or buy vitamins or talk with a nutritionist. As soon as I say, "free," I see them start to relax. They get calmer and more receptive to what I want to say. "It's free, so what have you got to lose?" I say.

Then I tell people I've been to a meeting myself. This really helps them. I say, "I've sat in on a meeting. The people there are the warmest, friendliest, most welcoming people you'll ever want to meet. Their program really helps people to lose weight, and it's called Food Addicts in Recovery Anonymous. It's a twelve-step program, kind of like Alcoholics Anonymous."

I explain, "Right now, you have a relationship with food that is taking you down a road you don't want to take. These people can help you change how you think about food. The really beautiful thing is that you can get a sponsor there. That's someone whom you can talk with every single day, who's walked in your shoes and knows what you're going through—as opposed to some skinny doctor who says, 'Oh, just eat less and have more apples.'" Patients usually relate to that, too, because I'm pretty skinny myself. They can see they're going to have someone who knows what it feels like to want a piece of chocolate, as opposed to talking with a non-addict like me, who can take it or leave it.

After I explain FA, I take out a brochure. I show them all the meeting locations in our city, and I mention the meeting times. Then I say, "There has to be a location near you, no matter where you live or work. Look at all these places!" They usually admit there's a meeting that they can reach near their house or office. "Just go and check out that meeting," I say, "and when I see you back here next month, tell me how you liked it." If there weren't meetings here, I'd suggest that it would be worth even a long drive to another city, just to check the program out.[3]

That's how I introduce people to FA. For the most part, patients go, and it's just exactly as I told them. They love it. When they're frustrated with having reached a plateau, they can break through and begin to lose weight again. They have renewed hope, and they're reinvigorated. Then they're able to keep from regaining the weight they lose.

I did have one patient, though, who didn't like FA. I was surprised, because she was the first person I'd ever referred who had that reaction. When I asked her why, she said, "I don't want to do what they're telling me to do." To me, that's a sure sign that she is an addict. She doesn't want to give up the food she loves so much. She's a person engaging in destructive behaviors who resents FA's ideas about what she should eat. She doesn't want to take suggestions from someone who's telling her how to be successful.

When you enter FA or have weight loss surgery, you're opening your life to a second chance. But if you take that second chance and continue to live just the way you did in the first go-round, you're going to get exactly the same results. You have to live differently and think differently to get different results. You have to make up your mind. You have to be a different person.

---

3. FA meetings are now held in Australia, Canada, Germany, New Zealand, and the United States. Members in countries or areas without the program can still successfully obtain and sustain abstinence. Please consult the FA website, www.foodaddicts.ORG, and contact us for more information if there are no meetings near you.

I mentioned that studies show that people who are morbidly obese have only a 1–2 percent chance of losing weight and keeping it off. That is a sad statistic, and it's why people are going for surgery. I believe we could really change that percentage if more people went to FA.

The problem is that FA requires work. It requires going to meetings and doing the Twelve Steps. It requires commitment and a change in priorities. In our American culture, when we have a problem, we want to go out and find something on the market that we can buy to fix that problem. In FA, though, you have to invest time, you have to make an effort, and you have to wait and be patient for the weight to come off.

I know that FA addresses many other food problems besides obesity. I'm just talking about obesity because that's what I treat. From my perspective, the ultimate solution for obesity is prevention. Until we can get prevention, I think that FA is the shining light. I wish more people knew of it. I'm doing my part by talking with my patients and putting information on our website. I also make sure to mention my referral to FA in the letter I send to my patients' primary care doctors. I hope that some of them will start making direct referrals, as well.

As I've said, I've been to FA, and the people I met there are truthful people. The patients I've referred come back to me, and they are truthful people too. I can validate what they say because I weigh them every time we meet. FA works, no question about it.

Every story in this book is a story of success. I believe that they are all true. You can trust what these FA members say about themselves. Absolutely.

CHAPTER 3

A Story of Recovery

We've talked briefly about food addiction and FA recovery, but we think we can most easily explain both by describing how they've affected our lives. In the story that follows, an FA member remembers her struggles with food and reflects on the physical recovery and peace she's found through FA.

I HAVE TWO FAMILY PHOTOS that I often show to others. In the earlier one, taken when I was five years old, I haven't yet lost my baby teeth. I am the cute little girl with the sparkly smile, standing with my mom, dad, and brothers. We're a perfect family.

In the second photo, I'm in the fourth grade, wearing a dress that is too small. I'm not yet overweight, but I'm almost five feet, five inches tall, which is my height now. The dress is cutting me under my arms. I look disgruntled, and my father looks angry. We don't look like a happy family anymore.

I used to think that whoever took the second photo caught a shot of our real selves. We were messed up, I thought. No one was happy with anyone else. My brothers first got into mischief and later into trouble. My dad was drinking and angry, and I was scared of him.

The negatives were true, but in recovery, I now see that my past wasn't all bad or all good. I like to say that our family was a normally dysfunctional one. I felt tense when my dad came home from work, but I also felt safe when he was there. My mom was the Rock of Gibraltar, handling any kind of problem with fairness and aplomb. There were issues, but we children were given a kind of love and caring that many others never have. Beyond my parents and siblings stood a network of aunts, uncles, cousins, and grandparents. All of us regularly went back to my grandparents' farm. We had a sense of home.

I felt a lot of fear as a child, but I couldn't name the feeling. I handled it first by trying hard to please. My mother always described me as the perfect little girl. "We never had to use any kind of discipline on her," she'd say. "We just gave her a cross look. She'd step back into line." My father still talks with amazement about the day he and my mother first moved me into my college dorm. I'd never set foot on campus before, but when we arrived, I could name and locate every building. I was scared to death, so I'd memorized the map of the entire school. "Get control!" was my approach.

Food was always a large part of my life. I don't remember a time when food wasn't important to me, but the problem I first noticed was my weight. When I was eleven or twelve, my folks brought the bathroom scale into the kitchen to weigh me. I remember the shock of seeing the numbers. I realized then that I was at least as heavy as one of my older brothers.

My mom was a great cook who dealt with food like a farmer's wife. She'd make fried chicken and everything that went with it. Basically, we're talking about flour and grease, and I loved it. Mom never wanted me to eat all that I ate. "Do you really need two sandwiches?" she'd ask. She worried, wanting to spare me the pain she had felt the one time in her life when she'd been overweight. She's been tiny since I've known her.

When I was around thirteen, I started to diet. I wasn't very successful then, but the summer before I left for college, I lost weight and got down to a normal size. I was probably about 135 pounds, but I gained 40 pounds by Christmas break. Since none of my clothes fit, I ordered a pair of farmer's overalls from the Sears catalogue. I was going to an old, southern university, where the guys put on blue blazers and ties when they went with their dates to the football games, but I wore those overalls for my entire four years. I found comfort by telling myself I was heavy, deep, and real: I was majoring in molecular biology, and all the other girls were taking fine arts classes on the other side of campus.

I think I was already a food addict before I left home, but college caught me in the perfect storm. I'd been the salutatorian of my high school class, but I believed that I'd merely fooled everyone into thinking I was smart. Every breathing moment during college, I felt inadequate, both academically and socially. When I ate, I felt better. This caused a bad cycle. My feelings of inadequacy made me eat, but the eating made me fat. Fatness made me feel more inadequate, which increased my drive to eat.

When I later heard food described as a drug, it made complete sense to me. Food affected my personality, as any drug does. As an undergraduate, I felt like an idiot inside, but despite my insecurity, I was no wallflower. Instead, I was well on my way to becoming the brassy, abrasive, and opinionated woman of my maturity.

I had a hard time when I graduated from college. In an economy with double-digit unemployment and high interest rates, I couldn't find a job. I also couldn't find clothes that fit me. I weighed 175 pounds and had moved back in with my parents.

My father had gotten sober in AA during my senior year in high school and had given me a framed Serenity Prayer for a graduation present. I'd been angry with my dad throughout the time I was growing up, but I took the prayer with me to college and kept it above my bed. Back home later and dealing with unemployment, I thought about the prayer. "I can't change whether or not I get a job," I decided, "but I'm going to take care of this situation!" I found a self-help book about how to get everything I might ever want, and I made that my bible. I resolved to pull myself up by my bootstraps. I was going to lose weight and exercise regularly. I'd keep up with the news every week. I made a list of all the museums I was going to visit and put myself on a diet of low-calorie prepared meals. I sent out hundreds of résumés, and when I'd lost about 30 pounds, I got a full-time job.

My new position made it possible for me to move to another city and get my own apartment. I did well in my company, and eventually I married and had children.

My bottom in addiction came when I had everything I thought I wanted.

I had always believed that there was something outside myself that would make me happy and change the script of my life. As I saw it, I had to go to a particular college. I went there, though it financially challenged me and my parents. College didn't fix the script. Then I wanted a job. I got the job. I wanted my own apartment. I got the apartment. None of this was enough. I needed a husband, children, a high salary, job promotions, a big house on the river. I got all of that and more, but at thirty-five, I was miserable. I had nothing left for fantasies—no idea of anything else outside myself that could make me happy.

In the midst of my misery, I was eating and going on diets. The periods in which I felt able to control myself got shorter and shorter, until finally I found myself back in a commercial weight loss program. I'd enrolled with friends, and eventually we figured that we were just paying that program to weigh us. Why not weigh ourselves? So we met regularly at a local grocery store, weighed ourselves on the public scale there, and then went out to eat at a restaurant down the street. One night, standing on the scale. I realized that in six months, I'd lost all of 10 pounds. The scale told me I'd gained 5 back. It read 176, and I knew down to my toes that it was never going down again.

At that point, I could not limit how much I ate for even one day. When my daughter asked me to read her a bedtime story, she interrupted my evening eating, and I begrudged her the time. Instead of calling on customers for my work, I drove here and there, bingeing in my car. *How high is this scale going to go?* I wondered. I could easily imagine it reading 200 pounds, but I knew it wouldn't stop there. Would it stop at 250? What would happen to me when none of my clothes fit and I could no longer buy the professional outfits required for my job? And when my weight doubled my husband's? What was going to become of me?

I was terrified, but I didn't give up. I knew I had something more than a weight problem. I'd read all kinds of self-help books and written mission statements for myself. I had a life problem, I thought, and I kept looking for a solution. One day, I found a book about compulsive overeating. It wasn't about FA and didn't talk about addiction, but it opened with the Twelve Steps. A light bulb went off as soon as I saw the First Step: "We admitted we were powerless over food—that our lives had become unmanageable." I knew that I was powerless.

I read the book, and that weekend my mom and dad came to visit us for my daughter's birthday. I told my dad that I thought I had his problem, only my troubles were with food. He talked about his drinking. He said he had a buddy who had been his friend for fifty years. "He'll still try to taunt me with a beer. He'll pull out a cold one and ask, 'Wouldn't you like to have a bottle?' He doesn't understand that I don't want one. The obsession and compulsion to drink have been lifted."

I wanted what my dad had. I was tired of fighting. I was eating against my own will. "Don't do it! Don't do it!" my brain would say, to no avail. I remembered following the instructions I'd once been given in a behavior modification class. I was supposed to cut a cookie into small pieces so I could savor it. I obediently put two cookies on a plate, laid out a placemat, fork, and knife, and divided each one into eight pieces. I fully tasted every bite and then got up and ate the whole bag. I did things like that all the time.

My dad also told me that if he'd only read a book and never gone to an AA meeting, he'd never have gotten better. So it goes with twelve-step programs. They give you hope, and then they humble you. The promise was that I could get rid of my painful obsession and compulsion, but I'd have to go to a meeting to do it.

That weekend, as I binged on my daughter's birthday cake, I knew I didn't want to ask for help. I didn't want to admit that I was licked. I did want the fulfillment of the promise I'd heard about through AA, though. I wanted to end the fight inside me, so I picked up the phone and found a meeting for myself on Monday night.

On Monday, I drove to the meeting place, sat in my car, and drove home without ever opening the car door. On Wednesday, I tried again. I told myself, "You've got to go, no matter what," and I followed through. Sitting with the people in the meeting room, I heard the term *food addict* for the first time. It made sense to me. At the next meeting I attended, the speaker told us that she had lost 80 pounds. I looked at her in amazement, thinking, *How is that possible?* She also said that she abstained from flour and sugar, which she said were drugs for food addicts. *What in the world did she eat?* I wondered.

The very next day, I tracked down the speaker and asked her to help me. At that point, I was afraid to eat anything, I was so close to another huge binge. She arranged for me to work with one of her friends in FA, and that's how, eighteen years ago, on July 12, 1995, I began my abstinence from addictive eating.

When I first joined the program, I felt a lot of fear. I was terrified that if I deviated from FA in any way, I'd end up back in my old ways of eating. I couldn't argue with the fact that I was a food addict. I remembered that when my cousin got pregnant and developed gestational diabetes, I worried I'd have the same problem. I was sure that I'd be unable to stop eating sweets, even for the sake of my unborn child. What is that but addiction?

Abstinence got me to a normal weight of 125 pounds and kept me there, but FA offers far more than a diet. I didn't just lose weight. I had to change. I couldn't hold on to my old attitudes and behaviors. If I'd had to live with the same tension I used to feel, I would never have been able to gain abstinence or keep it.

FA made it possible for me to change. Experienced members urged me to join an AWOL group, where I could study and do the Twelve Steps in sequence. AWOL stands for A Way of Life, and the Steps are actions that enable us addicts to develop the strength and clarity we need to stay abstinent.[4]

Because of FA and the Steps, I'm as free from cravings for food as my father is free from his past compulsion with alcohol. The unexpected miracle is not that I have lost 50 pounds and kept it off, but rather that my obsession and compulsion with food have been lifted. No

---

4. Please see the glossary in appendix 1 for a brief description of AWOL.

matter what else happens, I am grateful that I no longer have the impulse to eat addictively.

Of course, life is still life. My husband and I divorced some years ago. We are both doing well now, as are our children. I can truly say that I am very happily remarried, but it's not that my husband and I never quarrel or that my children don't occasionally get on each other's nerves. Rather, I am finally able to see imperfections and accept them. I can be angry with my husband or feel hurt and yet still know that I love him. When you love despite your aggravation, you truly love.

FA recovery stands at the foundation of my life and love. If I have job turmoil, I stay abstinent and it gets better. When I worry about my children, I weigh and measure my food, and the problems eventually resolve themselves. When money looks tight, I say to myself, *Just don't eat addictively, and you'll figure out what to do next.*

None of this means that I think a diet will save me. Abstinence is not a diet. What I'm really telling myself is that I must keep my recovery first and that continuous abstinence is my number one priority. This immediately reminds me that I have to ask a Higher Power for help, because it's impossible for me to stay abstinent by myself.

FA has helped me separate religion from spirituality. I have to have help. As soon as I am willing to try turning to a Higher Power for help with *any* aspect of my abstinence or life, I start to relax. I feel assured I will be given the strength and wisdom to deal with whatever is bothering me.

Today, I call on a Higher Power—God as I personally understand God. I have a kind of shorthand inside. "Thank you, God" is a prayer, but when I say to myself, *Relax!* that's a prayer, too. *Easy does it* is also a prayer. These make a bridge between me and my Higher Power, reminding me that I don't have to push. I can sit quietly and then, whether I tell myself to relax or I ask my Higher Power what I should do, I can be assured that answers and strength will come.

Chapter 4

More about Addiction and FA

W E WONDER IF, after reading a story like the one in chapter 3, you are left with some questions about your own relationship with food. Through personal experience, we have proven to ourselves beyond doubt that we are food addicts who will never be able to control our eating. You may not yet be similarly convinced.

If you are not, we encourage you to consider how long and hard you have battled with weight, food, obsession, or bulimia. Do you starve yourself? Have your struggles negatively affected your intimate relationships, physical health, or work?

You might also try an experiment to see if you can remain in control, no matter what you eat. Choose some of your favorite foods and a food plan or diet that seems healthy. See if you can eat moderately and then stop. Can you realistically see yourself continuing this for months or even years, free from obsession and steadily remaining at a healthy weight? If not, and your experiment with moderate eating ultimately plunges you back into old, destructive patterns of thinking and eating, you may well be a food addict.

Above all, given your relationship with food, you might ask yourself if it's viable for you to continue as you are now. Some of us were too frightened to face reality, but deep inside, we were uneasy. We sensed that we were in trouble. Maybe we knew that more weight would likely bring us to the point of a stroke, or we'd been warned that if we continued with bulimia, we'd need to cap all our teeth. We might have been told that our heart was in danger of giving out.

Health issues scared some of us into trying FA. Others of us came into the program because we could no longer bear the isolation and depression that accompanied our eating. For whatever reason, if you know that everything else you've attempted has failed, FA can help.

Abstinence and involvement in FA may look like big hurdles to you, as they did to most of us at first. Outsiders who are unfamiliar with FA often imagine that FA members are constantly struggling to avoid snacks and treats. They frequently remark that we must have extraordinary will power. They think that because our meal plans are restricted, we are deprived of enjoying food and joining in the many celebrations that are accompanied by eating. Our involvement in FA must require inordinate amounts of time, they say.

We hope you can put such worries aside. In fact, for food addicts who join FA and give it a thorough try, the program is liberating. Life is good when food is in its proper place. As was the case for the storyteller of chapter 3, abstinence brings freedom. Experienced members who stay committed to FA remain slender. Meals taste good, but food pales in comparison with the fulfillment of facing the ups and downs of life.

CHAPTER 5

Keeping an Open Mind

THE PERSONAL STORIES of FA members and the discussion of the Twelve Steps in the next two sections of this book will provide an intimate look at food addiction, FA, and the gifts of recovery. Before we move on, however, we want to clarify three aspects of our program: the importance of what we call the Tradition of anonymity, the use of a sponsor, and the many references to a "Higher Power" or "God."

Probably all of us first approached FA with feelings of uneasiness. We worried that the group might be some kind of cult. Even more fundamentally, we felt embarrassed or ashamed to admit that we might have a problem with food. We didn't want anyone to see us even nearing the door of an FA meeting.

We want to immediately reassure you. FA is a program of recovery, not a diet group. You will never be weighed or publicly humiliated. No one will demand payment of dues or fees. Above all, your privacy will be protected.

As do all twelve-step groups, FA recognizes the critical need for anyone approaching the program to feel respected and safe. We are guided at every level by the Tradition of anonymity. We do not reveal anyone's membership in FA, and we treat everything we hear at meetings as confidential. We believe that whether we are speaking with someone inside or outside of FA, there is only one story that any of us should feel free to discuss: the story that is our own.

Our trust in a mutual respect for anonymity is essential for recovery in FA, as is the willingness to find and work with a sponsor. FA sponsors are members who can draw upon their own experience of continuous abstinence to help someone who is newer to FA. Sponsors explain the boundaries of abstinence and suggest ways that we can stay steady when we might be most tempted by the foods we used to eat. They know something that newcomers don't yet know: how to stay continuously abstinent and free from food obsession, month after month and year after year.

In the beginning, newcomers phone their sponsors each day, but as they become stable and established in their abstinence, they call much less frequently. Ultimately, a sponsor's role is to help sponsees find their own Higher Power. Through a relationship with that Power, the newer FA member can gain the strength and clarity necessary to face life without leaning on food.

The suggestion that we might need a Higher Power to help us stay abstinent can loom as another large stumbling block. Many people new to FA have confused

FA with religion and offered a range of objections. Here are some of them:

I already believe in God. I don't need you to tell me about God.

I'd feel ridiculous asking God to help me with my breakfast, lunch, and dinner. God has many more important matters to handle.

There's no proof there's a Higher Power, and there never will be. I don't believe in God. Show me the scientific evidence for the existence of a Higher Power. Faith is wishful thinking. I've matured beyond the need for it.

I don't want to turn to a Higher Power. If there is one, that Power betrayed me. I didn't get any help when I most needed it. Where was the Higher Power then? Look at all the atrocities in the world. Why is there so much illness and suffering in the world if there is a God?

In the thirty stories that follow chapter 6, you will see that a number of FA members grappled with the notion of a Higher Power. In their stories they speak openly about their struggles to assure you that FA is accessible to anyone—believer, nonbeliever, or skeptic.

Please don't let the religious or spiritual terms in the personal accounts confuse or deter you. FA is not a religious program. In our meeting rooms, you will find people of all faiths, as well as those without any religious affiliation. FA demands nothing of anyone who wishes to participate except the willingness to keep an open mind. No matter what we believe or don't believe when we first come in, we stand together on only one foundation: our admission that we are beaten by food and our willingness to try asking a Higher Power for help. The rest is an experiment—a journey of discovery.

CHAPTER 6

To Our Families

ADDICTIVE EATING directly affects the food addict, but it also has an enormous impact on the addict's family. Perhaps you have a family member already in FA or you think someone you love may need this program.

This chapter is for you—the children, spouses, partners, and parents of people like us. We'll suggest how you might approach someone if you think he or she may be struggling with food addiction. We'll also talk about how life within a family changes when we join the program. These shifts can be difficult, especially in the beginning, but we hope that our perspectives will be helpful. Please be sure to read the opening chapters of this book first, as you'll need a basic understanding of food addiction and our program.

We'll start with the story of a man who began dating his future wife when they were both in college. They have been together for thirty-nine years, fourteen of them while she's been abstinent from addictive eating. We'll call them John and Amy. We asked John what it was like to be married to Amy before and after she found FA. He said,

> I'm trained as a scientist and believe in the rational world. The idea of making decisions—choosing what we do—was important to me, but my wife was a person who couldn't choose her actions. While we were dating she told me that she sometimes ate pints of ice cream at one sitting. I couldn't understand how that was possible.
>
> The issue of Amy's eating was almost a deal breaker for me as I thought of becoming more seriously involved with her. She gained and lost weight over and over. I could overlook 50 or 60 pounds, but a noticeable fraction of her relatives were hugely overweight. What if she put on 100 pounds or 200? I was terrified. I somehow knew that her problem was not temporary. It was not going to go away, and I didn't know if I could handle it. Could I love her unconditionally? Should I choose to go ahead with her if she had a kind of permanent disability?
>
> I loved Amy, and we did get married. By the time she and I had been together fifteen years, I'd seen her go up and down repeatedly. No matter how many times she lost the extra pounds, she gained them back. I know she felt like a failure. She'd go long periods without eating addictively, sometimes even several years. But then, she'd start. She'd eat too much or get into the wrong foods. The next day she might be okay. And then she'd eat again. And again.
>
> I don't really have words for describing how food affected my wife. "Depressed" is too mild. After she

ate addictively, she was lost and in a fog and desperate to avoid the reality of the moment. She'd eat more or watch television, trying to escape. The self-destructive nature of her eating scared me. Why would anyone do something so painful?

It's hard to be married to someone going through that kind of suffering and not be affected yourself. I felt despairing. She was not the only one who was going to be miserable on and on into the future. I got to the point where I had fear in the pit of my stomach. *When I get home from work tonight, what's it going to be,* I'd think. *Am I going to find her lying on the couch in the den feeling sick? "I'm not having dinner tonight because of all I've eaten," she'll say. Then I'll be on my own to cook, and she'll just lie there by herself or do whatever else she does.* I'm sure I was angry, feeling I was about to lose her again for a week or two weeks or whatever it took for her to get back.

I had no way of fixing any of this. I know now that there was nothing that I or anyone else could do, but early on, I did try to help. I wanted to monitor what she ate. I'd ask, "Should you be eating that?" or "Should we be buying this food?" or "Are you going to be okay if we go out to eat at that restaurant?"

I don't think it took too many times of having my head bitten off before I realized that wasn't my place. There was a line, and when I tried to monitor or control my wife, I got on the wrong side of it. It is not good to put yourself between a person and his or her addiction. You find out that you have nothing to contribute besides stating the obvious, which is not appreciated or helpful.

There is another problem with trying to be a monitor. It doesn't work. One of Amy's relatives is always about 30 pounds overweight. His wife barricades the refrigerator after dinner. He'll say, "I just want a little ice cream," and she'll say, "NO!" That wife never wins the war. She might win the battle for five minutes, but in the end, her husband always does what he wants. When I tried to monitor Amy, she got mad, and I felt like a failure as soon as she started eating addictively again. Nobody won.

Still, I have to say that there is something distancing when you can't be part of the solution to a problem. It was very hard. Once we had children, Amy never disappeared as a parent, but I can't say the same for her as a partner. She couldn't show up for me in a fully giving way. How could she? You have to be present for yourself before you can be present for someone else.

I am grateful that Amy found her way to FA. I was and am outside the FA circle. I still don't completely understand how the program works, but I've seen the results. It took a while, but Amy got stable in her abstinence. She's been continuously free from addictive eating and the old, terrible misery for so long that I can't remember how many years it's been. Her weight swings have stopped, and she's stayed slender.

To be honest, of course, I do have to admit that Amy's involvement in FA wasn't necessarily easy for me, especially when our children were young. Amy was committed to going to her meetings—three each week. During those times, I was home alone with the children. Dinner, baths, bedtime, and dishes were mine to do, as well as meals and activities during many Saturdays. One of our children had tantrums of frightening intensity, so I commonly faced major blowups while Amy was away. I was exhausted.

My time away at work might have been the least stressful part of my week, but my attitude towards FA has always been affected by what I know of Amy's misery before she joined the program and by what FA has meant for all of us. Our children are now young adults. Waking up in our empty nest, Amy gets out of bed early every morning. I'm sound asleep, not even conscious, but at 5:45, 6:00, 6:15, and 6:30, she's taking phone calls from newer FA members who want her help. She's generous and extraordinarily disciplined and committed. Service to others is an integral part of her life. I feel proud of her.

Because of FA, Amy is a very different person today than she was five or ten years ago. For the rest of us, being around her can't help but have a positive effect. Our children may not be paying a lot of attention to what she's doing now, but I really wonder about the influence it will have on them when they look back and remember it later on. They'll know that she was someone who put huge effort into giving to people in FA and to our community.

There is one other way that I've benefited directly from Amy's involvement in FA. As I mentioned, regularly and for fairly significant periods of time, I had to look after our children alone. They thought of it as "daddy time," but it was sometimes intensely stressful for me. Now I am glad, absolutely glad, that I had that time with my children. It built an intimacy between us. I became the father I wanted to be. During their adolescence, we faced some crises, and I was able to respond more calmly than would have ever been possible otherwise. I was a better parent because of the hours I spent alone with them.

When a spouse joins FA, the person's partner can have a hard time. For me, it's all been worth it. Minimally, looking at costs and benefits, I can say that the extra effort required of me was more than justified by what the program did for Amy and for our family. Would I rather live with an Amy who's eating addictively or an Amy who is abstinent?

The answer is obvious, but I don't look at our experiences that way. I feel that I am supporting Amy's spiritual growth. Seeing her day in and day out, watching how she lives her life, elevates me. As I guessed when she was young, her problems with food will never go away. She'll always be a food addict, but because of FA, she's no longer a victim of her illness, one day at a time. That provides me welcome relief, peace, and even inspiration.

We think John's description of his life with Amy before and after she joined FA is especially useful. As you probably already know from your own experience, there is, indeed, a line dividing food addicts and those who long to help them. Your impulse to manage your loved one's access to food or to confront your loved one with the damage he or she is doing is understandable and logical. Many members of FA ultimately come to appreciate such caring, but please don't forget that you and your loved one are dealing with addiction. When food addicts crave food, we find a way to get it, no matter how many obstacles you may put in our path, and when you pressure us, we tend to react defensively and defiantly. These are signs of our illness. We are afraid to give up the food we depend on to help us cope with our lives.

The daughter of one of our members, a young woman who joined FA seven years after her mother did, has suggested an alternative approach:

> People ask me how they can help when someone in their family needs this program. "Above all," I say, "don't pressure them or make them feel badly about the way they're eating. Offer them a brochure or pamphlet. If they ask questions, answer as best you can, but don't push."
>
> My mom never pushed me. Every now and again, she'd mention that I'd be welcome to come to a meeting if I'd like, but she never forced any FA literature on me. I'm grateful she basically left me alone. If she'd shamed me or we'd been fighting about my weight, I wouldn't have felt I could talk with her when I felt desperate.
>
> I called my mom one day when I couldn't stand struggling with food anymore, and she gave me the phone number of an FA member who was my age and lived near me. I don't know how I would have reacted if she'd told me what to do—suggested a person who could sponsor me or nudged me towards certain meetings, for example. It was better for me to talk with someone else. When I phoned the woman whose number she'd given me, I could honestly say I was bingeing and couldn't stop eating. That person helped

me get to a meeting, where I chose my own sponsor. I have a good relationship with my mom, but I couldn't have been as open with her.

We believe this young woman's mother took a wise approach. If you think someone you love needs this program, we suggest that you inform yourself first. Read the rest of this book and have a look at the FA website (www.foodaddicts.ORG), then be alert for a moment when your loved one is most open and discouraged—after a big weight gain, for example. When he or she begins talking a little about food and weight, you could casually mention that you've learned of a solution that has worked for many who've found that they couldn't control their eating.

Once you've awakened your loved one's interest in FA, offer to share this book and mention our website. This will enable him or her to find a meeting and contact us. Let your loved one take the initiative, rather than doing too much yourself. Alternatively, you might give this book to the doctor or counselor of the family member who's in trouble. See if the professional will have the conversation.

Perhaps you're reading this book because someone in your family has just joined FA. We know that can be challenging. When someone enters the program, life abruptly changes for that person and for everyone around him or her. New members are often on the phone early in the morning with their sponsors, and they laugh and talk at all hours of the day and night with FA friends their family has never met. They're at meetings three or four times a week. They say they can't eat at the restaurants that were family favorites or they don't want to go out to eat at all. It seems that spontaneity has been lost forever. Every meal they eat is measured; they won't share food from their plate with anyone else; they stop making the desserts that everyone loved.

No wonder families get upset! We understand, but we ask for your patience and flexibility. We food addicts have to take care of our recovery first—not because we are selfish, but because we face dire consequences if we do not and because we love you. We can't take care of ourselves, much less be present for you, if we are driven by our addiction.

FA members will always need time for FA. No matter how long we've been abstinent, we'll have to maintain a certain discipline regarding what, where, and when we eat. We can enjoy our lives with you and others in our family, but we need to bond with you over what we do, not over what we eat. We can't spend hours in the kitchen baking or organize an entire vacation around a series of special restaurants. We'll probably buy a birthday cake rather than making one, and when you have pizza at home, we'll need to eat our own measured meal. This will not diminish our enjoyment, and we hope it won't diminish yours.

Some issues take hard work. Relationships often have to be built or reestablished after years of emotional disengagement. It may take time for some family members to get over the anger they feel because of our past rages, deceit, or attempts to manipulate and control. Our loved ones may also need to look at any part they may have played in our mutual difficulties and misunderstandings, but we understand that we need to focus on our own shortcomings.

Sexuality can be an especially challenging issue for us and our spouses or partners. Because we hated our bodies or were out of touch with ourselves physically when we were eating addictively, many of us tended toward extremes. We may have made unreasonable sexual demands or, instead, denied our sexuality and refused any expression of it. Addiction distorted our relationships. As we grow in an understanding of our illness and the needs of our recovery, we try to make an extra effort to be present for our spouses. Your effort may be needed, too. You and your partner can work together to develop a healthier, more loving relationship. Within that context, sexual intimacy can again become possible.

As food addicts get through the cravings and exhaustion that accompany the early days of withdrawal from addictive eating, we become more comfortable and confident in our abstinence. Ultimately, you'll find us participating more, not less, in family life. As long as we are solidly abstinent and taking good care of ourselves, we can go to weddings and parties, on cruises and other vacations. Depression, mood swings, anxiety, and anger—the shortcomings that made us so difficult to live with—begin to ease. A good life can lie ahead. As each of us learns to better accommodate the other's needs, alternatives will be found that provide deeper satisfaction and even more pleasure for everyone involved.

FA promises a fundamental shift in personality for those who remain abstinent and continue to live in accordance with the Twelve Steps. Change takes time, but the spouses and partners of FA members who have been abstinent for many years almost always agree that the effort is worth it. A husband who met his wife when she was in recovery and never knew her otherwise offered the following observations:

I've sometimes talked with men who are dating FA women. Their concerns were the ones I initially had. None of us wants to lose the ability to be spontaneous or to feel *we* can't comfortably eat the foods we want to eat. I was initially sorry I couldn't share a glass of wine with my then girlfriend (who became my wife), but at a minimum, I certainly didn't want to feel self-conscious about drinking a glass myself when she was with me.

It turns out that none of these kinds of things are problems. My wife is able to talk openly with me and our kids about what she does and why she does it. The other day, our son said, "Hey, Mom, look at me! I'm having vanilla ice cream, and I love it so much, and I know you can't have it because if you did you'd be crazy." My wife said, "Yup. And I don't even want it!" We all laughed. So our family is in good shape.

There are advantages when someone is in FA. I point out that it's nice for anyone to know that his potential spouse won't ever be overweight! We have to consider ourselves, too. There's no doubt if I'd married someone else, I'd be at least 20 pounds heavier. Sometimes my wife might say, "Are you sure you want to eat that much dessert?" And I'll say, "Yeah. I do!" But she makes a healthy lunch for me every day, and I appreciate it. I stay slim.

All joking aside, I have what is most important to me in my relationship with my wife. Some people get stuck and blocked in their communication with each other. I was determined to marry someone who had the capacity for self-examination and growth. Because of meetings and AWOLs and having sponsors and sponsoring, FA members have a built-in mechanism that helps them look at themselves all the time.

My wife's access to FA was and is powerfully attractive to me. She has something most people don't have. Whenever she needs to, she can call any number of people in the program and talk about whatever problem is bothering her. I kind of wish I had that many people I could call.

When our children were babies and my wife had to go to a meeting I felt a little resentful sometimes. There are those sorts of inconveniences when you're married to someone in FA. We might have had to re-adjust a trip because my wife didn't want to miss an AWOL meeting or she'll be on the phone a lot. But I feel such things are logistical nuisances as opposed to being insurmountable problems, and all the benefits of her being in FA are blessings that far outweigh them.

Some people don't understand that FA is more than a diet. If the program were just a diet, my wife's behaviors would seem weird and potentially almost cultish. But all that FA does to support personal development and growth makes it really special—much more than a diet—and I appreciate the program in its entirety. FA is just a way to help people be better people.

*Thirty Stories of Food
Addiction and FA Recovery*

✧ ✧ ✧

Some Early Members of FA

✧ ✧ ✧

The early members of FA whose stories are presented in this section bear witness to the long-term, sustained recovery that the program makes possible. Each of these storytellers has maintained continuous abstinence for twenty-five years or longer.

May I Never Forget

✧ ✧ ✧

I'M EIGHTY-ONE NOW. Thanks to FA, I've been slender for more than three decades, but when I was forty, my life had become a misery because of food. I had a wonderful husband and four children, but during that terrible time, I didn't want to live. Each day before I went to work, I struggled to find something in my closet that would fit me. I was either driven to eat, struggling to keep from eating, or hating myself because I had binged again.

Bingeing gave me terrible headaches and stomach pains. I couldn't take off my shoes until I was ready for bed because my feet were so swollen I couldn't get them on again. The skin on my legs felt like it was going to split. I had high cholesterol and high blood pressure, and my joints hurt from arthritis. I weighed 235 or 245 pounds, and when I woke up in the morning, I'd see myself in the mirror, bent over like an old woman.

I'd been chubby since I was a child. Growing up was not easy for me. Our house was chaotic, and life felt scary. My parents had immigrated to the United States from Russia, and for them, a roof overhead, some food to eat, a coat to wear, and shoes on both feet meant a person had everything. I couldn't talk about any of my fears because they made no sense to my mother. Her family had been forced to hide from the Cossacks, who were murdering the Jews. If I ever tried to say I was afraid, she couldn't begin to understand. "What's the matter with you!" she'd say.

I was a thin, fussy eater until after my tonsils were taken out. Food began to taste better then, and I put on weight. I grew up an awkward, chubby kid. Later, as a teenager, I was a heavy, shy young woman who never felt like she belonged. I felt invisible.

When I was sixteen, I began to realize that food had a hold on me. That year, my father died of a heart attack. I adored my father, and I was devastated. During the period of mourning, when my close friend came to visit, she put her arms around me and sobbed, but I stood like ice, completely shut off from my feelings. While people talked, I sat silently, staring at all the desserts laid out on the table. I wanted to eat, but I was ashamed that I was even thinking of it.

I tried to lose weight right after that. My brothers had come home from the service because of my father's illness, and when they saw me, they told me to go on a diet. They said they were ashamed of me. As a good girl, I did what I was told. I weighed 178 pounds then, and my sister weighed about 200. We sent away for a diet from a modeling agency. My mother cooked for us— "garbage soup," we called it, because it was made with tomato juice and the tops of lettuce leaves and all kinds of other things. In six weeks, I lost 32 pounds. I looked normal, but I wasn't. I still felt I didn't fit in, that I wasn't enough.

I met my husband while I was thin. I was nineteen then, and we were married in less than a year. I got pregnant right away. Two years later, when we decided to have another baby, I was seeing a doctor who was very strict. He put me on a starvation diet, and every time I went in, he yelled at me. He said I was gaining weight. I couldn't believe it, because I was following the diet. I could hardly walk and was having a hard time, but no one sympathized. They thought I was a complainer, a *kvetch*, as they say in Yiddish. It turned out that I had twins.

I began to struggle terribly with food. My husband was twenty-five, and I was twenty-three. We'd had three babies in three years. I remember the three babies crying, two bottles heating on the stove, and the breadbox on the counter in front of me.

I didn't know then that I already had the disease of food addiction. I just thought I liked to eat. I liked to cook, I liked to bake, and I liked to feed people. I had a fine reputation among our neighbors and friends, who loved to sit down at the table in our house. We didn't have the money to cover the bills, but I always found money for food or eating out. I bought anything and everything I wanted to eat, and I fed my husband whatever luxurious fruits I saw in the store. When my mother came to visit and asked how much I'd paid, I'd shrug, "I don't know. I needed it."

My husband never complained about my gaining weight, but I hated the way I looked. I tried every kind of diet. I ate whole boxes of the candies that were supposed to take your appetite away. Hypnosis didn't work, and neither did the diet clubs. Though I was afraid of needles and pills, I tried one diet doctor after another. I didn't drive, so my poor husband took me wherever I needed to go. He'd come all the way home from work, get back in the car, and drive miles in another direction to take me to diet doctors in other cities. Sometimes he had to sit in the waiting room for hours.

Nothing worked. If I was tired, I ate. If I was worried, I ate. If I was late, or angry, or even happy, I ate. I could diet and take off a little weight, but the same cycle repeated itself endlessly. "One little bite extra won't hurt me," I'd say, or I'd scheme and begin to tweak the plan. Before I knew it, I'd gained back all the weight I'd battled for months to lose. Something was wrong with me, but I could only think that I was weak willed.

By the time I was forty, as I said, I no longer wanted to live. I had no hope. Then one day, two women from my neighborhood told me they were going to write away for information about a program just like Alcoholics Anonymous but created for people who had trouble with food. Everyone knew I was always dieting. I told them I was interested. The day they got the note back with the address of a meeting in a city nearby, my life changed.

As soon as I could, I went to a meeting of that twelve-step group, which was for compulsive overeaters. The meetings were not quite FA—they developed into FA as our understanding of addiction grew—but from my first contact, they gave me hope and the beginning of an answer to my problems. I was amazed to hear people stand in the front of the room and talk about the kinds of fears and uncertainties I'd always tried to hide. They said we had a disease, and they mentioned a spiritual solution.

I'm Jewish, and after the moment of relief that there were others like me, I began to feel afraid that the group was religious, that the people were going to try to convert me. I was wearing a Star of David that night, and without my saying a word, a Jewish woman suddenly came over and sat next to me. She put her hand on my knee. "Relax," she said. "Just listen. No one wants anything from you. We're only here to help each other." All of my tightness and fear evaporated then. Surely my Higher Power worked through her, because if she hadn't come to me, I don't know if I would ever have returned.

I started going to meetings right away. That program was new, so there was no one with sustained freedom from overeating and no unified definition of abstinence, but I was told to get a sponsor who could guide me. The sponsor I found was still overweight, but even so, she was God-sent. Because her husband was a recovering alcoholic in AA, she knew the AA program, and she shared it with me. Sometimes when I called, her husband answered the phone, and he, too, talked the AA program to me, inside and out.

From my sponsor and her husband, and from reading *Alcoholics Anonymous*, I learned about addiction and sobriety. I began to get the education I needed. I'd felt terrible about myself because I could not stop eating, but I was not a bad, weak person. I wasn't just an over-eater. I was more like an alcoholic. I was as powerless over my impulse to eat as alcoholics are powerless over alcohol. They can't have one sip of a drink, because even that much creates a craving they can't control, and they inevitably get drunk. My drugs were flour, sugar, and unmeasured quantities of food. One bite of any of them, and I lost control every time. If I could eliminate them from my diet, I could be free. I could have the equiva-lent of sobriety. I could have "abstinence," as we call it.

I was filled with relief, because I finally had a solution to my problems. I wanted recovery, and I learned more about it as my sponsor and her husband talked with me. "One day at a time" helped me immensely. I remember driving by a doughnut shop once, feeling my heart beat-ing like I had a lover standing on the corner. I thought, *Someday, I'm going to go in there and buy a whole dozen, and I'm going to eat them, all by myself. But not today.* As soon as I thought, *Not today,* the craving and obsession left me completely. I could let go of the doughnuts, just for that day, and the next day I didn't even want them.

My willingness to participate in my meeting was another turning point for me. My sponsor told me I needed to stand in front of the room and read one of the passages we always read aloud. She knew that if I wanted to remain abstinent, I couldn't let myself stay isolated. I had to be part of the group, she said.

I never wanted to be the center of attention, even when I was just with a few friends, so my sponsor's sug-gestion scared me to death. I had high blood pressure then. When the moment approached for me to read, I thought I was going to have a stroke, my head pounded so hard. My voice quivered and my hands visibly shook, but I stood in front of the meeting and did the reading. I felt I had to. I trusted it would help me stop eating, and if I couldn't stop eating, I knew I was going to die.

As I walked back to my seat that night, a woman reached out and took my hand. She'd been damaged by alcohol and shook all the time. "If you can do it, I can do it, too," she said, and for the first time, I experienced the privilege of helping someone else. No matter how painful it had been for me, I'd been helpful, and that was a wonderful feeling.

I have now been continuously abstinent for more than thirty years, but I wasn't just struck abstinent, as lightning might strike a tree. In the beginning, there were many days when I wanted to break my abstinence, and there were times when I was positive I would. One day, I planned a binge. I knew just what I would eat. In the program, we always talked about the need to speak with a member before we took the first addictive bite, so I called my friend to tell her I'd made up my mind to eat. She asked where I was. "In the kitchen," I said. "Why don't you go sit with your husband in the living room?" she asked. How simply she helped me! I went into the living room, sat with my husband, and did not break my abstinence.

I stayed open to all suggestions. I did not come into the program a religious person, but after my sponsor said I needed a Higher Power to help me stay abstinent, I sat quietly and asked myself, *What do you believe? Forget about Bible stories and anything you've read or been told. What do you believe?* It came to me that there is surely a Power in the universe. The sun knows when to rise and when to set. The leaves know when to fall off the trees and when to grow from buds. There's order in the universe and a Power that brings that order.

When I got up from the chair, I was ready to believe there was a Power I could turn to for answers, but it was only after I decided to trust this Power that I experienced it. We have to make a choice to trust.

I've especially faced this choice regarding my children. Early in my recovery, I worried all the time about one of my daughters. She was in a terrible, dangerous situation, and she called me every day, telling me she was afraid and asking me what she should do. I was heartsick. I had no answers for her.

One night, after my family ate dinner and left the table, I sat by myself in front of all the leftover food. I had a choice. I could eat, or I could call my sponsor. God helped me call my sponsor. She listened to me and then said, "Do you know what your daughter is doing? She's made *you* her Higher Power. Now, why don't you give your daughter to the care of your own Higher Power?" I remember breaking out in goose bumps. I put down the phone, went into the bathroom and cried. From the bottom of my heart, I prayed, "I don't know what to do, God. Please help me." Suddenly, I felt as though something lifted a heavy cloak from my shoulders. I'd gone back to the kitchen and was washing the dishes when I became aware of a voice singing. It was me. With all of my heart, I'd asked God for help, and my burden was lifted.

Not everyone has a sudden experience of a Higher Power. *Alcoholics Anonymous* describes the slow development of faith, but even with a sudden experience, we have to practice relying on a Higher Power each day. It's not easy.

At one point, one of my sons became addicted to drugs. I thought he would die—he could have, at any moment. I prayed for him all the time. "God, just for to-day I'm giving you the care of my son. Please watch over him." I never prayed specifically that God make every-thing right. Instead, day by day, I let go of trying to con-trol the situation. I stuck to my food plan. I asked God to be with my son. And I took action, making phone calls, doing service in FA, going to my meetings. All of this made it possible for me to stay abstinent, despite my worry, and God kept showing me that He could do a much better job helping my son than I could. Now my son's been drug free and in recovery for many years.

I learned a lot from my conversations with my spon-sor and her husband, and my early experiences in the program, but I knew intuitively that something impor-tant was missing. *Alcoholics Anonymous* is full of stories by people who no longer wanted to drink, yet every once in a while, despite my abstinence, I had what I called "the hungry horrors." For no reason, I wanted to eat as I used to. I knew I needed to find something that would completely take away my addictive desire for food, and I sensed the answer lay in the Twelve Steps.

I wanted recovery so badly that I faced my worst fears and did things I never wanted to do. I learned that some recovering alcoholics did the Steps through AWOLs (A

Way of Life)—a program that came to the United States from a treatment center in Canada. I met a woman in our program who could lead an AWOL group for us, but no matter how hard I tried, I couldn't find anyone to co-lead with her. If I wanted to do the Steps, I had to be a leader.

I was terrified, but God helped me co-lead the first AWOL. By the time we opened the second AWOL, word had spread. People were hungry for recovery. My co-leader and I opened the door to the church hall at the start of the second AWOL and saw two hundred people waiting for the meeting to begin. My knees almost gave out from under me.

As I continued to lead AWOLs, they changed me. Basically, I was a good person, but addiction brought out the worst in me. It made me impatient and angry. I was full of self-pity and negativity. Through doing the Steps in AWOL, I was able to let go of my anger at my mother and make amends to my husband and children. I learned to turn to God for help with every situation that troubled me. This gave me freedom from any urge to break my abstinence. Food became neutral for me. I didn't want to eat sweets or breads or huge quantities.

AWOLs changed the lives of everyone who did them, and we took the knowledge we gained into our meetings. Our meetings then changed, too. We spoke of ourselves as food addicts, rather than compulsive overeaters. We came to a unified definition of abstinence and emphasized the importance of doing the Steps in AWOL. We stayed abstinent and helped others gain abstinence. The program of Food Addicts in Recovery Anonymous (FA) developed as all of us grew in our recovery.

This is my thirty-eighth year since I first came into a twelve-step program and probably my thirty-fifth year of abstinence. FA and my Higher Power have helped me each step of my way. I lost my husband three years ago. It was one of the hardest times of my life.

My husband and I had been married for fifty-nine years, and it was terrible when he was gone. Sometimes I felt I didn't want to live, but food wasn't the answer. Eating wasn't the answer. The answer for me was to pick myself up and do what I needed to do. I asked God for help. I helped other people. I let go of thinking so often about how I felt. No matter what, I thanked my Higher Power for the gifts we'd received. My husband died peacefully and without suffering, in his own bed, right after we'd had a wonderful, happy vacation together.

Today, life is better. I miss my husband terribly, but I'm not lonely. I'm a blessed woman, with children who are a Godsend, and grandchildren, and even a great grandchild. I am not afraid of food, but I have a healthy respect for its power. I know that I'm an addict and that I can't play around with the substance that's my drug. There is no cure for addiction. One day at a time, for the rest of my life, I must stay away from flour, sugar, and unmeasured quantities, or I will have to go back to where I used to be.

Today and always, abstinence is my way of life, whether or not I'm in my own kitchen. No matter how I feel, I turn to God. "Help me, guide me, show me," I pray, and I make sure to give Him my thanks even in the hardest times. I never forget how much I hated being fat and how the compulsion to eat made me want to die. Through FA and with the help of my Higher Power, I lost more than 115 pounds, but that's not the most important part of my story. The miracle is that I have stayed slender for well over three decades, and that for many years I've not had even a moment of desire for anything other than my abstinent food—no matter what I've had to face.

Less Is More

❖ ❖ ❖

I GREW UP IN A BIG FAMILY. My mother died in her late thirties, when I was nine and my brother was six. My father was a good man, but he was left with seven children. He loved every one of us, and we knew it; though this was in the days before cell phones, we could always reach him by telephone. Still, it's impossible to raise seven children by phone. Basically, we grew up on our own. You can imagine the chaos.

I don't remember a lot of my childhood, but I know what I ate and how important food was to me. I went to the neighbor's up the street for Polish food. Two doors down from us, I got Italian food. The people on the first floor, right-hand side of our apartment building, had Jewish food, and across the street from us was the Irish food. I knew what everyone was eating and when they were eating it. I was the child who wanted to come to dinner and never go home.

I was always fat. As a teenager, I had a friend who loved diet pills, and I used to go to the doctor's to get the pills for her. She kept offering them to me. I refused, but, as they say, "If you hang around a barbershop long enough, you're going to get a haircut." I eventually tried the pills, and I loved them. They gave me energy and self-confidence, and they helped me stop eating.

I was 289 pounds when I started taking three diet pills a day, just as the doctor prescribed. They helped me lose weight that once; I got down to 200 pounds. I figured that if I found a man, life would be great, and with body beautiful, I went out to find one. The man I set my sights on was nineteen years older than I was and told me that he had a wife and son. He hadn't seen either of them in two years, so I took it to mean there was no issue, and we moved in together.

After my daughter was conceived, I prayed every day for a healthy baby. God granted me that prayer and my daughter was born healthy, but addiction came on me full force after her birth. Three pills worked, so four, and then five, seemed better. The pills made me want to drink more, which made me want to smoke more. In the end, they made me do everything faster. That included eating faster, and I took diet pills all the way up to where I weighed more than 350 pounds.

By this time, the sister I call my "maternal sister," who always took care of all of us, had bought a three-decker house. She gave me the apartment on the third floor, and I moved in. All of my resources went to support my addictions. I didn't pay rent or bills. The gas meter was taken out for nonpayment of my gas bills, and many times I was without heating oil. I went downstairs to my sister's house to shower, eat, and even to stay warm. I was enmeshed in her family in a way that I never should have been.

This went on for many years, and then, one day, I reached the end of my rope. I remember sitting at the kitchen table upstairs, holding my head in my hands. I said, "God, please, someday, make me normal without these pills." I knew I had a pill addiction. I also recognized that I had a problem with alcohol, but I still didn't know that I was addicted to food.

Prayer never falls on deaf ears. If we really want help and truly ask for it, we receive the help we need. God was always in my life, taking care of me whether I knew it or not, but after I prayed about the pills, God went to work, and the pills were taken away from me, little by little. Doctors stopped giving prescriptions because of legal pressures. One druggist closed his shop, and another was arrested. I could still get the pills on the street, but they were expensive. My one hope of a source was a doctor who would provide four months of pills, but if patients didn't lose weight, he wouldn't write a prescription for more.

During this time, I went to a bridal shower, and I saw a woman I'd known all my life, an old family friend. I was amazed by how beautiful she looked. She was an extreme dieter. Sometimes she'd been over 300 pounds, and sometimes she'd been down to 120. This time, she looked stunning. As soon as she came to my table, I asked her what she was doing. She said that she was in a program, not eating flour and sugar, and that she had met a wonderful man who was also in the program. He'd once been over 485 pounds. Now at normal weight, they were dating and very happy. I thought to myself, *She's thin, she's happy, and she's got a new boyfriend. Sign me up. I'm ready to go.*

My friend told me about a meeting nearby. I went as soon as I could, and there I first heard about our program of recovery from food addiction. I listened to the people who spoke from the front of the room. I remember one man in particular, who said, "The only exercise I do in the morning is to bend my knees." He was referring to how he got on his knees to ask his Higher Power for a day of abstinence, but I didn't have a clue what he was talking about. Still, I thought to myself, *I can bend my knees.* Others spoke of taking care of their children and their families.

I loved what I heard, but I went home from the meeting, and, as I had planned, I went to the food that was on my stove and ate it. Something in me had changed, though, and the food didn't taste the same. I promised myself I would go to another meeting.

That weekend, when I went to another meeting, my life began to change. I heard hope. God also had me hear something else I needed, because one of the members said, "Don't leave this room without a sponsor."

I approached the friend I'd seen at the bridal shower, and she agreed to work with me. She once told me that she and my sister taught me how to walk when I was a child. I always say that she taught me how to walk twice, because she became my first sponsor, my first guide, in the program. Standing outside the church where we'd met, she told me about the tools—the daily actions we take in order to abstain from addictive eating. She spoke of sponsorship, of the need to read literature and attend meetings, and, just as I was leaving, she held up her finger and said, "Oh, and no medication."

I was horrified, so I just turned and walked away. I had a plan, after all, which was to come to the program, lose 50 pounds, get my four months of diet pills from the doctor, and say goodbye to the program and all the people in it. I just needed to lose weight to get my pills.

So I went home and used the program as a diet. I was at least 350 pounds when I began. I don't know exactly how much I weighed because I couldn't find a scale big enough to weigh me. Being over 350 pounds and not eating flour and sugar (for the most part), while weighing and measuring my food (for the most part), I was bound to lose weight. The pounds fell off, and the doctor thought I was magnificent. I was his marvel child.

For three or four months, I continued to go to meetings. I heard people talk about how they took their children to school on time, how they cleaned their bathrooms regularly, how they stayed abstinent from addictive eating one day at a time, and how they faced all the stresses of life, though none of them looked stressed. They were smiling and obviously happy. I sat silent at each meeting, and every once in a while, I went on a secret toot. I'd have a drink, or I'd go to a bar and end the night by weighing and measuring my dinner at two o'clock in the morning. I was still taking pills and living a crazy life.

One day, my sponsor told me that I needed to participate in the meetings, explaining that I had to at least stand in the front of the room and read aloud one of the passages that are part of each meeting. That night, I raised my hand and was chosen for the section of *Alcoholics Anonymous* that describes how the program works. I began with the words "Rarely have we seen a person fail who has thoroughly followed our path. Those who do not recover are people who cannot or will not completely give themselves to this simple program, usually men and women who are constitutionally incapable of being honest with themselves."

I couldn't finish reading. I began crying and had to sit down. I thought, *My God, I can't do this program. I'm one of those who is constitutionally incapable.* At the meeting, I cried and cried and cried. And then I went home, and I cried some more. I knew that I had been lying through my teeth, but then again, I'd read in *Alcoholics Anonymous* that if I became honest, I would have a shot at recovery. I promised myself I was going to take that shot, so I called my sponsor the next morning and told her everything that I had been doing. She just said, "Who did you hurt? You only hurt yourself. So what are you going to do now?"

I have no doubt about who is in charge of our lives. My lying about the pills had bothered me most of all, and I reminded my sponsor of our talk outside the church, when she had said, "No medication." I understood her to mean that I should never take pills, but we finally figured out that she had actually said, "Oh, and meditation," which is one of our daily disciplines. I had heard what I needed to hear. God works miracles through people, but it's God who's in charge.

I decided to put the pills down and give this program my all. I was determined to do everything that was suggested and to follow the examples of the people I most admired. Soon afterward, I heard someone at a meeting say that she was going to ninety meetings in ninety days. I had come into our program resisting even the suggestion that I go to three meetings a week. How could I do that? I was a single mother! But when I was ready to really reach for my recovery, I thought, *Instead of taking a pill, I am going to go to a meeting every day.*

I was busy in my new life. If I wasn't at a meeting, I was talking on the phone to someone else in the program. If I wasn't on the phone, I was reading some literature or doing my morning meditation, or getting on my knees to ask my Higher Power for help. Above all, I joined an AWOL, a closed group for doing the Twelve Steps in sequence.

Once I was in AWOL, I hit a crisis and a turning point in my recovery. When I began in the program, I got away with a food plan that was quite loose. I would tell my sponsor that I planned to eat "two pieces of chicken," and that was fine. When I had to change sponsors, though, my new sponsor had another idea. She said, "Oh, no, you can't eat 'two pieces of chicken.' You need to measure four ounces of chicken. No bones, no skin. Put four ounces of chicken on the scale."

I thought I was going to starve to death. I was about 300 pounds, and I had been eating the biggest boneless chicken breasts anyone could find in a store—two of them. I depended on that chicken. I said to her, "Look. You've got the flour. You've got the sugar. You've got the booze and the drugs. You aren't getting the chicken. The chicken is mine. I'm drawing the line here. You people are just too much. You're going to push me over the edge." Of course, I needed to go over the edge—to let go of my dependence on food.

I cried and fought about the chicken. My sponsor just spoke nicely to me again. She asked me to do what she suggested for just one day: "I want you to ask God for help to measure four ounces of chicken on the scale and put it on your plate. Eat the meat. Say, 'Thank you, God, for an abstinent meal' and know that it is enough. Less is more."

My eyeballs rolled back in my head. I knew that less could never be more, but at last, in desperation, I did as I was told. To be willing to measure the chicken, I had to lean on God. Less chicken meant more God, and by the end of that day, I was full of God. My Higher Power had done for me what I absolutely could not do for myself. I actually felt God inside of me—the God of my own understanding.

Now I say there are two days that I'll always consider the best days of my life. One was when my daughter was born healthy. The other was the day that I was finally willing to let go of my obsession with food and put the chicken on a scale. I will never get over either experience as long as I live, because both were direct gifts from God.

Through doing the Steps in AWOL, we food addicts are given the gift of a personality change, and we experience many miracles. My prayers for recovery were answered, and my life became more normal. During the year and a half of my first AWOL, I got a full-time job and got off welfare. Over 200 pounds came off my body. My house began to become a home. I got a telephone.

My daughter and I started becoming a family. On the nights I was committed to going to a meeting, she'd get my coat beforehand and ask me if it was time to go.

Doing the Twelve Steps and living them each day, I felt like God was plucking me out of a muddy swamp and dipping me in a warm pond to clean me. Eventually, I decided to move. It was terribly hard for me to leave my sister's house because she had taken care of me for years. I felt grateful to her, but I believed my moving would be best for all involved.

I learned a lot from that decision. When we take care of ourselves and do whatever we need to do for our own recovery, it is best for everyone else, too. As it turned out, everything worked out beautifully. My sister had space for her own children when they needed it, and I moved into a home that was just right for my daughter and me.

Today, I am as grateful as ever for FA. There have been rough times, but I have stayed continuously abstinent. When my daughter became a teenager, she gave me a run for my money. Given the addictions in our family and all the signs of addiction I saw in her, I was afraid for her life. One day, she cursed and screamed in my face, "I can't wait to get out of this house!"

Instead of turning to food for comfort or escape each time I struggled with my daughter, I called others in FA to find out how they handled their own teenagers. I learned that I could ask God to help me stay strong and to keep my abstinence from addictive eating as my top priority. Abstinence and prayer allowed me to face what I had to, one day at a time. If I hadn't been in FA, I would have been in a bar and eating long into the night. I would have been drowning in my addiction. Instead, my daughter knew she had a mother she could count on.

Over the years, because of doing the FA program and being the person I need to be—a person in recovery—my relationship with my daughter has been transformed. I can't remember the last time we fought. I see her daily. She has two young children herself, and those granddaughters are the light of my life.

These days, I don't recognize myself sometimes. If I am angry or having trouble with something, if I'm uncomfortable or afraid, with every breath I breathe in God and blow out fear. I talk with God throughout the day. I say, "God, please help me." I ask questions. "God, how would you handle this situation, or how would you like me to handle it?" I try to see through God's eyes, or through other people's eyes even, so I can understand their experience.

My change in attitude has had a big effect on my relationships at my job. In the past, I didn't have the time of day for anyone I worked with, but now I enjoy the people at my office. When the papers pile high, the phones are ringing, and people are running out for cigarettes and getting annoyed, I stay calm. I look for the good side of things instead of focusing on the negatives. I talk with God, thank God, and I handle myself and the customers well. I appreciate them, and they appreciate me.

I wish that people in my family wanted this program, but they do not. I love them dearly. They have made their own decisions for their lives, and we accept each other's differences. I am not responsible for anyone else; I am just responsible for myself. So I keep my side of the street clean, hoping my own recovery will ripple out toward everyone around me. I try to share what I have received, but if there is no interest, I know I am powerless.

I'm fifty-five years old now, and I'm still slender. More than 200 pounds have come off my body and stayed off. I have faced deaths and births, showers and weddings, happy times and sad times. Through it all, I've turned to God and abstained from addictive eating—now for twenty-five years. Every day, my life gets better and my gratitude deepens. I'm still changing. God hasn't finished working on me yet.

A Rock to Stand On

✧ ✧ ✧

I CAME INTO A TWELVE-STEP program for food when I was twenty-six, and I joined FA when I was thirty-three. I am sixty-one years old now, so I've spent almost half my life in FA. The biggest gifts of the program are my abstinence and my understanding, at last, that I *have* *to* trust my Higher Power. I'm a person with only two options: fear, which would inevitably drive me back into my addiction, and trust, which is the basis of recovery.

My grandparents immigrated to the U.S. from Asia, and my parents were both born on the West Coast. After their marriage, my parents moved farther and farther east, until they ended up on the other side of the country. My brother and I grew up in a big house on a dirt road that was bordered by acres of beautiful meadows and trees.

I didn't understand how hard my mother's life was until I'd been abstinent many years. My father's work was his top priority. He was distant and accustomed to Asian patterns of relationship. My mother was more

American and was openly enraged. Our home was tense. My mother screamed and yelled, my father withdrew. I was afraid of my mother's sharp criticism, which was often directed at me, so it seemed best not to reveal myself or to attempt anything new. I grew up as a passive, hidden little girl, offering few opinions and spending much of my time alone, lost in books or studying.

More than any other emotion in my childhood, I remember fear. Because of my anxiety, I didn't want to eat, and I was thin for many years. Oddly, my one assertion as a young child was that I would never marry or have children. I was especially scared of men, and as far as I could tell, marriage looked like a terrible fate.

The physical and mental part of my disease became evident when I was in the eighth grade. We addicts don't live in reality, and when I noticed that I was developing curves, slender though I was, I believed that I was fat. The next year, I tried to solve this problem by a total fast. I ran every morning, worked out with the track team every afternoon, and took in only water for almost a week. The fasting made me feel strong and superior. I had a goal, and I accomplished it. I liked the sensation of dizziness every time I stood up, and I didn't worry about ending my fast with several servings of baked goods and sweets. Being a person of extremes, I repeated my fast the following year, bingeing on sweets again at the end. That was the last time I was ever able to abstain from eating for any length of time.

I had a life filled with opportunities, but I didn't know how to grow up. By the eleventh grade, I was intensely afraid of boys and men, of not succeeding, of making a mistake, of having to choose where to go and what to do. I couldn't understand how to make a decision. On what basis should I choose one place over another? I was afraid of all options. Food, especially desserts, helped numb me to my anxiety, so I ate as much as I could. My arms and legs became thick and heavy. I felt like a block of margarine.

I don't know how much I weighed when I graduated from high school because I was afraid to stand on a scale, but it almost doesn't matter. From the time I started blunting my feelings by turning to food in large quantities, my life narrowed. I twisted in and against myself, and I'm sure any doctor would have diagnosed me as clinically depressed. I couldn't brush my teeth or comb my hair. I wore dirty clothes and slept in dirty sheets. I disdained makeup and never learned how to buy nice shoes or match a skirt to a blouse. I felt unable to talk with my classmates and teachers, so I stayed silent most of the time. Worst of all, I began hearing a voice in my head that repeated over and over, "I hate myself. I wish I were dead."

After high school I didn't know what to do. Since my family was going to Japan, I went, too. My parents and brother settled in the north, and I enrolled in a university elsewhere. Instead of feeling excited, I was terrified, so I withdrew into intensive study and took four years of Japanese in a one-year program. The only students able to complete the course were from China (because they already knew how to write the characters), missionaries (who could speak Japanese), and me, because I studied like a maniac. I practiced writing characters and memorizing sentence patterns morning, noon, and late into the night, seven days a week. I also ate huge quantities of sweets, always secretly, and therefore often in bathrooms. I gained even more weight.

In many ways, the patterns I established in Japan played out for the rest of my life until I finally found FA. I was never at peace. The push to excel clashed with my feeling of certainty that I would fail. I could never meet my own pridefully high, perfectionistic standards. My urge to eat rammed into my equally powerful drive to be thin. I couldn't bear my feelings of anxiety and self-hate. I tried years of therapy, many kinds of diets, prayer, crystals. Nothing helped me stop eating and stay stopped.

I had two lives: one outside and one inside. I often looked all right on the outside. I came back to the U.S. and graduated from a good university here. I wrote a book. I returned to Japan and walked a nine-hundred-mile traditional pilgrimage. I had friends.

Inside, I felt increasingly unable to cope. My illness got worse. I ate larger and larger quantities of baked goods and candies, but they no longer blunted my terrible feelings. Sometimes I bit and scratched myself because I couldn't stand the pressure of my self-hate. I gained and lost weight, losing a little less and gaining a little more each time.

At one point, I found a twelve-step program for compulsive overeaters. By drinking dozens of cans of diet soda, eating pounds of low-calorie vegetables, and avoiding flour and sugar, I lost so much weight that I became emaciated. Then, after two and a half years of extreme thinness, I had one bite of a whole wheat muffin and completely lost control. From then on, I threw up after every binge, sometimes many times a day. Because of all I ate, I continued to gain weight, and though I was actively involved in the twelve-step food program, I was both bulimic *and* fat.

I found FA when, during a short period of remission from bingeing and purging, I was accepted into a graduate program. At that point, I wasn't at my top weight or in the worst of my depression. I actually felt hope for the first time in my life. I loved the school program and thought I'd be ready for a profession once I graduated.

I had always believed that if I were happy I wouldn't be driven to eat, but as I eagerly started school, I realized that my happiness wasn't going to keep me from eating. In an attempt to keep myself from bingeing on baked goods, I was eating huge quantities of vegetables and salad. I was barely in control. The bakery would be next. Finally, I saw through the wall of denial that stood between me and the facts of my life. I had always failed when it came to food, and I was going to fail again, despite every ounce of my will power, my feeling of happiness, and my every wish.

Hopelessness was my entry ticket into FA. By the grace of my Higher Power, someone took me to an FA meeting. I didn't like it. Back home, in the other twelve-step program, everyone praised me for my eloquence. In FA, of all the insults, I wasn't invited to speak because I wasn't abstinent. The food plan was horrendous. Plain meat. Plain vegetables. Hardly any salad dressing. Everything had to be weighed and measured. Nothing made sense.

Why measure celery or green beans when they had hardly any calories? What was the matter with an apple at three o'clock if my blood sugar had gotten low?

I came into FA because I had nowhere else to go. I was angry and convinced that it would never work for me, even though it worked for other people. I am still amazed that we don't have to like the program or believe that it will work. We just have to have an open mind and *do* the program in its entirety. When we're open and willing, FA always works.

The first morning I called my sponsor I belligerently told her I'd commit to my food plan for the day but I wouldn't guarantee I'd do it the next day. She said fine. I made it through that first day abstinently and called her the next morning. Again, I had a bad attitude. I gave her my commitment for one day only, but once more, she said fine. On the third day of my abstinence, my attitude changed. Instead of heaviness and anger, I felt happy and free. I was shocked when my sponsor told me my happiness was the result of my abstinence. In seven years of failure in the other twelve-step program, I had aimed to be happy and thin. I had never thought of abstinence as the ultimate, central goal, with happiness a by-product of it.

My euphoria in FA was short lived. By my fourth day, I was exhausted and my legs ached. I felt as though my skin had been peeled off, and I had to function without a layer of protection I'd always depended on. Through eating and purging, I'd tried to numb myself to the fear and insecurity I felt each day. Without food, my anxiety was almost unbearable. Worst of all, I was suddenly *in* my body, feeling and seeing that I'd become fat. Binge-ing and purging had somehow created a curtain between me and my hated body. Abstinence took that curtain away.

In FA, I met people who were slender and continu-ously abstinent, success that amazed me. After years of bingeing, severe undereating, and bulimia, I felt doomed to failure. This was arrogant in its own way. Why wouldn't the program work for me if it worked for every-one else? At the same time, I had a new humility. When my sponsor gave me a suggestion I didn't understand or didn't like, I reminded myself that I'd just crawled into FA. In contrast, she had five years of abstinence. Clearly, she knew something I didn't know. Instead of rebelling, I followed 100 percent of her suggestions.

I walked onto a different planet when I entered FA. Whether with food or drink, I'd always tried to fill my mouth with sweetness and my stomach with *anything*, so that I could escape my uncomfortable feelings. In FA, instead of having food that interested me and filled me up, I ate according to a plan given to me by my spon-sor. Each meal was starkly simple, with strict boundar-ies, so I could no longer make eating the focus of each day. When I also stopped drinking liters of diet soda and using packets and packets of artificial sweeteners, I was freed from my dependence on anything that I put into my mouth.

My sponsor helped me see that my abstinence in FA had to be my top priority. I had to accommodate my life to the needs of my recovery, rather than trying to cram recovery into my life. Struggling against my pride,

I finally cut back on my school schedule so that I'd be sure to have time to go to my committed FA meetings each week. I also had to stop isolating. Instead of withdrawing in silence to try to solve my problems myself, I learned to talk about my anxieties and confusion with my sponsor and others in FA. Since there were no cell phones in those days, I used pay phones that were scattered throughout the campus. My purse was heavy with dimes. I remember often phoning one kind FA member who told me repeatedly, "You can make it through today. Just don't eat one bite of food that is not on your food plan, and things will get better."

Early on, and most important, I was reminded to "ask God for help." My parents are dedicated Quakers and I was raised as a Quaker, but I had no feeling that there was any kind of Power that could help me. I did clearly understand that I didn't have the power to keep myself abstinent, though, so each morning, I obediently got on my knees to ask for the gift of a day of abstinence, and each night I knelt to say thank you. Whenever I had something frightening to face, my FA friends kept reminding me to turn to a Higher Power.

I followed all suggestions. I was willing to change many of my actions and attitudes. A schedule that was too intense to support my abstinence? I cut back on my schedule. The unwelcome suggestion that I gain weight when I got too thin? I accepted a heavier food plan. A conflict between an FA meeting and an Asian American community event I'd been looking forward to attending for weeks? I went to my FA meeting. An uncorrectable problem with my fertility because of my years of undereating and bulimia? I sadly accepted the consequences of my illness.

Because of FA, my life got better. I learned to accept responsibility and to think of the needs of others. I led meetings, stayed in contact with other FA members, did the Steps in AWOLs, and eventually led AWOLs myself. For the first time in my life, I practiced gratitude and appreciation. I thanked my parents for their help and generosity, and I did all I could to be a good daughter to them. I groomed myself and wore clean clothes. I found and held a job. The depression I'd experienced since high school disappeared completely once I got abstinent.

Throughout the years, I did ask God for guidance, and I thanked God for the many blessings I received, but I had a problem. I didn't really believe there was a Power that would completely take care of me. To be more precise, I didn't believe there was a Power that would take care of me exactly the way I wanted to be taken care of. I felt I had to succeed, whether at school or in a job. My security depended on good results, as I defined them—not good results as God might define them. At the deepest level, I wouldn't let go of my own agenda. I was unwilling to depend on and trust in God's good care.

Though I progressed in my recovery, my footing had not fundamentally changed. I had never completely let go of my fear. This became clear within my first five years in the program, when I completed my degree in graduate school and got my first job. I was put in charge of a college's health insurance program. I am terrible at handling details, and as I floundered, my anxiety intensified to the level of panic. Fear blocked my ability to think, and instead I reacted, making foolish errors.

One morning, in the midst of this scary time, my sponsor asked, "Are you paying your installments and putting them into the bank?" I thought she was referring to the need for daily actions that ensure continuous abstinence, so I mumbled that I was going to meetings and making phone calls. "No," she said. "Are you practicing gratitude? Each day, if you look for all the things that make you feel grateful and you thank God for them, you'll see God and be with God throughout the day. That will take away your fear."

After our conversation, I did thank God to some extent, but mostly I got through my difficulties by leaning on a supervisor. My sponsor was asking me to strengthen my footing by depending on spiritual help. Instead, I relied on tools like meetings, phone calls, aid from another human being, and my own will.

As the years went by, at the deepest level, I kept trying to live life on my own terms. Whenever I failed to succeed, I tried harder. If that didn't work, I tried even harder. If that didn't work, I quit. This was fine until after about ten years of abstinence, I got a job that was beyond my experience. I could have tried as hard as possible, accepting the results and trusting that a Higher Power would either turn a difficult situation around or lead me to a different job. Instead, I became paralyzed by fear. I felt sure I couldn't succeed, but I couldn't quit, because my sponsor urged me to keep trying. "Ask God for help and accept the results," she said, yet again.

In the end, because I wouldn't turn to a Higher Power with trust and acceptance, I fell apart. Every morning, I woke up in anxiety, dreading the rest of the day. I obsessively fantasized that a twenty-ton truck would run into the back of my car and break most of my bones. I didn't want to be dead. I just wanted to be incapacitated. I longed to be given an escape from my job by the need for a year or two of physical rehabilitation. I almost broke my abstinence. At a reception one night, I looked at some cake. I knew one bite would be catastrophic, but I didn't care.

Physical abstinence did not keep me from feeling so desperate and frantic that I was nearly driven back into my addiction. I am grateful to the Higher Power that kept me from the cake, despite myself, and to my sponsor, who wisely suggested that I start my program over, from Step One. Accepting that I was in no shape to help anyone else, I let go of all my sponsees, stopped leading my AWOL, ceased speaking at meetings, and began again. I gave notice at work, but my employers asked me to stay, and they put some supports in place that helped make it possible.

God took care of me. Four years later, I felt I had to leave my job when my supervisors were not pleased with my work. Painful as that was for me, I felt intensely grateful for my changed attitude. My sponsor encouraged me to hold my head high, because, she said, I was abstinent and had tried my best. I didn't allow myself to listen to the old voices of shame and self-criticism. Instead of carrying on about feelings of "pain," I spoke of myself as being "uncomfortable."

Most important, I kept abstinence my top priority by making peace of mind, not my job, my biggest concern. Asking my Higher Power for guidance and following through as I was guided, I left the job, but with a severance package I never imagined possible. That support gave me almost a full year of freedom, during which I wrote, played the piano, and gave service in FA. A great life!

Since that time, I've had several other jobs, one of which, again, I did not match and had to leave. My mother died suddenly, and as each year passes, I realize more acutely how much I love and miss her. My father is now ninety-five and struggling with the loss of his cognitive abilities. For all my love, I can't spare him his pain and anxiety.

God helped me, and continues to help me, face such life situations abstinently. I've never had a sudden spiritual experience that profoundly altered my experience of life all at once. I've grown slowly. My faith has been faltering, but I've always tried my best, and as *Alcoholics Anonymous* promises, our best is enough. God builds on whatever faith we have to make it stronger.

When I was about twenty years abstinent, it came to me that I had never been willing to believe that God could restore me to sanity in *all* areas of my life. I was still afraid of men and marriage. It took me all those twenty years, but at last I fully took Step Two and became willing to trust that God could help me think and keep me safe. Some months later, I began dating a man I'd broken up with four years before. I'd never have chosen him for myself, but God chose him for me, and we married about a year and a half later. I have never laughed as hard as I laugh with my husband. I have never before loved anyone or trusted anyone as I love and trust him.

Today, I've been abstinent for twenty-nine years. Thanks to my Higher Power and FA, I'm slender but not too thin (five feet, two inches tall and about 107 or 108 pounds). My weight is stable, and I've had no episodes of bulimia. When we are willing to let go, God gives us a life beyond what we could ever think possible. I am a writer now, and I work with my husband on our family farm. I cannot imagine a better life.

Gratitude and faith are easy when life goes my way, but the road inevitably gets bumpy sometimes. I know I'm vulnerable to fear and self-hate, and I can't afford either one of them. I'm a person who can't face my life by myself. I have to have a hand to hold and a rock to stand on. God gives me a hand to hold. My trust and reliance on God's hand give me my rock.

The Open Door

✧ ✧ ✧

I WAS BASICALLY RAISED by my mother. Although my brother and I had a father, he was a political organizer and was not home. Most of the time he could not live with us, so my mother performed the Herculean task of raising us while carrying two jobs and going to school.

Money was very scarce in my home. In one community where we lived, I was not aware of being poor because everyone was poor, but when I was in about fourth grade, we moved to a wealthy place that had a better school system. I discovered then that children in the neighborhood had things called snacks. They had refrigerators that were filled with food and dressers that were filled with clothes. They had closets with hangers, each with a dress or a blouse. This was foreign to me. I had one set of clothes to play in and one set of clothes to go to school in. That was it.

In the transition from a poorer environment to a wealthy one, I learned that there were boundaries and that I didn't know them. There were ways of living I didn't understand. Children made fun of me because I didn't know the rules. I wore outside boots into homes with carpeting, and I accidently burned a neighbor's table when I put a pot of pudding I'd cooked on top of it. I wasn't invited back to that house again.

I think if I had shared my sadness and sense of deprivation with my mother, she would have dealt with it lovingly, but when I came into the world, the first thing I ever said was "no." This was shortly followed by "I can do it myself." Words to share my feelings of aloneness and loss were not in my vocabulary. I became self-sufficient and invulnerable, or so I thought. The other children taunted and teased me because I didn't have the right clothes or know all the rules, but that didn't bother *me!*

I found another way to buttress myself. Our family valued education and the arts, so, though I didn't have a big wardrobe, I was given piano and ballet and painting lessons at the settlement house. I wasn't particularly good at anything, unlike my brother, who was excellent at many things. I've since learned that everything takes practice, but I was never someone who wanted to practice. Fundamentally, I was lazy, so I took the approach of believing that my lack of accomplishments and any other problems I had weren't my fault. I wasn't a good ballerina because I stopped taking ballet before I went up on toe. That was the ballet master's fault. I didn't do well in certain grades or writing certain papers because the teacher didn't teach well. I wasn't a good pianist because my mother didn't make me practice.

When I became an adult, food assumed a central place in my life. My brother might have been brilliant, but I was a good eater. Food gave me solace and a sense of accomplishment and possibility. It led me to an understanding of my culture and religion.

I'm a Jew. As I saw it, Passover and the holiday feasts were critical to a Jewish home. Because I had to create those feasts, I certainly needed to experiment throughout the year to make sure that the food would be appropriate. To this day, there are dishes that my children can't stand to see. I was a food pusher. I made the food, and they had to eat it. "Don't you want this?" I urged. "Of course you like it. No? All right, tomorrow I'll make it with a little more cinnamon." I don't know how many recipes I had for noodle pudding.

Of course, I also had many recipes that were not Jewish. I prided myself on my interest in other cultures, but in fact, the diversity of cultures in my life came from my cookbooks. I had floor-to-ceiling bookcases in every room in my house, and the kitchen and dining room bookcases held cookbooks from all over the world. When I first came into FA, letting go of my cookbooks and all but a few of my baking pans and utensils was terribly hard. How I grieved! I literally cried when I got rid of my cheesecake pans—all twelve sizes of them. Without them, I didn't know who I was. If I wasn't reading about how to make something, trying to make something, or fantasizing about the crowds that would one day love my catered food and pay me a million dollars for it, who was I? Maybe I was an ordinary mother. Maybe I was a housewife. I could not admit in any way, shape, manner, or form that I was "just" a housewife, but that's who I was.

I began FA when I was thirty-five. By then, I'd lost the ability or even the desire to take care of myself. I didn't like sugar as much as I liked flour and grease. There was never a day in my house when the butter wasn't on the counter, ready for spreading. I'd had three babies in less than five years. By the time the last baby was born and was about six months old, I'd decided it wasn't worth it to dress. I lived in nightgowns and housecoats, which fit over my fat. They were comfortable and convenient since I was always nursing one child or another.

I was haunted by fears and was afraid to leave my house. I never answered the door or the phone. I thought if I left my home, someone would try to steal my children. If I drove, a car accident might kill them. I might run into someone and she would see that my clothes didn't fit me anymore. She'd notice that my hair was thin. So I stayed behind my door and watched everything that I ate. I was sure I accounted for every bite, and I could not understand why I weighed 190 pounds. I must have weighed myself sixty-two times a day. I'd get on the scale in the bathroom, but I didn't like what it read. The bathroom had a tile floor. It seemed best to take the scale out onto the smoother, wooden floor. That had seams in it, though, so I'd put the scale on top of a chair, which was just one plank of wood, and then I would climb up on top of the chair to see my weight.

All the while, I kept telling myself I wasn't really fat. I wasn't 200 pounds, after all. I was only 190. I didn't like my appearance, but the real truth was that I loathed myself, not really because of how I looked or what I ate but because I wasn't who I thought I should be. I should have been someone who would be able to open the front door, walk out, and live in the world successfully. My deepest, darkest secret was that I couldn't open that door. I could not walk out into the world, much less live in it successfully.

One morning, I decided I needed to have the piano tuned. No one in the family played the piano. We had it because I thought every cultured home should have a piano. I called the piano tuner, who came over at two o'clock in the afternoon and found me in my nightgown. She showed me a program from a concert she'd played. The photo of her in the program did not match the person in front of me. The picture was of a fat woman, and the woman before me was thin. I said, "You don't look anything like the woman in the photo." She replied, "That's because I'm in a twelve-step program for food addiction. Would you like to know about it?"

I was furious that she alluded to food and that she would think I might in any way be interested, so I didn't answer. She thought I misunderstood and elaborated. "It's kind of like Alcoholics Anonymous. Have you ever heard of that?" Of course I had. My mother is a Gestalt therapist and had worked with alcoholics. When she asked me if I wanted to know more, I said no, showed her to the door, and slammed it shut behind her.

The moment the piano tuner left, I went upstairs and looked up her organization in the phone book. I decided I would give a meeting a try. The only problem was that it was in the next town. That meant that I had to take a ten-minute drive. I felt like I was being asked to go to California. When I walked into the meeting the next day, I was covered with sweat and my hair was plastered to my face. I was terrified.

At the meeting, the woman telling her story was thin, but she mentioned that her daughter was morbidly obese. She said, "I just put my daughter in God's hands every day, and I'm not afraid anymore." I thought, *Oh, my God, she's not afraid for the welfare of her child. I want that. I don't want to be afraid all the time.* The world lit up. My heart opened. I asked the woman to sponsor me, not even knowing what that meant. She said she was sorry, but she had so many sponsees she had no time. I left the room crying, sure that she thought I was ugly, that I wasn't dressed correctly, that once more I wasn't enough.

I know there is a God because the next week, I went to the meeting again. I could not have gotten there under my own power. I can't say that I had an open mind, but agoraphobia and all, I got into the car and I drove to that second meeting. During that hour and a half, I felt safe. My fears abated.

I began attending the program, but I kept doing things my way. I heard someone say, "Take what you want and leave the rest," so that's what I did. I took what I wanted, and I left the rest. Most of what I didn't want involved what we call the tools, the actions we take to stay abstinent, like using the phone to stay in contact with other members of the program each day.

I was also unwilling to change my attitudes. All the talk about quiet time and God made me uneasy. I didn't think it was anyone's business what I thought of God or what I didn't think of God. I also didn't agree when people in FA told me not to coddle thoughts of food.

"Don't let sugarplums dance in your head," they said. I thought they were silly. I could bake as much as I wanted to bake. I lived in a fantasy world, dreaming of myself as a great caterer and imagining the wonderful rewards that my cooking would bring me.

One day, I thought I had truly arrived. I was triumphantly slender, and I was asked to cater chocolate brownies for a party at a prestigious law school. After I delivered and served the brownies without a problem, I took the next logical step. There were no chocolatiers near me in those days, and finer chocolates were accessible only through catalogues. I consulted mine and ordered 10 pounds of Belgian chocolate for my next cooking adventure. I was never asked to cater anything again, of course, but I was ready.

Once the chocolate arrived, I wondered if it would be as good as the catalogue said it would be. I tasted a bit to be sure and knew that I had broken my abstinence from addictive eating. I figured I'd get right back on track. After a couple of days, I told my sponsor that I had broken my abstinence but that I was fine again. I put the chocolate in the freezer because I knew if I had it in the freezer, I wouldn't touch it. Unfortunately, I did touch it. I went back and ate all of it. I ate all night long, padding back and forth to the freezer. I was desperate not to eat, but I couldn't stop. When the chocolate was gone, I took the foil and paper it had been wrapped in and threw them away in a neighbor's trash bin so my husband wouldn't know what I had done.

The program got me to my goal weight, but as the incident with the chocolate proved, I wasn't cured. "Thin isn't well," we say, and I proved that true. Weight was not my real problem. My problem was that I continued to fantasize about food and to focus on it. In FA, I was asked to fundamentally change my attitude. I had to let go of making food the center of my life and of pushing it on my children. I wasn't ready for any of that, so I ate again. And again.

One day I was eating a meal when my son started howling. Without thinking, I hit him with my fist and knocked the wind out of him. He looked at me with his big eyes and cried. We were both stunned. I was never raised with violence, and yet I hit my child. I realized then that I had the alcoholic rage described in *Alcoholics Anonymous*. My fury came from nowhere. I never thought that I would be capable of abusing one of my children, but whatever made child abusers harm their children lived in me.

Sobbing, I called someone from FA, who told me, "The only answer is abstinence." I cried about my unmanageable life, my love for my children, my shock that I had hurt one of them. She said again, "The only thing you can do is to get abstinent." She assured me that if I were abstinent, everything else would fall into place. She said I had to put my recovery first.

The next day, I went to a meeting, and I got abstinent. I didn't count my days of abstinence. Instead, every day, all day long, I said, "Thank you, God, I'm abstinent. Thank you, God, I'm abstinent. Thank you, God, I'm abstinent." I'd been told that a person with a grateful heart doesn't eat, and it is true. A grateful person is never driven to break his or her abstinence.

In the beginning, I had a checklist, and every night, I looked at my list of the tools we use to stay abstinent. Did I make phone calls to other FA members? Did I get on my knees in the morning and ask for another day of abstinence? Did I take my quiet meditation time? Did I call my sponsor to talk about my food plan and my day, and did I eat three weighed and measured meals? Did I read the *Twenty-Four Hours a Day* book in the morning? Did I read a little bit from *Alcoholics Anonymous* at night? Did I go to a committed meeting? Did I get down on my knees to say thank you to God for a day of abstinence?

I made a check after every question, and I felt like a million dollars. I had a huge sense of accomplishment. I couldn't play the piano like Vladimir Horowitz. I wasn't able to tune a car. I didn't dress beautifully. My children didn't receive all A's in school. But because I had taken care of myself and my recovery, I went to bed without any feeling of fear.

One day at a time, for twenty-eight years now, I have continued to stay abstinent. The suggestion that I turn to my Higher Power for help has been key to my recovery. At first, I didn't understand why people kept saying that I should "ask God for help." What did "God" have to do with whatever problem I was facing at the time?! I was desperate to remain abstinent, though, and I knew that my feelings of fear and anger could drive me back to the food, so, alien though it was, I did keep asking God for help.

Slowly but surely, through my own experience, I came to understand that there was a Power that could help me.

That Power made me feel satisfied after finishing what felt like one miniscule meal after another. It allowed me to contain my anger, to accept my children for who they were, and to make phone calls to FA members I'd never met so I could talk about feelings and situations that were troubling me. No voice boomed down from heaven saying, "I am God. You are abstinent. Listen to me." Instead, I discovered that if I wanted help, I had to ask for it. Whenever I've asked, especially in the midst of turmoil, fear, or loneliness, I've been given an answer— sometimes one as simple as "Wait." And I've learned, of course, that I must always say thank you.

As I practiced the FA program, my life changed radically. I got a small job that eventually led to several promotions and a position of major responsibility. At one point, my organization sent me to New York City for a conference. I bought my first briefcase and went to the train station with my husband and children. As they waved goodbye, all my bravado left and my heart sank.

Once I reached the city, I found my way to the hotel. First on the schedule was a huge welcoming meeting. Before I went in, I called an FA member to help me remember the principles of the program, and then I consciously turned to God and walked into the room. In all my life, I could never go into a room of strangers without feeling terribly afraid, but this time I entered quietly. I walked through the crowd with a smile. No one came up to me, no one wanted to know who I was, but I did not run away. There was a big, open door into that room, and thanks to FA, I walked through it.

These days, I live in a smaller home than I used to have. I've divorced and remarried. My children have grown and live in other countries and places. I have a fulfilling job. My life is full and rich and deep because I put my program and recovery first. At sixty-two years old, I'm in the love affair of my life with my own husband, and there's not a day that goes by that I'm not grateful for all that God has done for me.

The Gift of Desperation

✧ ✧ ✧

FOR ALMOST HALF MY LIFE, I've been standing in front of twelve-step meetings describing myself as a food addict. Many other things have changed, but the fact that I am a food addict will never change.

Food plays a big part in my family history. Every one of my siblings has turned out to be a food addict, too, but no one was obese when I was growing up. There were six of us children, and there wasn't enough food available for any of us to get really fat. We had three good meals a day, but we ate up any baked goods as soon as they came into the house. My mother couldn't keep bread on hand it went so fast, and when we needed to make a sandwich for lunch, we often had to go to the corner store to get some. We never went hungry, as we could always find cereal, which eventually became one of my main binge foods.

I was the oldest of the six children and was very responsible, but I never felt that I measured up. Though we all had brand-new shoes and uniforms on the first day of parochial school every year, I always felt that my clothes weren't quite as good as the other children's—my blouses weren't as white or weren't ironed as well.

Inside my family, I was insecure, too. We children didn't necessarily understand what we'd done wrong, but we were sure that in some way we were in the wrong. I believed that if I were good enough, if I did enough work, my parents would love me and my father would be pleased. I never felt I succeeded in earning my parents' love. There was no end to how badly things could go, I thought. I expected catastrophe, yet on the surface I carried on, smiling, doing the ironing, and watching my five siblings and five or six of my aunts' children, as well. I was trying to get attention as the "do good" girl.

I grew up with a stocky little body that grew into a fatter body over the years. Despite being the good little girl whose parents were deeply involved in the church, I started picking up sailors when I was around thirteen. I also began smoking addictively, and I quickly escalated from one cigarette to two packs a day.

After high school, I went to nursing school, where I started drinking alcoholically. I distinctly remember crawling up the stairs and sleeping with my hand on the floor to stop the bed from spinning. I also discovered the food in the cafeteria. I loved starchy, heavy food.

I am an addict who could never give up food. I stopped smoking in nursing school. Drinking lost its allure before I was twenty-two. But from early on, I was never able to get away from the food. My life was not all that bad. It's just that the normal, daily activities of getting up, going to work or school, and interacting with people frightened me. I had to have something to take the edge off of life. I needed food. It put me into a fog.

I was five feet, seven inches tall, and after nursing school, I probably weighed about 150 pounds. I looked nice, but I didn't know it. When a young Marine came calling, we began to go out. We ate a lot, drank a lot, went to bars a lot, and I ate even more than I drank. He told me I wouldn't get pregnant because he had some disease, and though I was twenty-one and a nurse, I believed him. I became pregnant, and, accompanied by my sister and a friend, I went to Florida to have the baby. I gave that child away for adoption some forty-five years ago.

When I came home, I reunited with a man I'd dated before, and we married. There I was, a young bride in my own kitchen, cooking just as I had for my birth family. My husband and I were just two, but I made enough for six or seven. I could bake without recipes, and my weight started going up and up. I remember drinking sweetened condensed milk when I was breastfeeding our first child. It's thick enough to hold a spoon upright and so sweet that it's used for making candy, but it wasn't sweet enough for me.

I had one daughter and then, a proper Catholic, got pregnant again, right away. In my fifth month of that pregnancy, I began to go blind and become paralyzed. I had a caring, gentle obstetrician, but I didn't even value myself enough to let him know what was happening until my bladder stopped working. Within days, I'd lost almost all of my vision and couldn't walk. I ended up in the hospital with the first episode of what was then diagnosed as multiple sclerosis. That was one of the only times in my life that I lost weight without trying.

The hospital discharged me after a month, but I was still weak. I used to have to sit in the room where my twelve-month-old daughter was playing, since I couldn't see well enough to be sure I'd find her if she left the room. God forbid that anyone try to help me, though! I had to have control over something in my life. My sister-in-law came one evening, and before she arrived I'd cleaned the house and made her a meal.

The multiple sclerosis eventually went into remission, but my marriage with my husband was not going well. Hoping to boost our relationship, we moved to Colorado and ended up in a mobile home park with horseback riding, golf courses, tennis courts, and swimming pools. It could have been a Hollywood set: a beautiful location, two young children, two cars, and a husband. I was the same person I'd always been, though, and I became even more isolated and miserable than I was before. I went to bed with several bowls of cereal at night, trying to mask my unhappiness by eating. I had such anxiety attacks that I lasted only two or three days in a hospital job I found there. At the same time, just as when I was young, I was the responsible citizen and the one people called on when they needed help.

We moved back East, where I grew up, and I kept getting bigger. Sometimes I lost 30 of the 80 pounds I needed to lose, but I gained them back, and more. Food took its toll, and eventually I reached 200 pounds. I had to diet hard to stay at that weight. I tried commercial weight loss programs, hypnosis, and acupuncture. Nothing worked for me.

I know now that I didn't need a diet. I need a fully developed program for food addiction. I'm like a drug addict, but my drug is food. I've asked a heroin addict why he continued to shoot up. When he said, "I'm trying to duplicate the first hit," I thought of myself. I've walked around the kitchen looking for the perfect bite. Was it in the pantry? Was it in the refrigerator? I never found it. No matter what I ate, the food never met my expectations, and I had to keep eating, keep looking. I used food to numb myself to reality.

I first found my way to a twelve-step program for compulsive overeaters through one of the other head nurses in the hospital where I worked. I had uncles on both sides of my family who were alcoholics, so I was familiar enough with the issue of addiction to want to go to a meeting. At my first meeting, I learned that I was not bad, immoral, or stupid. I had a disease. I was ready to hear that wonderful message. Then I thought, *What do those skinny little girls know about my life?* I got a sponsor who gave me a food plan, but I called her only once in a while.

The program I'd found wasn't FA. It didn't have the disciplines I needed, but, to be fair, I also have to admit that I wasn't willing to change. I didn't avoid all sugar, and I measured sloppily. I'd weigh out a protein portion and cover it with greasy drippings from the pan. Still, by occasionally going to meetings and sometimes calling a sponsor, I lost 60 pounds in the first six months. I was amazed, and I traveled here and there pontificating about the program. I admitted that I was powerless over food, and I told everyone else to do what I was doing, but I wasn't willing to make phone calls, really use a sponsor, or use any of the other tools. I was around the program, rather than in it.

In my second six months in the program, I battled to keep from gaining back all I'd lost. I wasn't as obese as I had been, but I heard a constant litany of jealousy and anger in my head. I was filled with destructive emotions. Still, all the while, I kept the house clean, raised my children, and tried to be pleasant with my husband. Outside I smiled, but inside I heard a cacophony of horrible voices. Kneeling in church one day, I suddenly thought, *I would never speak to anyone else the way I speak to myself. I don't deserve this. There has to be a solution.*

Around that time, I heard a speaker who had been 500 pounds. She weighed about 160 at that point. Desperate, I asked her to be my sponsor, and she gave me the FA program. In FA, we sometimes talk about G-O-D as the "gift of desperation," and that's the gift I received. My children were twelve and fourteen years old then, and I knew that if I wanted to be fully available to them as a mother, I'd have to focus on my recovery. I gave up many other activities so that I could commit myself to four meetings a week, and I approached FA with all the energy that I used to devote to eating and self-destruction.

I'd lost a lot of my ability to function professionally by the time I reached the program. I'd been working as an operating room nurse and had helped prepare women for childbirth, but I was at the point where I could only handle one patient. Working as a private duty nurse for a woman in a coma was perfect for me. To stay abstinent, I needed to have close contact with people in FA, and I made a lot of phone calls to other members every day. If my patient had ever come out of her coma, she'd have only known me as the woman with the phone at her ear.

The first day, the first week, the first month in which I was freed from addictive eating were miracles to me. I began to learn about the power of God. My thinking gradually became clearer, and I had the energy to walk through some serious situations. We'd been living in a place owned by my parents, and they evicted us. The house that belonged to us had been wrecked by the students we'd rented it to. The neighbors hated us, and the ceilings were falling down, but we moved into our own house and started to renovate. Our children were unhappy and upset. They'd had to leave their friends for a neighborhood where they couldn't easily make new ones. Life was not easy, but no matter what happened, I didn't eat addictively.

The program's tools saved me. I was a chronic food addict, and I needed every aid to recovery, including the long phone conversations and the help I received at meetings. I joined one of the earliest AWOLs, in order to study and do the Twelve Steps. I was so eager for recovery, I left vacations to come back for those AWOL meetings. They were like water to someone lost in a desert, and I didn't miss one.

Going through the Steps in AWOLs, I found some integrity. I was with others who, like me, were riddled with fear and insecurity. I also found a Higher Power—a

God who loves me and wants my well-being. The experience of having God at my side, in my corner, and at my back reassured me. Until I was thirty-five years old and came into this program, I never felt safe, particularly in relationships. I had no friends from grammar school or high school, and I kept in contact with no one from Colorado. I didn't have the energy to make friends and felt too vulnerable to reach out. I couldn't take an interest in anyone else. With the safety I felt with the God of my understanding, though, I found I could show up for life and for other people.

When I was five years abstinent, I came down with tuberculosis. I was so weak that I had to choose my activities carefully. I could either wash my hair or take a shower, but I couldn't do both on the same day. I had to go to God often in order not to fall back into seeking relief elsewhere. God made me feel safe because He gave me the grace and the grit to face my life as it was. There is a dignity that comes when we don't allow ourselves to become consumed by circumstances, knowing that we will come out on the other side as a whole person, however hard our lives might be. This is only possible for me when I have contact with a spiritual entity, with God, whom I understand as having a sense of humor and loving me.

I've lived a real life. At one point I fell and fractured my skull, which reactivated the multiple sclerosis. I was unemployed for almost two decades, and my husband became sick. Through it all, I stayed abstinent. I've learned over the years that food does not bring solace. Addictive eating brings destruction.

The program's tools—the actions we take to stay abstinent—and its Steps and Traditions have always sustained me, giving me a blueprint for living. I've stayed in good touch with FA members and have done a lot of service, trying to help others in their recovery and offering my skills to the organization as a whole. Service has saved my life.

Today, I use all of FA's tools. As one of my friends says, the one I don't use might be the one that is most necessary. My meditation time is as essential to me as air and water. I work with a sponsor who has helped me come to a deeper acceptance of myself as I am. Rather than criticizing myself or feeling ashamed or blamed, I can be grateful for awarenesses and feedback. They help me grow. Both sponsoring and being sponsored are gifts. I can open up and be vulnerable to my sponsor and my sponsees.

FA has taught me that I have to be absolutely honest in the way I eat. My food plan calls for four ounces of protein, and that's what I weigh out on my scale—4.0 ounces, not ever 4.1. The only thing I can do perfectly in my life is to weigh and measure my food. For the rest, I bring my human self to the situation and try to do the very best I can. The willingness to try is an asset of my recovery and another of God's gifts.

I've been abstinent for thirty-one years. My Higher Power has helped me keep 80 pounds off my body and given me a joy that "passes understanding." At sixty-five, I decided to drive a motor scooter. My husband keeps saying it's time for me to quit, but it's out in my driveway now. I'm in loving communication with my children, and I have a fairly sophisticated, challenging job.

Each week, I walk into a variety of facilities dressed in a professionally appropriate suit, with the confidence born of having a thin body. I can be in relationships now. I can be confident without being arrogant. I feel deeply and can put my feelings in perspective, first and foremost with the help of the God of my understanding. The disease of food addiction is powerful, but recovery is more powerful still.

I Am Enough

✧ ✧ ✧

MY FIRST SIGNIFICANT experience with food happened when I was thirteen, at the celebration of my bat mitzvah, a Jewish coming-of-age ceremony. My mother had made me a beautiful party, with about sixty guests. I was a skinny, scrawny little girl. I remember standing next to a crockpot full of forty or fifty little cocktail hot dogs. My next memory is of the inch or two of grease in the bottom of the empty pot. Using a single toothpick, I'd completely finished off the entire dish by myself, one hot dog at a time. I was stunned and ashamed.

I believe my mother was a food addict. I was terrified of her. She had a temper, and I remember her volatility and screaming. Apparently, my older sister was missing one day because she hadn't let my mother know that she was playing at a friend's house. My mother drove to get her and put her in the front seat of the car. She smacked and beat my sister all through the drive to pick up my father from work. My other sister tells me that I was sitting in the back, a witness to the beating.

I am not surprised that I don't remember the incident, because of the intensity of the fear I've felt. I was the good kid in our house. I saw what happened to my older sister, who had more of a defiant personality. I was so afraid of my mother's wrath that I became quiet. My sisters thought of me as a goody two-shoes, but I was just trying to protect myself.

I was afraid at school, too. When I was in early elementary school, I started stuttering. I am a controller. I want to pretend that I am all right, all the time, and this has never been helpful to me. I think my phonics teacher was supposed to address my stuttering, because when I was in the fourth grade, she brought me to a little room lined with pictures. Under each image was a simple word: *cat, dog, elf, land, big, little.* The teacher asked me to walk around the room and read each word aloud. I was a good reader, and I was smart. I didn't make a single mistake, and I don't think I stuttered once. I remember thinking, *Yay! I fooled them.* And that was the end of any help or intervention for my stuttering. I had too big a need to be perfect.

I've often been afraid to speak, so I remember feeling a lot of frustration. In school, I never got the credit I would have gotten if only I'd raised my hand. My anxiety that I would stutter kept me from answering teachers' questions even when I knew the correct responses. I was so terrified of public speaking that I skipped an entire year of speech classes in eleventh grade and had to repeat the course in my senior year.

It is amazing that I now speak so often from the front of the room at FA meetings. I still stutter sometimes, and my immediate thought is *I shouldn't be so nervous,* or *I sound like a babbling buffoon.* FA has taught me that these thoughts don't serve me well, so I say to myself right away, *It's okay. You're okay,* and then I pray, as I often do, "God help me accept myself as I am." I try to think, instead of getting lost in my feelings. I remember a saying I've often heard in FA, "I am enough, I have enough, I do enough," and I say to myself, *Well, at least you're talking, and that's better than staying mute and keeping your thoughts to yourself. At least you're speaking.* I've learned to practice these thoughts when I start to stutter, and I go ahead and keep speaking anyway.

I was no angel when I was a teenager. I'd been an all-A student before, but I started smoking cigarettes and drinking with my friends when I got into high school. I was good at forging my parents' signatures on my excuses. "My daughter woke up with a sore throat. Please excuse her tardiness," I'd write. I got a boyfriend and had a great time until he broke up with me two months later. I spent the next three years trying to manipulate him back into my life. By the time I was seventeen, I was depressed enough that my parents sent me to a psychiatrist.

My food addiction makes me need and want to have something in my mouth all the time. I stayed thin until I was eighteen because I was smoking and drinking. When I went off to college, I gained 20 pounds my first semester, which terrified me. I had a mental breakdown that fall. I didn't do my assignments. I just partied, drank, started doing drugs, and ate and ate and ate—not happily. I was insecure, naive, and I wanted to be accepted so badly that I didn't even recognize an insult. My roommate once said that I was okay "even though" I was Jewish, and I felt only relief that she approved of me.

Many unhappy years followed. I had to choose a major but had no idea what I wanted to do. Nursing sounded prestigious, so I went to nursing school. I was probably 15 or 20 pounds overweight then, but I was obsessed with my body. I might as well have weighed 300 pounds. I hated how I felt and barely passed my exams and clinical rotations.

Once I graduated, I got a job as a psychiatric nurse and moved back in with my parents. Eating made my life miserable. I ate ferociously, as though each plate held my last supper. I remember my mother looking at me and saying, more than once, "You'll never be thin."

I have a photograph of myself from those days, when I was twenty-two or twenty-three years old. I looked like a frumpy old lady. I was afraid to weigh myself, so I rarely got on the scale. I might have been only 5 or 10 pounds overweight for most of that time, but I felt fat and ugly and stupid. I hated myself, and I was always thinking, *If only I could get thin, then I could be confident and secure.* From the day I turned nineteen until I came into FA when I was twenty-seven, I continually told myself that thinness would save me.

As time went on, I was dominated by my relationship with food. I was always dieting, always starving myself and trying to lose weight—unless I was bingeing. I felt too inhibited and insecure to function socially without food and alcohol. Most of the time, I binged on the weekends and tried to undo the damage by starving on

Monday and Tuesday. I remember fasting all day one Monday until by four o'clock in the afternoon I couldn't bear it. I had a little piece of cheese and some lettuce, and that opened the floodgates. I went from fast-food restaurants to grocery stores, and I ate straight into the night.

When I was twenty-five, my mother was diagnosed with ovarian cancer. Just before then, I'd enrolled in a commercial weight loss program. I'm five feet, five inches tall, and they weighed me at 146 pounds at the time. They put me on a diet of five hundred calories a day. I remember curling up in a fetal position on the floor of my apartment, crying, almost every night of the five weeks I did that diet. I didn't understand that I was grieving my mother, and I didn't have the food to numb my feelings. I lost 24 pounds, but within a week of the diet ending, I'd already gained back 7 pounds. I was furious at the waste of my time, money, and energy. Already, I was back to my old ways, nearly finishing off whole boxes of cereal. I couldn't ever get to the bottom of my bowl. Leftover cereal required more milk, and leftover milk required more cereal.

The failure of the weight loss program left me desperate. One month after my mother's diagnosis, I went to a twelve-step program for compulsive overeaters. I had tried it briefly a few years before, and I wasn't really open to it when I went back. I knew that I didn't want to be fat, but I didn't think I had a food problem. I thought I had a weight problem. I was judgmental at first, looking at everyone's bodies. No one was thin yet, but on the other hand, one of the women who got up to speak said she weighed 300 pounds before she'd come to the program. She was still heavier than I wanted to be, but she certainly wasn't 300 pounds.

I wasn't ready right away, but I heard someone talk about her feelings of self-doubt. That gave me the sense that I belonged. I went to more meetings, and then I found FA. I thank God for the gift of willingness. I got an FA sponsor and was able to follow her suggestions because I wanted to be thin more than I wanted to breathe.

I felt afraid of the food plan my sponsor gave me. I'm an undereater as well as a binger, so deep down I felt sure that I wouldn't be able to lose my extra weight. I considered the possibility that I might even gain weight while eating three meals a day. My sponsor promised that I'd lose my extra pounds and keep them off if I stayed in FA and was willing to change. I consciously chose to believe her, though my deepest conviction was that I would do as I always did: lose some pounds and gain them all back. Even though I didn't feel sure that FA would work for me, I felt relief. I told my mother exultantly, "I'm sick!" I was thrilled that I wasn't a weak-willed glutton and a pig, as I'd always felt I was. I had an illness and a book that described it: *Alcoholics Anonymous.*

When I ended my first abstinent breakfast, I remember thinking, *Oh, my God, I want to eat again.* The food wasn't enough. Then I remembered people at my meeting saying, "Ask God for help when you need it," so I did. I had no idea what would happen, but I prayed, "God help me." The words that came to me then were "Get up and do your dishes." That thought didn't come from me! I got up, did the dishes, and for the first time discovered that I didn't have to eat just because I wanted to eat. I learned that the impulse would pass if I didn't act on it. In the past, no matter how hard I tried not to eat, I failed every time. In FA, I saw that if I asked God for help, I'd receive it, as long as I took action.

I had one spiritual experience after another after I joined FA. One night, in the dead of winter, I had to drive past a doughnut store. I could practically smell the doughnuts. I was terribly afraid my car would turn into the parking lot, but I said to myself, *If all the people at my meeting last night can resist the temptation to eat right now, then I can, too.* My car stayed straight, and within four or five minutes, I no longer wanted to eat. I was amazed.

One of the early pamphlets had a big influence on me. It said that we should associate the first addictive bite of food with all the misery we've ever known. I held on to that pamphlet with two hands, as if it were a life raft, and I did what it suggested. I kept remembering what my life had been like before abstinence and the FA program. I had tried and failed to be thin for years, but my troubles went way beyond my obsession with my weight.

I was among the walking dead. I'd been imprisoned inside myself, partly by my anxiety about stuttering, but a lot because of my fear of living. I wasn't able to be honest and vulnerable, to let anyone know that I was scared or didn't understand something. I was a know-it-all, a psych nurse who told others what they should do. People loved me because I was a good listener, but I hardly ever talked about myself. What could I have said? My way of life was based on making whoever was in front of me like me and accept me. I did whatever it took to gain acceptance.

I had been like a horse with blinders, but after I got abstinent, I could look to the left and the right, and I could see. The world looked beautiful. It took me a long time, but I began to be able to make decisions and choices, to know what I liked and didn't like. I started having opinions. As I shared at FA meetings, I learned that no one wanted anything from me. I could be honest and still be accepted.

When I was twenty-seven years old and four months abstinent, my mother died. She had been ill for two years. I had accompanied her to her chemotherapy appointments, and at the end, I stayed overnight with her in the hospital, where I helped take care of her physically.

The FA program got me safely and abstinently through my mother's illness and death, mainly because of my meetings. For a year or two, I drove all over my state to attend many meetings a week. I broke into a sweat as I drove, because in those days, we had no navigational systems or Internet maps, and I was afraid of getting lost. Each time I had to go to a new town, I called the local police and got directions to the meeting place. I traveled for miles, because I was terrified that if I didn't, I would go home and binge on pasta. For an hour and a half, at every meeting, I heard warm, friendly people talk about how they lived without hurting themselves, asking God for help. I shared honestly, too, and that helped me remember how grateful I felt that I was not eating addictively.

Some years after my mom died, my dad got Parkinson's disease. As the illness progressed, we saw that he needed more care, and we finally had to move him to a nursing home far away. I hate remembering that awful time. I'd go to bed each night thinking about my father. I cried and prayed, "God, please watch over Dad. I put him in your loving hands. Please let the nurse's aides be gentle and kind. Let them treat him nicely, because I can't be there. And God, please help me to fall asleep."

The pattern of discipline I learned in FA helped me to visit my father every week and to look for the positive in the situation. I appreciated my stepmother, who was with him every day. The program also taught me not to have unrealistic expectations. I accepted that my father had lost the ability to talk, but I knew he could listen, so I told him stories about my husband and daughter. Above all, I kissed him and thanked him for how kind and nonjudgmental he'd been.

FA helped me deal with every aspect of my parents' illnesses and deaths. One night before my mom died, when she was in terrible pain, I ran away to exercise and left her alone in the house. I didn't know how to be with her. That memory haunted me for years. Later, I learned in recovery that I could talk with my mom's spirit and apologize for having left her. I like to think that she heard me, but I know that I also made up for my shortcomings with my mother by being a loving daughter to my dad. Instead of running away, I learned to tell my father how much I loved him and how sorry I was that he was suffering.

Abstinence wasn't always easy. My insecurity made it hard for me to make decisions, so in restaurants I used to struggle, wondering if I'd eaten the right portions. Before FA, I had sometimes eaten too much and sometimes not eaten enough. How much was the right amount? I remember a particularly hard time when I took my father out to eat one day. I was full of feelings about his situation, and I went back and forth, trying to decide how much rice I should have, changing my mind in the middle of the meal. Later, my sponsor helped me see that I needed to separate my food from visits with my father. I ate ahead of time, and then I could concentrate on feeding him and being fully present.

Indecision is crippling, and I've learned that I need to trust my recovery and turn to God when I go out to eat. I always weigh and measure my meals when I'm home, but when I'm in a restaurant, I ask God's help in choosing an abstinent meal and deciding how much to eat. Once I've decided, I put the portion that's not mine on another plate. I don't touch it or think about it anymore, and then I'm free to enjoy the meal and the people I'm with. I've learned to say, "God, I completely put this meal in your hands" and to remember that if I have any doubt, "Less is more." If I err on the side of having less food, I'll have more recovery. It's rare that we can get full portions of salad or vegetables in a restaurant, and there's always more protein than we should eat, so "Less is more" has kept me abstinent.

The FA program has helped me in every area of my life. It kept me abstinent during the joy of my bridal shower and wedding, and then through my pregnancy and the birth of our daughter. When I became pregnant, I consulted with my doctor, and my sponsor adjusted my food plan. There was never need for me to eat flour or sugar. It was hard to get up in the middle of the night with a crying baby, but I was grateful that the food I'd eaten during the day was enough to get me through until breakfast. I could be a good mom by focusing completely on my baby, and whenever I was hungry, I prayed a prayer that was and is one of my favorites: "God, you fill me." I still say those words whenever I feel empty or hungry.

For many years after the birth of our daughter, I tried to get pregnant again. Once I miscarried at seven weeks. My husband and I went back and forth to the fertility specialist for one unsuccessful attempt after another. I prayed my way through all those years of intense disappointment and sadness. I practiced being happy for my FA friends who were having babies, and again and again I turned to God. I prayed for gratitude that I was already blessed with one child, and I asked for the miracle of a baby or the miracle of acceptance.

There's a passage in *Alcoholics Anonymous* that promises "we will not regret the past nor wish to shut the door on it," but to be completely honest, I do feel regret that we had only one child. I wish that our daughter had a sibling. I still have a sadness in my heart sometimes, but I know that our daughter is fine. She has many close friends, and my own life is full and wonderful.

I could never have pictured my days as they are now. I've returned to nursing after decades away from the field. Even fifteen years ago, my current job would have terrified me, because I'm the only nurse in a school of six hundred children. Some of them are diabetic, and others have seizures. I can face this responsibility only because I have finally learned to ask for help from God and from other people. I'm not too proud to say, "I don't know" or "I don't understand. Please explain that to me again." But I go to God first, and then I turn to other people for support.

My abstinence has made me free. I am grateful I know absolutely that I am a food addict. I will never be cured, and I can never afford to give thoughts or fantasies of food any time in my head. My weight is just right. I struggled more against my impulse to undereat than any wish to overeat, so it was very hard when my sponsor wanted me to gain 3 or 4 pounds. I don't resist her anymore when she has suggestions about my weight or my food plan. She is helping me stay healthy.

Today, I am fifty-seven. I have been abstinent continuously for thirty years, and I can let myself feel joy. That wonderful joy is the major gift of my recovery.

Despite All Circumstances

✧ ✧ ✧

*Despite every difficulty, these FA members became
abstinent and have maintained their recovery
through illness, isolation, and challenging
life circumstances in the past and present.*

I Had to Be a Man

✧ ✧ ✧

I'M IN EXCELLENT HEALTH TODAY. When I first came to an FA meeting, I was 80 pounds heavier. My cholesterol was about 300, and I was prediabetic, with a sugar count of 130–140. After fifteen years of abstinence, my cholesterol is around 153–160, without the help of any medications. My sugar count is 75 or 80, and my blood pressure is 110 over 70. I feel like I'm on borrowed time, since doctors expected me to die of a heart attack long ago.

FA has helped me lose weight and keep it off, but it's done a lot more than that for me. I feel peaceful today, though I struggled for years. Growing up, I felt deprived. My parents were immigrants from Syria who had known hardship. My father worked in a factory for long hours and low pay. He and my mother had been hungry before, so they didn't spend money easily. Our family never went out to eat, never took a vacation, never had snack foods or sugar in our house. My mother and father were different from the parents of everyone else I knew. He was fifty years old and bald. She wore a kerchief around her head. I was ashamed of them. I came to learn later, through the Twelve Steps, that I was most ashamed of me.

As a young boy, I was driven by enormous fear. I stuttered terribly in elementary school and even into high school and college. I was afraid I would fail, but I knew I had to perform. My mother wanted me to be a man. I grew up hearing her saying to me in Arabic, "Are you a man? Are you a man?" I had to be a man.

The pressure to be successful and respected became central in my life. I worried constantly about school. Would there be a test? How could I pass it? In my family, we calmed our fears by eating, and by the time I was five or six, I was demanding a big snack every night before I went to bed. Today, I think of this as a form of self-medication, because I couldn't get to sleep without eating. My disease was already taking shape.

Food became an important part of my life. As a child and a high school student, I'd come home from classes and head right for the refrigerator. I hated having any feeling of hunger, so I always kept myself full. The moment I felt the least bit empty, I ate again. I put myself to sleep every night by visualizing a mountain of Chinese food that would fill me and give me comfort and keep me from feeling empty inside.

I began to become aware of my body. When I was with my friends, swimming in the river or taking a shower at school, I noticed their muscles and sinews. I was round and heavy. I'm only five feet, four and three-quarters inches tall. By high school, I weighed 150 pounds. When I left for college, I was up to 186 pounds. In graduate school, I was about 215, and when I came into FA, I was 220. I was always fatter and shorter than I wanted to be. My lack of height was a painful part of my struggle to measure up as a man.

I tried so hard to succeed and perform that I never learned how to relax. In my junior year in high school, I suddenly lost the ability to study and started flunking my classes. I somehow patched myself together, but this happened again, more severely, when I was in college. I was nineteen then. I was doing well and my life was fine, but I came home for a weekend and my father told me he wanted to leave my mother. I started crying and couldn't stop. I cried all through the weekend and for the next ten weeks when I was back at school. I finally saw a psychiatrist, who kept saying, "You've got to get off the potty." I couldn't understand what he meant. I guess he was trying to tell me to grow up, but it wasn't so simple. I would have gotten off the potty if I could have.

I took the only solution available to me at that time, which was to drop out of school. I wanted to go into in-patient treatment, but I was told I wasn't sick enough, so I ended up seeing a psychiatrist two times a week for nine years. He helped me put myself together enough to function.

As I look back at that episode in my life, I see it was a real opportunity for me. I think my Higher Power was calling out to me. He was telling me that I couldn't keep denying what was inside me and putting myself under such pressure. Later I understood that there were parts of me that I needed to understand and accept, but the immediate trigger for my breakdown was my realization that I couldn't control everything in my life. I broke in two when I saw that I couldn't stop my father from leaving my mother.

As it turned out, my father didn't leave, and I went on in school. I managed to graduate from college and got into a PhD program in history, which I left after I'd gotten a master's degree. Then, a few years later, I received a fellowship for a master's in playwriting. This was hugely important to me. I wanted to be a playwright, though I'd denied this for years. Around this time, I also met and married my wife.

Within a few years after I'd gotten my second master's, I was a young father with two lovely girls and a beautiful wife. Responsibility comes easily to some men, who seem to relish it. In contrast, I was dragged and pulled into getting married, having children, and buying a house. My responsibilities frightened me, but once I had them, I barreled into the world. I had to make a living for my family, so I buried the imperative inside me to write. I made my choice, but I was an empty, unhappy man.

From age thirty-two to age fifty-three, I progressed into full-blown food addiction. It was as if I were an orange, trying to fit myself into the mold of an apple, and I could hardly bear it. I'd get to work at eight in the morning and stay until nine or ten o'clock at night, going back and forth to the vending machines. My wife had stopped cooking for us because I was never home at dinnertime. I ate huge take-out orders by myself and then started getting up in the middle of the night to eat.

I was full of rage, and my cholesterol was sky high. Fear had me.

I finally got to a point beyond what I thought I could stand, so I started seeing a psychiatrist again, trying to understand what was wrong with me—why I felt so empty and why I couldn't stop eating. One day I even asked my teenage daughter why I ate so much. She didn't know, of course. All my children could do was suffer for me, and when I finally found this program, they were its champions. They knew exactly what their dad needed.

One day, I was sitting in a client's office. He had a huge belly, and he told me in the midst of our conversation that he'd had heart bypass surgery. I lit into him. "You're going to kill yourself. You had that surgery and now you're so fat? What are you doing?!" He turned to me. "Who's talking?" he said. "Look at you!!" I had to admit he was right. His wife was in a twelve-step program for compulsive overeaters, and when he offered to find out about it for me, I was glad.

My client gave me the program's literature, and I saw that it was full of references to God. When I went back to see him a month later, I was honest. We lived in an area with many Irish Catholics, and the program seemed like something for them, not me. I told him that I didn't want a religious program and that I thought I could deal with my problems on my own.

One year later, I was back in my client's office. He was fat, and I was fat. I looked at him, and he looked at me, and I admitted that I couldn't stop eating. I had to do something. He suggested that we go to one of his wife's meetings, and I agreed. I'm grateful to that man and his wife. They were angels to me, though they're no longer in the program. Through them, I found my way to FA.

I weighed 220 pounds when I went to my first FA meeting. I sensed that people were trying to be honest and come to terms with their own lives. I'd finally found a place where it was all right to face the truth and talk about the emptiness I felt. This was a huge relief.

I did have two issues. Number one, I didn't want a sponsor. The women who stood up to introduce themselves as sponsors scared me. They seemed like army sergeants, and I didn't want the discipline they seemed to require. *I can sponsor myself,* I said to myself. *I'll be okay. I can get someplace with this on my own.* And in fact, I sponsored myself for three months and lost 20 pounds. I was delighted, but I wasn't sure how it happened.

My second concern was that I didn't like the God talk. People sharing about their abstinence would often mention their Higher Power or God. All that God talk came from fantasy land, I thought. How could an intelligent person believe in God? *Let them talk about God*, I decided. *I don't need God.*

I remember a beautiful expression we used in the old days: "If you don't get the program, the program will get you." There I was, full of self-will and on a diet, when I heard a young woman at a meeting say, "I love my abstinence and my Higher Power." She had a warm, loving look in her eyes. She was authentic, and I knew it. Afterward I went up to speak to her because I had no idea in the world what she meant. All she said to me was, "Just keep coming to the program. Just keep coming."

As I see it now, God was again calling to me. As I moved forward in the program, that part of me that couldn't surface all those years, my real self—that part of me that is the Higher Power in me—was pulling me. I was being ushered and led, even though I wasn't aware of my own desire to connect with something greater than myself. I only knew that the program felt right for me.

After my conversation with the young woman, I began to listen to a few of the people who had been scaring me. They were all women, because there were hardly any men in those days. I often felt odd as the only man in the meeting rooms, but those women had something I wanted. After a while, I finally understood that they were integrated within themselves. For decades I'd been a consultant, focused on helping executives align their behaviors and values. Looking back, I'd have to say, "Physician, heal thyself!" Until I'd been in the program for a while, I had no idea how far I was from being integrated myself.

The women who drew my attention were not executives. They were ordinary people. I had no idea what they meant by God, but I knew their wholeness had something to do with a Higher Power. I wanted to be like them—to be able to live according to my values. I wanted to act with love and kindness, but I came into the program feeling guilty about my behaviors and ashamed of myself as a man. Those women were each full people, connected with all aspects of themselves.

It's impossible to do FA without a sponsor. I finally found myself one. She had six years of abstinence and had lost 140 pounds, and I owe her everything. She started out by talking to me about abstinence and addiction. "Nothing goes into your mouth that you haven't planned and weighed or measured," she said, "but remember, too, that the disease of food addiction is activated before we break our abstinence. We're already in trouble when we start thinking like addicts and acting like addicts. Get to know your disease!"

I was grateful to my sponsor. I paid $100 for fifty minutes of attention from a psychiatrist, but my sponsor talked to me for free, fifteen minutes a day, seven days a week, 365 days a year. I'd lived long enough to be able to appreciate true giving. I was amazed by her generosity. I also often fought with her. I had difficulty accepting suggestions about what I wanted to do and what I wanted to eat.

One memory stands out. During my early abstinence, my sponsor agreed to my use of tabbouleh, a somewhat complicated Mediterranean dish, as the grain in my meal plan. I happily ate it for lunch and dinner. After six months, when she told me I shouldn't have it any longer, I put up a fight. For all my arguing, I could have been a lawyer. I went on and on, praising tabbouleh's healthy qualities, but she kept saying, wisely, that she wanted me to eat more simply. Finally, I told her I couldn't give it up. She told me I'd have to if I wanted her to sponsor me, and that was the end of our conversation. I was furious.

Sitting in my bed later, I regretted the tone of our talk, so I called her back. "You know," I said, "it's God's will that I have that dish." She answered, "I don't think so," and I went back to sitting in my bed, still thinking. At about six o'clock the next morning, it finally came to me that I was crazy. My sponsor had taught me how to eat. My bingeing had stopped. She had helped me take 80 pounds off my body. I'd become more loving to my wife and more attentive to my children. I was going to throw all that away and drop my sponsor because of tabbouleh? *You are one sick fish*, I told myself. The experience made me aware of the severity of my addiction. It showed me how bound I was by food and how much I was run by my own will.

I called my sponsor to apologize and let her know that I thought she was right. "There's only one issue," I said. "I have six quarts of tabbouleh in my refrigerator. That's $54.00 worth of food. Can I finish it?" She suggested I give it away, and when I couldn't find anyone who wanted six quarts of tabbouleh, I put it all down the garbage disposal. I expected regret, but I experienced instead a feeling of freedom I will never forget.

My sponsor helped me become abstinent, but she also opened the door for my relationship with God. Early on, she'd suggested that I get on my knees every morning to ask for a day of abstinence. I told her I couldn't, because I didn't believe in God. She was insistent. "Why would I kneel?" I said. "Who would I be praying to?" She suggested I kneel as a symbolic gesture of my powerlessness over food. I could do that, because I knew by then that I was powerless, so I knelt every morning.

One day while I was kneeling, I had a tremendous feeling of relief. For the first time in my fifty-three years of life, all my worries seemed to go away. This lasted only a few minutes, but it reminded me of what I'd heard other FA members say about their experience of God.

I wasn't escaping. Instead, I was freed from concerns about all the problems that had seemed so important a few moments before. I knew what was truly important: my two wonderful children and my relationship with my wife. This was a beginning experience of a Higher Power.

I had another experience three years after my mother died. Once, on my way home after a meeting, I stopped my car at her house and suddenly felt a tremendous sense of joy. Before, I'd had that feeling only when I accomplished something I thought was glorious or I'd done a great job. It was always associated with my own achievements. This time, the feeling just came upon me, unrelated to anything I'd done. It was another moment when I was open, and I began to think that I was sensing God inside me.

These two experiences happened because I was surrendering the food and my self-will. By that I mean I was abstaining from foods with flour and sugar and letting go of my attachment to quantities and complicated mixtures. I was trusting that whatever I planned and then put in my mouth would be enough—a challenge for someone who had so long been afraid of feeling empty. I remember the first time I couldn't get the exact foods I'd written down on my food plan. I'd gone to a luncheon, and all that it was possible for me to eat was a salad and an apple. I had to give up my usual protein and grain portions, but I ate what I could, and to my amazement, I felt full.

That was a great learning for me. I realized that hunger and craving were a part of my mind. They were rooted in a spiritual hunger and emptiness.

I've had the most trouble letting go of quantities. Every once in a while, when I feel empty inside, I still long to have a full stomach again, but the feeling passes. I've also learned the importance of simplicity. In the beginning, I'd mix this with that, but my sponsor insisted on what she called clarity: maximally simple food. She didn't want me to mix potatoes with rice or create combinations of vegetables. I've found that she was right. When my food is clear, my mind is clear. If I were to eat complicated foods again, my life would become complicated. What I eat affects how I think and how I live.

It took two years for me to let go of food and trust that I could stay in this program. I always felt that my disease was strong and active, but after two years I was much more free of the food. I'd say it took me four years to let go of my rage and six years to let go of my fear. Now I feel anger and fear sometimes, but they are minimal.

I'm still a very emotional man. I have a lot of feelings inside, perhaps too much passion. I have to accept my feelings—let them be there and run their course and dissipate. I ask God for help and know that the answer for me is to let go of my feelings, just the way I let go of food. When I'm upset, it helps to look beyond what is bothering me to all the things that are really important in life.

I'm a playwright now. It's nothing I can make a living from, but I have the satisfaction of writing full-time. I have wonderful relationships with my daughters and a friendship with my former wife. I find joy in helping my children. I've also taken my sister into my home. She is terribly ill with cancer and needs my care. Why wouldn't

I do these things? I don't do them because I should or have to. I do them because I want to show up and be present for the people I love. I belong, and I feel happy and thankful for the gift of belonging.

I'm a work in progress, but I'm getting better. When I came into the program, I knew one voice: the voice of my self-will and fear. In FA, I've learned to hear another voice inside me. It's much deeper and steadier. I call that the voice of my Higher Power. I love that voice. It has said to me, "Be kind. You're basically a kind man, not a rageful one. Be giving. Be of use."

FA has made it possible for me to let go of my attachment to food so that I can hear the deeper voice. The voice coming from my self-will said, "Eat, eat, eat, and you will feel okay. Stuff yourself, and you won't feel empty." The voice of my Higher Power tells me, "Don't eat. Live!"

You've Got to Be Willing

✧ ✧ ✧

MY PARENTS ARE CANADIAN. My mother was about fifteen when she had my brother, and my father was only two or three years older than she. I was born two years later and was eventually followed by a little sister. We children weren't planned or expected, but we were wanted.

I recall a lot of financial difficulty and arguments about money at home. My father was a truck driver. When he came back on weekends, life was good. My mom would go grocery shopping on Friday, which was payday, and food was abundant. During the week, the food petered out, and so did my mom. I was afraid of her. She withdrew and held in her feelings, and then she'd suddenly explode.

When I was young, I was told, "You keep eating like that, and you're going to pay the price." I remember a world in which there was only me and food. One day, I stood in our garden picking and eating raspberries until I'd cleaned out a whole row of fruit. No matter if the

berries were dusted with dirt or cobwebs, I ate them all.
I was in a trance. Years later, when I had gum surgery
and was given Percocet for the pain, I suddenly realized
that I was in the same trance. Food was a drug for me,
especially sugar, and those berries were filled with sweetness. I never felt full, though, no matter how much I ate.

When I was about thirteen, a boy I liked said that I
had one of the best bodies in the school. The following
year, when I went back at the end of summer, another
boy mentioned that I'd gained some weight. I was just
maturing and was probably only 5 pounds heavier, but
I was determined no one would ever say that about me
again, and thus began my dieting.

The Scarsdale diet was the first I tried. I did it during
the summer. I also started running, so when I returned
to school, I was very thin. Then I discovered bulimia.
My parents had been talking about separating, though
I knew they loved each other and us, and I was devastated. I remember I ate until I was sick at dinner one
night, and I decided to throw up to relieve myself of
the physical discomfort. When I walked out of the bathroom afterward, I'd had a revelation. Nothing mattered
anymore, and I'd found a way to eat as much as I wanted
without gaining weight. Between the bulimia, dieting,
and running, I lost more pounds. People noticed and
began to express concern, but I didn't mind. The thinner
I became, the faster I could run.

Meanwhile, life fell apart at home. My parents separated, and we lost our house. I needed to get a job, so I
found one at a chocolate store. I was running, bingeing
at the store, purging in the bathroom, stealing money,

using laxatives, and getting even thinner. At that point, I was five feet, five inches tall and weighed about 112 pounds. I don't know why, but I blacked out quite regularly. A cloud would come over me. My teeth would chatter, my body tingle, and I would lose consciousness.

There were more troubles at home. My father moved far across Canada for another job, and my mother decided to take my sister and join him. When my brother was eighteen and I was sixteen, we were left alone in the house with only our bedroom furniture. The realtor selling our condominium was a family friend, so he'd debrief us and tell us when he was going to show it.

My life was a mess. I was dating a twenty-five-year-old man at the time. Someone once asked me, "What's a twenty-five-year-old want with a sixteen-year-old?" You can imagine. The man was a cocaine addict and an alcoholic, and he was obsessed with me. He took me out to restaurants and dressed nicely, but he was awful. I was repulsed, but I couldn't get away from him because he followed me everywhere.

After my parents sold the condo, my brother and I went first to live with my grandfather. I commuted all the way across the city, trying to finish classes and graduate from my old high school, but the twenty-five-year-old kept me out until two and three in the morning. When my grandfather decided he'd had enough, he sent me to my parents, who lived hundreds of miles away.

I hated my new life. I lost all my friends and couldn't keep up at school. My father was working, but we had no money. Our television sat on a cardboard box. My mother, sister, and I slept in one bed. I worked in a bakery, taking whatever food I could steal or buy to eat in the woods. I remember standing among the trees eating pies with my hands before I went home to throw up. I started running and taking laxatives again, which caused me to lose control of my bowels. All this because I was struggling with 10 extra pounds! When I lost that weight, I began fainting, and then the twenty-five-year-old cocaine addict traveled across the country and found me.

Leaving was the only answer I could see, so I ran back to the city where I'd grown up. Though I had a place to stay originally, it wasn't long before I stood at the city transit station with nowhere to go. My grandfather wouldn't have me back, but God was working in my life, because a friend's family took me in. I appreciated everything they did. They even helped me get into a nursing program at the local university, but eventually I was driven back to my old double life. People in the family began to write notes on the food in the refrigerator: "NO." I purged in their basement and clogged their toilet.

Finally, I moved out. I was dating a man I'd met who was six years older than I. He came to my apartment one day when I had just finished eating a dozen doughnuts. I had flour all over my face and was sitting on the kitchen floor, curled up in a ball. I loved this man, but I wanted him to go away. He was banging on the door and looking in the window, thinking I was cheating on him, so I finally had to let him in. I was a mess, but I said, "I'll be with you in just a minute." I went into the bathroom, threw up, and took a shower. When I came out, I had my makeup all done, and I was dressed up—the girl he knew. "Okay," I said, "I'm ready." He was horrified, but we never spoke of it. We just went about our day.

I had a nice figure at that point. I was still running, and I looked great, but I would rather have been dead than fat. I always tried to stay about 10 pounds underweight. My ultimate goal was to eat everything I wanted without gaining any weight. The purging worked to keep me thin, but there was a feeling of unrest in me, an unsettledness that was part of my illness. I was always dissatisfied with my life. I went to therapists to try to stop bingeing and purging, thinking that would make me happy, but no one could help me stop. I found psychics. I thought my job was the problem. I needed more excitement, more money.

At one point, my girlfriends and I signed a lease for a condominium so we could live together and have fun. There weren't many jobs for nurses then, but I had a solid position, plans with my friends, and a boyfriend who was a nice man—at one point, we were even engaged. Life was going to be good. Instead, an opportunity came up to work as a traveling nurse, and in a heartbeat, I threw all the other opportunities away. I went first to St. Thomas, in the U.S. Virgin Islands. Things would be different there, I thought, and they were for a little while. I was running and enjoying the sun, but then life turned again, and I began bingeing and purging. I ended up getting involved with four men, three of them alcoholics, and I betrayed my boyfriend in Canada. I didn't even want to be with those men. Finally, I needed to leave. That was the answer. So I returned to Canada.

Over the next years, I went back and forth as a traveling nurse, trying to find stability in a life I'd ruined by my negative attitude. Each time I found a place for myself, I decided it wasn't good enough. I'd leave, realize that I'd made a mistake, and try to return, but I'd destroyed what I had and couldn't go back. I'd have to go somewhere else to restart my life.

St. Thomas. New Orleans. Florida. New Hampshire. I kept coming and going, ending up in the same place: bingeing, purging, and being with men I didn't like. My world got smaller and smaller. I had no friends. I began to wonder, *Who would know if anything happened to me?* Eating impaired my thinking. I had no access to good judgment about people. When I wanted something, I was determined to get it, come hell or high water. I didn't care who I hurt or how I affected others. I wanted what I wanted, and I steamrolled over anything necessary to get it.

I finally ended up in New England. I was twenty-four, approaching ten years of bingeing and purging, and I'd begun to have suicidal thoughts. I tried another two therapists without luck, but, eventually, by the grace of God, I ended up in the Boston area and in contact with FA.

As I attended FA meetings around the Boston area, I grew desperate. The women my age who were abstinent were happy and grateful, but I was stuck in my same misery. I was approaching my twenty-fifth birthday and was looking at nothing but another year of bingeing and purging. I didn't want to be twenty-five and living as I'd always lived, so I found a new sponsor and a different level of willingness.

I'd never understood before when people told me, "You've got to be willing." They meant, "You've got to do this program when you want to eat. Do it instead of eating." I remember curling up in a ball, in agony I wanted to eat so badly, but instead, I picked up the phone and called an FA member. I don't even know what we talked about, but by the end of the conversation, I'd lost the compulsion. For the first time, my urge to eat passed without my giving in to it. That was the beginning of the sixteen years of abstinence I have today.

With abstinence, I began to reflect on my life. I got into an AWOL and started seeing the mistakes I'd made. Addiction is a disease of negativity. When I was eating addictively, I hadn't appreciated my life. I'd had a good job and a nice boyfriend and dear friends, but none of it was good enough for me. I wanted more. I wanted better. I'd grown up in one of the most beautiful places in the world and hadn't even been aware of its beauty.

For some time, I was torn by a longing to go back to Canada. I finally understood that my old boyfriend was a nice man, and I obsessed about trying to reunite with him. Instead, I was told, "Grow where you're planted." I had no family and no friends in Massachusetts. All I had was FA and the people in it. I was afraid, but the program sustained me. AWOL and AA's Big Book, *Alcoholics Anonymous,* helped me finally understand what was wrong with me. I was an addict, though I wasn't chasing a drug as much as I was chasing a feeling. I was running after excitement and happiness and my own twisted ideas of what I thought was living, and I ended up in the same awful situation every time I moved.

My sponsor said, "Now you're going to learn how to let go." She meant that I needed to let go of food, let go of the impulsiveness inside me, let go of anxiety and fear, let go of chasing after some vision of a better life. I stopped calling my ex-fiancé. I'd hurt him every time I'd seen him because I was unable to commit to our relationship. I stopped moving, so I could complete the entire cycle of an AWOL—all Twelve Steps. I made a commitment not to date for a year and stopped training for marathons so I could stabilize at a healthy weight.

In the program, we talk often about the need to let go. I didn't know how, at first. Now I see that it was as simple as following through on my commitments. There's a physical level to letting go: eating what I'd committed to eat and not one bite more, resting instead of running, giving myself the space to look at myself instead of chasing after yet another man.

There's another part to letting go, though. As I kept following through on my decisions, I had to continue to turn to my Higher Power. Once my sponsor and I determined that something wasn't good for me, I had to be honest with her, myself, and God. I couldn't allow my fears to make me question my commitments. Indecision can be a kind of insanity for me, so whenever I wanted to change my mind, I had to pray, "God, take away these thoughts." Then I'd focus on thinking about other things. This became the foundation of my life. God took my obsessions, but I had to keep giving them back to God, especially my impulse to move.

In the end, letting go of food and running was easier than letting go in other areas of my life. My biggest obsession came after I married. I had met a good man, and we had two children. While I was pregnant with our third child, we decided we didn't want to have any more. The decision was not made well. I remember lying on the table waiting to have my tubes tied after the birth of our son. I felt scared that I was making a mistake, but I couldn't open my mouth to say, "Stop."

We did fine with three sons, but I kept thinking, *I didn't get my girl.* Then it occurred to me that we could try to get pregnant again—I could have the surgery reversed. In quiet time, I powerfully felt the urge to try again. This became a painful obsession. For one or two years, I prayed and did everything I'd learned to help me let go of my wish for a daughter. My husband was willing to try for my sake, but against his own wishes. He was clear that he did not want another child. My two attempts to have the surgery to untie my tubes caused such pain in our relationship that I canceled my appointments. Each time, I picked up the obsession again.

No one had the answer for me. I talked with my sponsor and various members of our fellowship. Some people said, "Practice being satisfied." My physician encouraged me to go ahead if I truly wanted another baby. Because the desire was so strong in me despite my efforts to let go, I thought the impulse must have come from God. Nothing fell into place, though.

In my last attempt at surgery, my husband and I went to an infertility doctor. The conversation took an unexpected turn when he became aware that my mother had suffered from cancer in both her breasts. The doctor said he was sure he could undo the tubal ligation, but he suggested that I get genetically tested for breast cancer. Soon after, I had an MRI and my annual mammogram, both of which revealed that I did have breast cancer. Genetic testing confirmed that I was genetically positive for the cancer. That was the end of my obsession with having another child. Following all the recommendations, I had a double mastectomy. The surgeon also removed both my ovaries, since I apparently faced a 40 percent risk of ovarian cancer.

It would have been terrible if I had gotten pregnant. What I see in my own story is that I wanted what I wanted. I think I misinterpreted God's will for my life, believing that because *I* couldn't let go, God wasn't removing from me the desire for another child. I didn't understand that it sometimes takes many years before we can know and accept God's will. Looking back now, I think it wasn't God's will for me to have another child. I had to have the cancer treated, and a safe pregnancy was impossible with the kind of chemotherapy I needed.

I'm grateful that I didn't eat addictively despite the diagnosis, the surgery, and the chemotherapy. I put the FA program to the test. I decided that I would not change anything that I normally did. I would get up and get on my knees to pray for the gift of abstinence and for help during the day. I would eat as I normally eat, avoiding special diets and supplementary foods. I couldn't take calls from sponsees who telephoned every day, but I continued to work with those who'd been abstinent awhile and called only as they needed me. I said to myself and to God, "If FA can't walk me through this time in my life when I need it the most, then I'm not going to do it anymore. What is the point of having a program that only works when I'm healthy?" I decided to finish my AWOL and kept attending meetings throughout my chemotherapy.

My doctor was amazed by the results. Chemotherapy basically destroys the immune system and radically drops the count of the white blood cells. Patients have to build up their white cell count before the next treatment. I recovered so quickly and well between treatments that my doctor thought I was taking medication to bump up the formation of my white cells. I was glowing. He called me a poster child for recovery.

I prayed through every step of my treatment. I wanted no barrier between me and God. The doctors suggested Ativan for nausea before I even began the chemotherapy, but I realized I didn't need it. I was just nauseated from anxiety. After the mastectomies, they put me on a pain pump for the first forty-eight hours. When I came home, I didn't take Percocet because I didn't need it. I'd had it once before, when I broke my wrist, and I remembered that I'd always wanted the next dose. I'm an addict. I can't handle those kinds of medications. Instead, I took Tylenol, and I rested. Pain regulated my activity. When I got sore, I needed to lie down. I didn't need a pill.

When I was first diagnosed with cancer, I got on my knees and surrendered to my situation. I prayed, "Please, God, let me go through this gracefully." Whenever I was afraid or didn't want to go through the chemotherapy again, I just said, "God help me." My sponsor had survived breast cancer herself, and she gave me a prayer. She told me to say, "God, I want to live. I love my life." That prayer meant that I needed to get up and be with my children, go to my FA meetings, talk with people in the program, plant my garden, live my life.

I felt that I was carried. More than asking God for help, I found myself thanking Him, in awe of all I received. My brother and two of my girlfriends in Canada left their families and came down to America to help me take care of mine. People I didn't even know brought food to my house. The women at work donated their vacation hours so that I could get paid during my time off. They also signed me up for a fund that sent me $1,000. I felt God's presence and was filled with gratitude.

I didn't have perfect faith and stillness, of course. No one is perfect. We had just started painting and redecorating our house before I was diagnosed with cancer. I wish we had put the work on hold during my treatments, but I insisted that we continue. My husband did the painting, and I did the decorating, room by room. I think now that I lost track of my priorities. I wish, instead, that I'd trusted God more and stayed quiet. I want to listen better to the voice inside me that says, "Wait" or "Just sit still." The disease of food addiction never tells me to wait. The good, sound decisions that I don't waver on take time to make. They are the ones from God.

Today, I know I have to slow down. I can take quiet meditation time in the morning and then jump up and run around yelling at the children as I try to get them out the door. What is the point of the quiet time then? I need to appreciate and talk with God throughout the day. Otherwise, I get a lot done, but I end up feeling empty and unhappy. All I have is a checklist and a series of accomplishments. I don't like myself.

I have a great day only when I am conscious of God and have gratitude. I ask God for help. Then I trust God to give me direction and guide my actions, and I do whatever I think is the next right thing for me to do. I so often felt crazy in the past. My addiction impaired my judgment, and I wasn't able to trust myself. Now I believe in intelligent faith. God's guidance makes sense. My sponsor used to say to me, "God gave you a brain. Use it!"

Though I have been abstinent continuously for more than fifteen years, I never want to take my abstinence for granted. I am abstinent because God is in my life. My weight has basically stayed the same. I look normal, at 125 pounds, and I'm free from any obsession with food. This means that I am also able to recognize possible signs of trouble. When I am too drawn to a particular food or seasoning, when I think about it too much, I don't put it in my food plan. I don't want to eat it.

I fell on my knees this morning to be in God's presence, and I took quiet time before I began this story. I wanted God to work through me. It's scary to let go sometimes, but I can accept God's will in my life today. It's been three years since my cancer treatments. I am healthy now. I have three beautiful sons, a loving husband, and a wonderful life.

Peace in Any Storm

✧ ✧ ✧

WHEN I WAS GOING to get married, my husband and I planned a beautiful wedding in a park in the city where we lived, and I said, "I'm going on a diet. I just want to be 199 pounds. I don't want to be 200 pounds." I was five feet tall and about 225 pounds at the time, and I tell you, that made a lot of sense to me—199 pounds was all I needed to be.

Except for my christening outfit when I was a baby, every white dress in my life had to be made for me. My communion dress had to be made because I was chubby. My confirmation dress had to be made because I was chubby. And my wedding gown had to be made because I was morbidly obese.

When I decide to diet, I'm the kind of person who gains 25 pounds, so the pre-wedding diet didn't go too well. In the end, my sister-in-law had to take my wedding gown apart and put it together again so I could get into it. The only obstacle on the road to a beautiful wedding was me.

I've actually led several different lives. During the polio epidemic in the 1940s and 1950s, I got sick. I was a child, and there was no vaccine then. I've learned since that only 15 percent of those who got polio survived. No one expected I'd live, because I couldn't eat or swallow. My lungs were also affected, so I couldn't breathe. Everything in my throat was paralyzed.

I lay in an iron lung for nine months. When I came home from the hospital, I was thin—the only time I've ever been thin until I joined FA. I didn't stay that way very long. My mother was a stay-at-home mother, and she was an excellent cook. Our family's Italian, and everyone believed the cure for my health problems was to feed me.

I grew up having two dinners every night. My older sister lived in the apartment below us. When we were little, her oldest son and I used to meet on the stairs at dinnertime. He'd head upstairs for his second meal, and I'd head down. Spoiled rotten and surrounded by delicious, homemade cooking, I grew up thinking that I should be indulged for the rest of my life. When other people didn't cooperate, I indulged myself. Nothing was ever enough for me. Whether I was eating or, eventually, drinking, drugging, being with men, or shopping, I never had enough.

I got through my childhood and grammar school years looking for a pat on the head and a smile, but when I got into high school, something flipped. I grew into a rebellious young woman who got into plenty of trouble. I was grounded at home, night after night, and I ate to blunt my anger.

After high school, I became a hairdresser and worked at a salon on one of the most exclusive shopping streets in our city. I didn't have the money our customers had, but I shopped where they shopped and bought what they bought. Perish the thought that I was less than they were.

My body size was passable then. I dressed well. My hair and makeup were always good. I was probably only 30 or 40 pounds overweight, so the package wasn't all that bad. But I ended up in an affair with my high school boyfriend, who was an emotionally abusive alcoholic.

I didn't know how to deal with my boyfriend, so I did just what he did. I didn't like the drinking in the beginning, but it turned out to be just like eating, and then I loved it. I had the same experience with drugs. I was afraid and didn't like them, but everyone was doing drugs, so, before you knew it, I was smoking grass, cleaning grass, rolling grass, and then getting free grass because I cleaned and rolled it for someone else.

I was in my mid-twenties when I broke up with my boyfriend. I was free! I could have turned my life around then. I could have gone to college. Instead, I went nuts, and all hell broke loose. I was out every night. My mother was still alive, may God rest her soul, and there were many times that it was four in the morning before I crawled home. She'd be up waiting. I'd go to bed for two hours and then get up and go to work.

As an adult working woman, I was getting bigger and bigger, and angrier and angrier. My rage scared me. I knew if I ate, it would numb my anger a little, so I went ahead and ate. Because I ate, I got bigger, which infuriated me, and that made me eat more. I felt like a gerbil in a cage.

During that time of misery, my mother got sick. In four months, she died. When my family was in the funeral parlor, I said to my brother, "Why can't I put Ma in a glass coffin like Eva Peron and leave her in the living room?" My brother turned white as a sheet. He had no idea what to do. At twenty-eight years old, I wasn't a child, but at that time, the glass coffin made perfect sense to me. The scary part of my life before my recovery in FA was that everything I did, no matter how crazy or how self-destructive, made sense to me.

My father had back surgery a week after we buried my mother. He ended up in a wheelchair, paralyzed and in a rehabilitation hospital, and there I was, a food addict at home alone. My addiction progressed to an even more deadly level, and I gained 40 pounds in three months. I had the personality to match. At 220 pounds, I was with my father in the hospital one day when I got frustrated. I was screaming like a maniac when the security officers came.

I met my husband in the bar where my cousin worked. He was ten years younger than I was. After we'd dated a while, he came to the house with a diamond. I said, "What's this for?" I was living at home, and my father was paying all the bills. I didn't see any reason to accept a proposal, but eventually I realized I really loved him and didn't want to be without him. We're going to be married thirty-two years soon.

After we were married, my husband became, surprise, an alcoholic. He also picked up cocaine. He ended up in a rehab program, where I learned about Al-Anon and heard of a twelve-step program for compulsive overeaters. I went to one meeting and didn't go back, but something drew me. I called the program's main office to get an updated meeting list every three months.

My husband got clean and sober, and within a year, he was going to three AA meetings a day and calling a sponsor regularly. He learned to physically remove himself when I went nuts. He'd go to the upstairs bedroom and lock the door, further infuriating me.

I was 280 pounds, and one morning, as we say, it was all over. By ten o'clock, I'd eaten myself sick. I didn't know what I could do for the rest of the day if I was too sick to eat. I thought of throwing up, but I didn't, and then, in desperation, I decided to go to a meeting.

I was introduced to the FA program that night. I was a mess. I walked into the room hopeless. I'm proud, and it was awful for me to cry in front of anyone else, but I cried the whole meeting because I heard my own story in the one the speaker told. When I went to talk to her about something non-program related, I cried again. She responded by saying gently, "Here's my phone number. Call me in the morning, and on your way home tonight, get some plain, nonfat yogurt and a piece of fruit." I made it home with only the yogurt and fruit, which was amazing. Already God was working in my life.

The next morning, I got up and called my sponsor at some ungodly hour. She gave me a food plan for the day. I measured the yogurt and sat down to my breakfast, which I couldn't eat. The yogurt was horrifying. I managed to eat my banana, and then I called my sponsor again, hysterical.

I had just spent $420 on a commercial weight loss program, and I'd decided before I went to the FA meeting that if it didn't work, I was going to have to give up. I was devastated. *Not one more diet,* I said to myself. *I'm not going on anymore. I can't. I'm done.* So I was crying as I talked. "You don't understand," I told her. "I have to be able to do this. I have to, because otherwise, I'm not going to be able to go out of my house anymore."

My sponsor gave me a suggestion that helped me tolerate the yogurt and finish eating it. I will never forget the awe I felt that night when I knelt. I couldn't go down on both knees because of my size, but I knelt as best I could to say thank you. I couldn't believe that I hadn't binged between my meals that day.

Over the next five days, I went to five meetings, mostly in a series of different towns. In fact, for three weeks, I probably went to a meeting every night. I couldn't imagine staying home and keeping the commitment to my abstinence. I figured if I wasn't home, I wouldn't eat, and I was right. I'd eat dinner, go to the meeting, come home, take off my makeup, and go right to bed.

My sponsor told me to get on my knees twice a day: once to ask God for an abstinent day and once to say thank you. I am Catholic, but this didn't come naturally to me. Who was I talking to? I didn't know, so I just said, "Please, please, let me be able to be abstinent. Please help me do this." Every night, I was in awe, because I was still abstinent.

At one of my first meetings, I heard someone speak who was calm. Everyone at that meeting was calm. When they got up to speak, their hands weren't flying all over the place. They didn't raise their voices, and they didn't swear. *How do you get to be like that?* I wondered. I didn't think about losing weight, because I didn't think it would be possible for me to lose weight. I just wanted to stop eating like an animal, and I wanted to be calm.

Later that first summer, I decided to change sponsors, and I asked the calm person I'd heard to sponsor me. She said yes and then started to talk to me about preparing my abstinent meals. I remember thinking to myself, *My God, I'm such a good cook, and now I've got this little Asian woman sponsoring me and telling me what to do with food?!* That was the moment when I began to understand my powerlessness. It didn't matter what I thought I knew, because everything I knew had failed me. Nothing I knew had worked.

That night, I gave up, and I opened myself to suggestions. There were many. When I complained to my sponsor that the people in one of my meetings were in a clique and no one talked to me, she asked, "Do you talk to them?" I had to admit I didn't, so she set me to volunteering in a service position that made me talk to them.

I remember walking into my Thursday night meeting and seeing my sponsor sitting in the front row. Each week, she'd give me a big smile and pat the open seat next to her. I'd say, "Not tonight," and sit behind her. I really was basically willing, but looking back I think there were moments when my sponsor should have gotten combat pay. I'd kick and scream, but eventually I'd do what I needed to do.

One day, I called my sponsor and told her, "I had such a nice day yesterday! My life was all in order." She said, "You're going to have more of those." My sponsor was right. I came into FA desperate and hopeless, a ball of rage. I'm not that person anymore.

I am full of hope now, though at the moment, my husband is completely unemployed, and I can't work. He's getting unemployment, thank God. I am on Social Security disability payments, and I'm turning sixty-five in a few months. It gets scary, but I know the way my God works for me. One door gets closed, and a bigger and better door gets opened. If we have to live in a hall-way, with all the doors closed for the moment, we're still in a good hallway.

This is not the way I was. This is me allowing God to work in my life. This is me getting all the barriers be-tween me and God out of the way—the food, the drugs, the alcohol, the sex, the gum, the cough drops, the soda. Today, there's only me and God.

I'm still human, of course. I still get afraid. Now the symptoms of polio have come back, and they're much worse because I'm older. My life is difficult at times. My limbs are weak. I get tired, and I drag my right leg. My whole right side is kind of paralyzed. I froze my lungs on my right side, and my vocal cords don't move. You'd be speechless with amazement if you saw me take the voice test. I can make all kinds of noises, even though my vo-cal cords are not moving. Somehow my body found an-other way to talk. But I'm having trouble swallowing, and I can't eat some foods anymore.

There are other problems. I don't breathe that well. I don't get enough oxygen, so I don't have much energy. I'm going to a neurologist, because the biggest effect of the type of polio I had is that the neurons in the brain die. Here I am, getting older, and like anyone else, I worry about dementia, but I've already got some dead neurons in my brain!

I am sustained by my faith in God. I am going to be okay. There's no cure for my symptoms. There's no surgery. The only "cure" is prevention, so when I'm tired, I lie down. I eat the right foods. I don't abuse myself by smoking or drinking, and I haven't been overweight for years. I weigh myself regularly, and I stay petite at 117 pounds. I don't run away anymore. I've talked with a CPA, and I've done my financial planning. Above all, I've made amends to people dear to me—people I hadn't talked to in years—and now those relationships are restored.

I've been abstinent for nineteen years. Without the FA program, I surely would not have the life I have now. I know from the core of my soul that I would have no life. One bite of bread, and all I would care about would be food.

In FA meeting rooms, you hear the word *grateful* over and over again. Just feeling grateful is not enough, so in my own little way, I try to give what I have to someone else. I do this by sponsoring, co-leading an AWOL, getting a newcomer's number and giving him or her a call. If I can help just one person, then I'm doing my job.

I'm more than grateful to FA. It has given me freedom and peace. When I was in the iron lung, the power went out in a storm once. Suddenly I wasn't breathing. The generator came on, thank God, but I grew up paralyzed with fear whenever there was a storm. Five years in the program, and I got better. I drove to my meeting one night when the wind was snapping branches off trees and said to myself, *When I'm doing God's work, I'm going to be okay.* And I was fine.

Today, I eat solely because I have to put fuel in my body. I was a prisoner in a prison of my own making for far too long. Now I have comfort. I have calmness. If I stay abstinent, I'll keep my freedom, and I'll always have peace in the middle of any storm.

Inch by Inch

◇ ◇ ◇

I GREW UP IN IRELAND. My father was an alcoholic. He kept coming home drunk, or not coming home, and there was no money. My mother slept in my bed because she didn't want to sleep with my father, and he would come into the room looking for her. I wanted to run away but couldn't. I had nowhere to go, lying there, wanting to leave but loving them at the same time.

I was an addict from the age of seven. Food was a shining light through all the hard circumstances of my life. I knew I could cope if I had the comfort of food. It was the way out for me. There was no other way I knew. I can remember sneaking into my father's store before anyone else woke up and sticking my fingers into boxes of chocolates. I was six or seven years old then and already unable to stop eating certain foods. Later, when we were on a family holiday once, we stayed at a farm. My father told me to stop eating the potatoes at dinner, but, as embarrassed as I was, I couldn't, and I ended up doubled over in pain from the bulk of what I'd eaten.

With all my eating was a sense of fear and self-hate. I was raised Catholic, and at age six, when I made my Holy Communion for the first time, I had to wear a pretty little dress. Photographs were taken, and my mother sent me over to my grandmother's to pick them up. When I saw my face in the photos, with all the freckles and ugliness, I was devastated. I can't remember anyone ever telling me I was ugly, but I hated myself so much I felt physically sick. I had to eat something to stop the pain I felt about my ugliness.

For a while, my father managed a pub, with our house connected. He drank all the profits, and one Christmas night, some men came with hammers and nails and barricaded the pub from the house. My father was drunk and went to hit my mom, so she took my three brothers and me and said we were leaving. We started a ten-mile walk to my auntie's. My mother told me later that she had lost hope, and as we walked over the bridge across the river, she thought about drowning us all.

We moved a lot because of my father's drinking. We had to leave another house we'd had, and then we were on the waiting list for council housing and had to move again while we waited for an opening. I tried to fit in as the new kid on the block each time we moved. I desperately wanted to be liked. I wanted to prove that I was somebody who belonged.

When I was thirteen, my youngest brother, Jim, was hurt in a car accident. That devastated our family. I was meant to go to the shop to pick up my father's birthday cake that day, and I refused to go, so my brother went instead. On the way, he was knocked down by a car and was left in a coma for five months. He was physically and mentally damaged for life and has needed daily care ever since.

When Jim was hurt, my father went back very badly on the drink and my mother had a nervous breakdown. She ended up having to go to the hospital, where she had electric shock treatments. I was left looking after my other brothers while my mother and father and Jim were in the hospital. I loved my brothers very much, and I tried to look after them, but my mechanism for survival was eating a lot of food.

In my teens, I began to put on weight. I got quite pudgy, and people started commenting, but I couldn't stop eating. I was back and forth on diets when someone at school mentioned that I could try to make myself throw up. I did it once. It was scary and strange, so I stopped and thought I wouldn't do it again. I'm a true addict, though, and the behavior escalated. I did it once in a blue moon, and then I did it every week, and then every day. I started to lose my hair and had nosebleeds. I ended up being fat *and* bulimic because I ate vast amounts of food and couldn't throw up at the pace that I was eating.

Meantime, I'd gotten in with the crowd that wanted to have fun. We'd listen to music and go to dances. When I was sixteen, I started to drink and ended up in a relationship with a man who was an alcoholic and a gambler. He used to beat me up. I knew I didn't want to be with him, but for months I hadn't the guts to finish the relationship. My life from age sixteen to age twenty-four was drinking, eating, drinking, eating, and trying to keep my head above water.

After I graduated from a secretarial college and had worked for a while at my first job, I decided to go with a friend to England. *Wouldn't England be nice*, I thought, *with its gorgeous men and red pillar post boxes for letters. I'll sort myself out there, and I'll be better.* I was at a low point then, depressed, losing control of my drinking, and embarrassing myself.

I moved to England, but of course I took all my feelings and addictions with me, and life didn't turn out the way it did in the black-and-white movies I loved to watch. I got a job in an office. Being a diligent worker, I moved up the ranks a little bit, but I had to keep eating and drinking. I ended up in a relationship with another sick alcoholic who beat me. I stayed with him because I hated myself so much I couldn't bear to be with anyone better than I was.

The food and the alcohol didn't work as well anymore. My rage and self-hatred had nowhere to go. They didn't go down the toilet when I was roaring up with bulimia, and the cigarettes weren't helping. When my partner hit and kicked me, it released some of the hate I had inside, so I started to punch myself in the stomach or face and to scratch myself at night. It's scary when the drugs you've used for sedation all your life stop working.

One morning, I felt I couldn't go on. My decision to get help was the beginning of a sequence of events that started to open up my world. I picked up the phone and made a call to directory inquiries to ask them for all the numbers of eating disorder units in the United Kingdom. Soon after, I made contact with a twelve-step program for compulsive overeaters and went to a meeting.

That night, I cried my eyes out, and for the first time, I heard someone speak who might have been me, telling a story of self-hatred and an inability to stop eating.

It took many years and a few more relationships with abusive, alcoholic men before I found my way to the doors of FA, but I began my journey of recovery with my first phone call and the meeting for compulsive overeaters. Before then, I had always felt I had to brace myself against the world. I knew there was a God, but I had no faith. I just had me, trying to control myself and everything and everyone around me. I thought I had to pull my socks up and get on with it, as the captain of my own ship. I am grateful to the food program I first joined because it introduced me to the Twelve Steps. I got a glimmer there that faith in a Higher Power meant I had to get out of the center of the universe.

For about thirteen years after I first found some kind of help, I went in and out of just about every twelve-step program in London: AA, Al-Anon, Nicotine Anonymous, Adult Children of Alcoholics, and the food program I'd already discovered. I used to think that food addiction was just a physical illness, but it's a mental and spiritual illness, as well. It's deadly. I tried to kill myself with an overdose of pills one night.

I found FA partly because of someone I met at a convention held by the program for compulsive overeaters. I had an epiphany at that gathering. I'd thought all morning about a big bread roll full of sandwich filling, so I bought one and ate it. During the lunchtime break, a woman who had talked in one of the sessions about abstinence and weighing and measuring her food sat down beside me. I looked at her tray and suddenly heard the words in my mind: *End it. End the relationship with food. There is something better.*

The woman at the convention wasn't in FA, but my conversations with her led me to an Internet search, and I found the FA website. When I rang the number to get information, I told the person who answered that I was desperate. "Can you tell me what to do?" I asked. Once she began talking about abstinence and eating simple foods, I started arguing right away. On and on I went about sauces and this and that—I'd read lots of books, after all—but I was struck by her response when I said that I wanted my obsession with food removed. She told me, "That's only possible by having a relationship with a Higher Power, and you can't have that relationship unless you stop leaning on food. You have to eat simply and put food obsession aside."

Talking with this woman and others in FA, I knew the program was for me. I was desperate and willing. Willingness didn't mean I wasn't afraid or that I didn't cry some days. It meant that I followed all the suggestions I was given, despite how I felt.

From my first day of abstinence, I experienced freedom. I didn't have to worry about being fat or getting fatter. I didn't have to obsess over whether I had eaten enough or too much. I was given a structured food plan, and each day that I committed what I was going to eat to my sponsor, I felt safe. I believed the FA people I talked with. All of them said the program was working for them.

I was a stickler for rules, so when I was encouraged to make phone calls to other FA members each day, I made them religiously. I was terrified not to, since I mistakenly believed I'd be thrown out of the program and lost, if I didn't. The phone calls saved my skin. In twelve-step programs, people get better by going to meetings with others in recovery, but there were no FA meetings near me in England. I had only the people I talked with on the phone, but contact with them was enough to keep me abstinent. When I felt afraid, no one said, "There, there, have a little bite of something. It doesn't matter if you have a slip." They were living in the solution, so they told me, "Okay. You feel afraid. What action are you taking today? Breaking your abstinence is not an option, so what are you going to do about your fear this day?"

After a while, the happiness I'd felt because I'd become thin and free from food obsession gave way, and the depression that had plagued me all my life came back. As I made calls, I kept asking people how they stayed abstinent. FA friends told me that feelings were just feelings. Actions were most important. They said I couldn't wait for the feeling that would help me take an action. I had to take an action, which would link me to the right feeling. Above all, they talked about a Higher Power. Everyone I spoke with clearly had an understanding of a Higher Power, but the thought of depending on one was alien to me.

I've changed. Today, I know that as a food addict, I am mentally and spiritually sick. I'm vulnerable to depression, and I have to have help. Without the program, I become a prisoner inside myself. The cure is spiritual. FA's Twelve Steps always direct me to God—to a Higher Power who can restore me to right thinking and stabilize me.

Every now and again when I first wake up, I still have the feeling that I don't want to go on. I hate myself. But I've been in FA long enough to know that self-pity is one of my big character defects. It's part of my illness. So I pray for help, I make phone calls to people in the program, and I act my way into freedom by ignoring my feelings and getting on with my job. I do the work at hand, saying thank you to God for each task.

I had that old, negative feeling the other day, and that night, I consciously surrendered myself to a Higher Power. I said, "Here I am. My disease has reactivated. I know you're all powerful and only you can relieve me and soothe my mind. You can help me." I went to bed, and as I lay there, I felt peace, as though I'd physically let go of something. The next morning when I woke up, I was a new woman, lighter in my head and in my body. I felt alive and happy to be alive.

I see the contrast between that night and the next morning as the difference between my illness and recovery: I can be completely despondent one day, and the next I am grateful and happy in my abstinence. The cure isn't anything I had been in the habit of putting into my mouth—food, alcohol, antidepressants, lithium, valium. I've had plenty of all of those. The cure is in my actions of faith and the principles I follow. To stay alive, I need my Higher Power, and I need contact with other people in FA. It's not enough for me to sit alone and pray.

I'm grateful I can feel pain today. When I get through difficult times and the hard feelings that come up for me in relationships at work and at home, I reach another place, where I feel mature and strong. I ran from any sort of discomfort most of my life, but now I can stand on my own two feet, in my own two shoes. I can lift myself up, with the help of a Higher Power, and I can face all the difficulties that life throws at me. The feeling of being mature and strong makes me know that I can face whatever might happen next. I'm not as afraid as I used to be, and I don't have to keep my world so small anymore. Slowly my life is opening up, though I've a long way to go.

I hardly know how to describe my life now. I always felt stupid. In recovery, I didn't let those feelings stop me, and I decided to go on in my studies. I wanted to prepare myself to move on from my job someday, so I began a course of study at home, mainly through online classes.

The exams and study have been difficult. In the past, I would have given up at the first hurdle, but because of my Higher Power and FA, I'm consistently showing up for each step along the way. Someone in the program said to me once, "Inch by inch, it's a cinch; mile by mile, it's a trial." I am a good worker and a good student now. I'm learning how to sit down at my desk to face a difficult assignment. When I come up against something that I don't understand, I don't hit myself in the face, as I used to. I ask God for help, and I stay put. I keep the book open.

One of the biggest changes I've experienced happens when I look at myself in the mirror. I actually have moments when I could hug myself, because I think I look pretty darn good. I'm five feet, five inches tall. I've been almost as low as seven stone (98 pounds) and as high as fourteen stone (196 pounds) when I was bulimic, but now I'm just right.

I've been abstinent for over six years. As I look back, I know that there was a Higher Power in my life because I didn't die. I should have died the night I kicked the man I was living with. I was retaliating for his beating, and he took a knife to me. I should have died even before then, when my mother lost hope and wanted to drown herself and us children. Given my feelings, I should have died by my own hand.

I believe I had an inner strength that God gave me, but I owe my life to FA. It's helped me find a home inside myself and a resting place in my Higher Power. I have no words for my gratitude. I see the world through different eyes than those of the young girl in her Holy Communion dress who hated her own face. Today, I know that good things are coming.

To Thine Own Self

✧ ✧ ✧

FOR YEARS, I believed it would be impossible for me to find freedom from food. I'm considered petite—1.5 meters, or about five feet tall. Petite people have to eat less in order to stay small. I could never be satisfied with less, I thought, so I would have to battle my weight for the rest of my life.

I grew up in a city in south Germany, one or two hours from the Alps. My father was a social worker, and my mother was a therapist. When I look back at my childhood, I see that I already had the spiritual and mental aspects of the disease of food addiction. Nothing showed on my body, but I was filled with anxiety. I had an awful fear that I would be an outsider and that other people would forget me. I had nightmares as a young child. Until I was eighteen or even older, I was afraid to sleep alone in my room in the dark.

When I reached the age of twelve or thirteen, the fight with food and my weight began. First, I learned and paid attention to calories. Then I exercised and ran.

I tried not to eat after 6:00 p.m. I put off eating breakfast. I skipped dinner, so I wouldn't have as many meals. I used diet products and diets, but I couldn't follow the plans for more than two days because I didn't have the patience to cook all the meals.

I knew a lot about myself. I'd read my parents' many psychology books and had learned about addiction, but nothing that I knew helped me once I got a craving. When the hunger started, I had to eat. From morning to night, I fought my cravings for food.

At the age of sixteen, I got desperate. For the first time, I stuck my finger down my throat and made myself throw up. I knew this was called bulimia, but I couldn't understand why psychologists considered it a disease. It seemed like the answer! I was excited, but also afraid, because I knew that I had crossed another line, so I told my mom right away.

That year, I started psychoanalytic therapy, two sessions a week. I went for three years, though I rarely managed to keep myself from bingeing and throwing up between my appointments. I loved my therapist, but I never talked much about my eating. Once, she asked me what I ate when I binged, and when I told her, she was horrified by the quantities. "Oh, my God!" she said. "If you continue eating like that, you will have to go to a clinic!" She had no idea I had been eating like that for years.

My therapy ended because my insurance coverage stopped, and my disease got worse. I started planning my binges. I shopped at a variety of supermarkets because I was afraid to buy huge quantities of food in one place every day. Throwing up was hard for me, but I did it two or three times daily. First I was living with my parents and then with my husband, so I had to lie to get food. I was ashamed and stressed, trying to keep my bingeing and bulimia secret.

In the end, I got up each morning only because I wanted breakfast. My husband and I had a daughter. We'd welcomed her birth, and I had friends, but I had lost the feeling of love or connection. The world seemed like it was made of paper. It wasn't real. I wanted to fall asleep. I wanted to feel numb. I wanted peace. I'm grateful I never wanted to die, but I knew I didn't know how to live. There was no place on earth where I felt at home.

I found the FA program after I'd been in a psychiatric clinic for several weeks. I'd entered the clinic voluntarily because I felt I couldn't take care of myself anymore. While I was there, I began using the caps of water bottles to cut my arms until I bled. The pain of the cutting made me feel at least a little alive.

When I got out of the clinic, I had to see a psychiatrist. He suggested that I go to a self-help group. I thought, *Never! I know so much about myself. I'm a smart woman. Why should I ever do that?!* He was supposed to help me. Why did he make such a crazy suggestion? Still, I decided to try just one meeting and then tell him it wasn't right for me.

I called my mom, because she had worked in a twelve-step clinic for years, and she found two different twelve-step food groups. I ended up phoning FA for information. I couldn't understand why the woman I spoke with was so friendly, but I went to her meeting. She'd said, "You can always come!"

I can't tell you how grateful I am to the FA woman who first spoke with me, because I don't know what would have become of me if I hadn't met her. She was an American who was studying in Germany, and her FA meeting consisted of me, her, and only one other person. I was in such a sea of misery that I couldn't concentrate, and I didn't understand a lot of what she said, but I felt like I'd come home. I knew I'd heard something I needed and wanted.

I didn't ask the woman to sponsor me right away. I thought I was supposed to go to more meetings first, but mainly I wanted to eat all the foods I thought I would have to give up. I went on a three- or four-day binge and discovered I didn't enjoy the food anymore. After just one FA meeting, I knew too much.

I asked the American woman to sponsor me, but several weeks later, she moved back to the United States. There were only fifteen or twenty FA members in all of Germany at the time, and only two of us in the meeting in my city. That person left the program, and I didn't have another FA meeting near me for five years.

In those days, international calls cost about five dollars a minute, so I had to get a German sponsor. I found a strong and committed FA woman who lived far away from me. Sometimes I took a five-hour train ride and went to her meeting. I also had a few phone numbers for members in the United States.

One day, my husband told me he had cancer. After his treatments, he said he wanted to rethink our marriage. I despaired the night he told me. I couldn't call anyone in Germany because it was late, so I took my plastic phone card and tried to make my first call to the United States. My English was not very good at the time. I'd only studied it in high school and had never used it since.

The first person I called wasn't home. The second person answered, but I was afraid and didn't know the language enough to lead the conversation. In the back of my mind I heard: "Eat and forget. Eat and forget." I didn't want to eat, so I'd called, but all I could say was, "Hello." There was silence, and the person asked, "Who are you?" I was so scared. I said, "Someone from Germany."

I tried to explain my problem, but I couldn't say much, and I didn't understand a lot of what the woman said. At the end, she told me one thing. She said, "I'll pray for you." In her voice, I felt a kind of love come through the receiver of the phone. I was so frightened, I hung up without saying goodbye. My hands were sweating. It had been hard for me to share my inner feelings in a language I couldn't really speak, but I felt much better after the call. I wondered, *This person thousands of miles away, across the ocean, why does she say she'll pray for me?*

The phone call carried me through the night abstinently. The next morning, I called my sponsor, and I was all right. In the years to come, I shared this story with others. I told them how, later on, I phoned the United States many times, and how every time, I hoped I would get an answering machine. It is hard to talk with someone in your own language when you have not met. It's even harder using a language that's not your own, but I made the effort. I wanted to get answers, to understand.

Since my first sponsor was a strong, committed FA member and was from the United States, I thought I could find strength with other people from America. I'd heard that we might try AA when there were no FA meetings available to us, and I was able to find English-language AA meetings on an army base nearby. In the beginning, it was hard for me. I had to talk with the guard and show my passport before I could enter the base. I always explained that I was going to an AA meeting. I had problems with alcohol, too, but I wouldn't call myself an alcoholic. I'm addicted to food. I went to AA because I was looking for strong meetings.

The AA members accepted me. I sat with them for months and didn't say a word. I just listened. In the beginning, I didn't catch much of what was said, but gradually I began to understand more. There were a lot of AA old-timers at those meetings, and they talked about the book *Alcoholics Anonymous* and how they used the Steps to face their daily lives.

After a while, my German FA sponsor left the program, and I found another sponsor. By that time, I'd been through one or two AWOLs. In Germany, we did the AWOLs in our own language on the phone. Once a month, we all traveled from wherever we lived to the middle of our country, where we met for a meeting together. My third AWOL was led by Americans and was in English. Since then, I've been doing AWOLs in English, and now, at last, I'm leading one in German for people in my own country.

FA works long term. For thirteen years, I have been in a slender body. I came into the program when I was twenty-four, and I am thirty-seven now. I weigh 48 kilograms (about 105 pounds). I've been about 40 pounds overweight, when I was pregnant. I've also been bulimic and over 20 pounds too thin. I didn't have a huge weight loss in the program, but when I share my story, I always say that if I added all the pounds I've lost and gained, it would probably be 90 pounds or so—and certainly being 20 pounds underweight was extreme.

It's wonderful to be the right weight, but the complete freedom I have from food is even more important to me. I had horrible food cravings the first month of my abstinence. The vegetables, salad, proteins, and fruits I ate tasted terrible in the beginning because I was used to eating lots of sugar and fat. Now I am completely accustomed to abstinent food. I like my meals, but I don't look forward to them. I never thought I could eat three meals and be satisfied.

Becoming abstinent, or "putting down the food," as we say, didn't mean that I could easily face my life. The hunger I felt all the years before the program was really spiritual, not just physical, and without food to numb my feelings, I felt worse at first. I wanted to jump out of my skin, I was so nervous. Always, I wanted to get away from myself and to change whatever situation I was in, instead of trying to change myself.

Newly abstinent, I had to be patient. In our meditation book, *Twenty-Four Hours a Day,* there's a description of a mountain before us. We can only see a stony path ahead, but if we continue on our way, we can reach a higher place and look back one day on a wonderful view. After a while in the program, I saw that wonderful view. The Twelve Steps filled my spiritual hunger, and the longer I stayed abstinent, the better my life got.

FA has helped me find out who I am and how to live. For years after my husband and I divorced, I tried to date men. The first time I did a Fifth Step and talked honestly with my sponsor about myself and my life, I cried and cried because I was afraid I was homosexual. She thought that was fine, but I didn't, so I kept trying to date men. Two or three of the men even asked me to marry them, but I refused. It was just not in my heart.

In FA, we remind ourselves, "To thine own self be true," and I recall this when I think of my coming out. It was very hard for me to be true to myself, and coming out took years. I wondered if being lesbian was natural. I was afraid that I might be abnormal and that I was somehow not following God's plan. Perhaps being gay was a kind of illness.

I don't know why I had such doubts, because I was not raised to be prejudiced or nervous about homosexuality. My parents had gay friends, and I was never with people who weren't accepting, yet I was afraid. I did end up meeting a wonderful woman, whom I married, but during the first two years of our marriage, I sometimes had fits of doubt. I remember my sponsor becoming impatient with me for questioning again and again whether I was lesbian. Finally, she said, "Stop doubting yourself! Even if you have occasional questions for the rest of your life, accept. You made a decision. Follow through on it now and see what happens."

The people in FA and FA AWOLs helped me to be true to myself. They reminded me to think of what makes me happy and not to worry about other people's opinions. I have followed through on my commitment, and I've been happily married for five years. I love my wife. Of course, it's been challenging sometimes, but I've learned that whenever I have a problem, I have to look first at myself and examine my own attitudes. There is a lot for me to see.

For years, I have had trouble with anger. When I was married before, I sometimes felt so angry at my husband that I went into another room and hit myself. Once I tried to hit him, too. Today, because of FA AWOLs, I have choices I never had before. Now when I get upset, I don't have to try to get rid of the feeling. I understand that when I fight anger, it gets bigger and comes back twice as hard. Most of all I hurt myself when I go more deeply into anger, so instead, I turn to God for help. I ask for the wisdom and strength to stay quiet or to say the right words. I pray to know that, in truth, no one can hurt my inner self, and I say that I want to be shown how to be helpful and loving.

I got very sick this year. I was nauseated day and night. For nearly three months, I felt horrible. At one point, I lay on the couch, praying for God to take me away. I felt so awful, I didn't want to live in my body anymore. Even then, I was able to stay abstinent, thank you, God. Working with my sponsor, I avoided having anything made with flour or sugar and I didn't eat between meals.

Challenging life situations like that long bout of nausea help me strengthen my faith. One of the readings in *Twenty-Four Hours a Day* suggests that we wear the world "as a loose garment." This is my favorite text, because it teaches me that the world is the world. I have to accept. There are things that happen that make me uncomfortable, but within myself, I can always turn to God. In that place of peace and love inside myself, I am safe. If I go there, to God, one day at a time, I will never be driven to eat addictively again.

Asking for Abstinence

✧ ✧ ✧

MY STORY STARTS many, many years ago, in the South, where I was born into a military family. As far back as I can remember, I had issues with food. When I was very young, I used to get up in the middle of the night and "sneak"—that's the word that was used of me—sneak into the refrigerator. I'd eat, and when I got through, I played. I broke things on the shelves and stirred ingredients like my mother did when she prepared meals. I vividly remember the spanking I got from my father when he returned from the late shift one night and found me in the middle of my mess.

That was not the first time, and it certainly wasn't the last, that I took food. My mother says that she couldn't turn her back on me. Baby aspirin, Aspergum, and laxatives tasted sweet to me, and she had to hide them all. I spent a lot of time looking for them. Later on, our dinner table became a war zone. My parents had been through the Depression and a world war, and we were told to eat what was put in front of us. I had an aversion to certain foods, and I wouldn't eat them, no matter what. Then came my father's rage. And shouting. And my tears. Often I'd throw up and be sent to my room.

When I was still a young girl, we moved to Europe. My mother and father began drinking more heavily. They did the best they could, but they were the children of alcoholics, and, as I came to understand later, they were alcoholics themselves. In Europe, when I was about seven, I had the misfortune of being sexually abused by my brother. I couldn't go to either of my parents or say anything to anyone about how ashamed and hurt I was, how awful I felt about my body. The only comfort I found was in food. The abuse continued until I was about twelve, when one night my brother brought another boy into my room, and I found the strength from somewhere to say no.

As I grew up, I began to believe that I was a bad person. I'd begun babysitting, and I took food from people's cabinets and denied it later. I couldn't understand myself. My mother impressed upon me that I was a liar and a sneak. Obviously, my behavior was affecting my family, but I didn't know how to stop.

I eloped when I was seventeen and ended up in another state, far from my parents. I expected them to bring me home, but instead they told me I'd made my own bed and I'd have to lie in it. My father had beaten me, and after our marriage, my husband began physically abusing me. I was in a bad situation. I had such low self-esteem, I thought I'd done something to deserve the violence, and, again, I felt I had nowhere to turn.

I left my parents' home in September, and by December, I'd gained 30 pounds. This was during the sixties, and as life would have it, my husband eventually got drafted. My disease was full blown by then. I was bingeing all the time. Trying to keep the weight off, I'd learned how to smoke and had discovered diet pills. Bulimia followed.

At one point, I decided to stop eating, or at least to limit myself to one piece of food a day. Smoking, taking the diet pills, drinking diet soda, and starving myself, I got down to 97 pounds. I was five feet, five inches tall at the time. I remember standing in front of a mirror, concave from my breasts to my waist. I had just a small amount of flesh protecting my female organs, and yet I thought, *If only I could lose 5 more pounds, I'd be okay.*

After a while, I couldn't get any more pills, and I went back to eating with a vengeance, gaining back all the weight I'd ever lost. Life went on. My husband was killed in Vietnam, and I married again, choosing what was familiar in a man: drinking and rage. I got pregnant right away. My second husband's job took us to Europe, and there, while he drank, I ate. My food addiction got worse. Before I knew it, I was pregnant again. I hadn't used birth control pills because I didn't want to reveal my stupidity by asking any questions. I was sure that I was stupid. My only hope was to hide it.

My second child was born in England, which made him a British citizen, which qualified him for the National Health Service, which qualified me for the National Health Service, which gave me access to diet pills. I got hooked on pills again and hit new lows of depression. I weighed 250 pounds and ordered everything I wanted to eat from bakery trucks that came by the house. When I told one of the ladies I knew that I had stayed up for four nights in a row crying, she recommended Librium. That seemed like a good idea, so I went to an American doctor and politely told him how depressed I was. I didn't mention the diet pills, and when I started combining the antidepressant with the pills, I lost the ability to function.

My husband came home in a fury one night. Finally finding some courage, I called my mother to tell her that I was leaving and discovered for the second time that I wasn't going to be able to go back home. Thankfully, my husband decided to ask for help with his alcoholism. He never drank in front of me again, though he continued to use alcohol.

I could finally see that my husband had a problem, but I had no idea that I had one. He needed help, not me. I did finally go to a twelve-step program for compulsive overeaters when we came back to the United States. I weighed 267 pounds at the time, and I was trying to diet again. Our budget wouldn't allow me to pay for much, so I was attracted by the promise that the meetings were free. The members seemed nice, but I was frightened by their talk of God. As a practicing Catholic, I had my own religion. I didn't need theirs.

I politely left the first meeting with a promise to return within a week, though I knew I'd never go back. During the almost thirty years that followed, I tried every diet known to man, enrolling in commercial programs and free weight loss groups. At one point, my husband even took a part-time job to pay for the fees.

When I was fifty years old, weighed 250 pounds, and had lived through twenty-seven years of gaining and losing, gaining and losing, I finally walked back into a twelve-step program. This time, I was led to FA. I had no hope, but someone had told me the program worked. Sitting in the back row at the meeting, I looked at a tiny, petite woman speaking from the front of the room and heard her say that foods with sugar and flour are addictive. I felt as if someone had hit me between the eyes with a two-by-four.

The woman explained that an alcoholic can't go into a bar and have one drink. An alcoholic is lying to himself if he says he can and lying to others if he ever makes that claim to someone else, because an alcoholic can't ever stop at one. I'd had trouble with alcohol, but for some reason I didn't believe I was an alcoholic. Instead, I knew immediately that food was my drug. I'd never been able to go into a bakery and eat one cookie. It wasn't possible for me to have a single piece of chocolate. But how could I give up flour and sugar? *What do these people eat?* I thought. *How can they make a sandwich?!*

I listened carefully and decided that I would try to avoid flour and sugar. In a fog, I heard nothing about finding a sponsor, but I went the next week and the next, and finally I asked someone to sponsor me. She gave me a food plan, and when I started, I made an agreement with myself. My father used to say, "A man is only as good as his word." I had been known as a liar and a sneak, and I was determined to follow the food plan for ninety days. I didn't cheat, I didn't sneak, I didn't lie. I was scared to death to do anything other than what my sponsor told me to do, and at the end of ninety days, I had lost a significant amount of weight.

At one of my meetings, a speaker held up an enormous pair of pants that he'd once worn and said, "I graduated first in my law school, and I'm the only one that didn't get a job. Then I came into this program and lost over 200 pounds." He was in a normal-size body, and as he talked, I thought, *If he can, I can.* But I asked my sponsor, "Do I have to do this for the rest of my life?!" She answered, "What is the rest of your life? Your life is just today. Stay in the day." So I stayed in the day, and pretty soon I had six months of abstinence. By my ninth month of abstinence, I'd lost 110 pounds, and I was in a normal-size body, too. I stood up to share my experience then, and I cried because I realized there was nowhere else for me to go. This was the only solution that had ever worked.

I got abstinent because I followed the suggestions that my sponsor gave me. Every morning I got on my knees and asked God if I might have an abstinent day. I took half an hour of quiet time for prayer and meditation. I read our literature, wrote postcards to FA members, and made phone calls to people with long-term abstinence. Through these actions and others, I stayed close to the program and fellowship.

These disciplines reminded me of where I'd begun. My father was a military man, and he gave us children a time to eat, a time to go to bed, a time to do our homework, a time to do this, a time to do that. I learned military time before I learned regular time, because my father gave us orders. "You be home by 1800 hours," he'd say. I couldn't wait to get away from all of the regimentation, and yet by the time I came into the program, my life was out of control. I slept, and I ate, and I read books, and I did whatever I wanted to do whenever I wanted to do it. I needed to be told to stay in touch with program members, to eat my meals at reasonable times, and to make meetings a priority. I was grateful for the order this brought to my life.

The program my sponsor gave me was far more than a list of things to do each day. The core of my experience of recovery was that I began to have a personal relationship with the God of my own understanding. This was completely different from religion.

The first morning I got on my knees to ask God for a day of abstinence, my husband looked across our king-size bed and said, "What are you doing?!" I answered honestly when I told him that I didn't exactly know what I was doing and didn't know if it would work. I had gotten on my knees whenever I was in a Catholic church, but I never prayed, "God, help me with my weight" or "God, get me out of this situation I'm in." I thought God had sick children to take care of. He was too busy to bother with me. Besides, I was afraid of God. I was a liar, a cheat, a thief, a glutton—my mother told me so. I wasn't someone worthy to be in the presence of God. I was supposed to ask God's help for others and handle any of my own problems by myself.

Still, I did as I was told, and after many days of getting on my knees, I realized that there must have been a Higher Power who was helping me. *You could be abstinent for a week,* I thought. *You could probably be abstinent for six weeks. But it's more than six months now and you're still abstinent.* How could that have been possible unless there was a Higher Power who heard my prayers for help?

After a while, I completely lost my embarrassment, and I began talking to my Higher Power out loud. I discovered that when I prayed silently, I'd start to think about my grocery list, or I'd remind myself to tell my husband this or that. In the silence, a party would start in my head. So instead, I went into a room alone, and all the other voices were drowned out when I had my conversation with God out loud.

By then, I'd started asking God for help with things other than my abstinence. I was practicing—starting a relationship by talking about little things that I knew didn't matter. At work, we had various parking lots, and often we had to park in what we called Never Never Land. I started saying, "God, show me where it is you would have me park." It was uncanny. I'd go to the lot nearest the door, and so often, someone would pull out, leaving me a perfect space. Some days, of course, no one did that, so I'd park in Never Never Land and say, "Okay, God, you want me to walk today." In a way this was silly, but it helped me develop my relationship with God.

Through FA, God became real to me. I was hard-hearted and harsh when I came into the program. I remember my own sponsor saying to me, "Your rage and anger scare me." That made me cry, because I don't remember ever wanting to frighten anyone, but I had seen rage and anger work for other people, and I guess I thought I should use them, too. I also know now that a large part of the reason for my rage was that I had so much hurt inside of me. But when I took quiet time in the morning, it was as if someone's arms were wrapped around me. I felt love for the first time during my quiet time. I never felt loved before, and I could not give love, either, because I protected my heart. My ability to feel love and give love came from my quiet time, from my Higher Power.

The FA program and the FA fellowship changed me completely. The process was slow, but I began to be able to trust. At one point, I met an FA member who was visiting from another area. When we talked, she looked me in the eyes and listened to everything I said. No one had ever listened to me so carefully. She had a grace and calmness, a sincerity that mesmerized me. She was a beautiful person, and I wanted what she had. Her example encouraged me to go on in my recovery.

I began to phone this woman, and when we spoke, her peacefulness soothed the rage inside me. Once when my mother was visiting, she went shopping and came home with all kinds of candy and honey and jellies and jams, none of which I could eat. When I saw the bottles and packages on the counter, I was crazed with anger. I wanted to scream at my mother, but instead, I picked up the phone and called my friend. She listened and then spoke to me sweetly, sharing the story of a healed relationship with her own mother. I calmed down, grateful for the possibilities she showed me.

I did the Steps of recovery through AWOL groups and received the gift of new ways to see my life. I looked back and finally understood that my parents were ill from alcoholism. I realized that I was not a bad child. The Steps gave me new actions, too. Instead of focusing on how my mother treated me, I looked at myself and made amends for my own behavior. Today, my mother and I have a relationship. It's not as close as the one I'd always hoped for, but we are much closer than we have ever been. Though she never calls me, I am able to pick up the telephone to reach out to her.

AWOL and my Higher Power also freed me from the anger I felt at my brother, who moved into our town last year. I'd stopped thinking about what happened between us, but seeing him shook me to my foundation. Fear covered me, and I felt an old rage that I had never shared. I had told my sponsor and my husband about my childhood, but I had never talked about how horrible I felt, how betrayed.

I couldn't avoid my brother because we attended the same twelve-step meetings, and each time we were together I hated being in the room with him. *Alcoholics Anonymous* says that resentment cuts us off from God and threatens our abstinence. I experienced the truth of this as my rage continued. One day, I told a friend in the program an outright lie. In my recovery, I don't lie, and I saw immediately that my disease had reactivated. I got on my knees and told God I couldn't go on.

I didn't know what to do, but I was completely honest with my sponsor. I hid none of my reactions or feelings, and I continued to do the Steps in AWOL. Then it came to me to ask God to help me see my brother as God sees him. Surely God loved him. Gradually, my vision changed. I remembered my brother as a young boy, and I saw him as someone who had been hurt. My brother had been abused, too, and he'd gone down the path I had taken. He was beaten by alcohol, drugs, and food, and he was sick. I saw myself in my brother. I remembered how patiently and kindly I'd been treated in FA, even though I'd been ill, and slowly God lifted my anger.

Today, I have what I call outrageous joy. I have two sons in recovery. They do not drink or drug, and they work hard. My husband is drink free and cigarette free because of twelve-step programs, and I love him dearly. We've moved to be near my grandchildren, who are the biggest pleasures in my life. All this, and I wear a size six or eight petite, as I have for years. In a few months, I'll reach my fifteenth year of abstinence and almost fourteen years of life in a normal body. I don't turn to food for comfort anymore. I go to God.

I am the only FA member in our state, but I am excited about the possibility of developing meetings here. I'm isolated, and I need to be with others in our program. I've just gotten back from a two-and-a-half-hour drive to one small FA meeting, and I'll soon be driving several hundred miles to another state to support a person who has started a meeting there.

It's nothing for me to spend five hours in a car or a day in an airplane in order to give FA service somewhere else. This program is a precious gift. Whenever I offer my help, it strengthens my own recovery and allows me to give back at least a little of what I've received. It's my way of saying, "Thank you, God, for the gifts that you have given me." Besides, it gives me that outrageous joy.

Body, Mind, and Spirit

✧ ✧ ✧

O NE OF MY THERAPISTS once told me that he had never seen a client whose moods changed more rapidly than mine. I was seeing him because I regularly thought about suicide. "In the blink of an eye, the bottom seems to fall out of your life," he said, "just because of someone's look or some little straw that breaks. The chemicals in your brain are not in balance. I know you are seeking some kind of normalcy without your medications, but that will never be possible for you." I was taking two antidepressants and two anti-anxiety medications at that time, and I'd been on medications and in therapy since I was about nineteen.

For as long as I can remember, I've had moments when everything changed in a flash. I was suddenly in a pit somewhere, hopeless. The next line in the script was *You should eat. Go eat.* Food is a temporary fix, after all. If you feel terrible and you eat two or three bowls of ice cream, eventually all you notice is the ice cream.

Sometimes today, I still have sudden lurches toward despair, but I use the FA program when the bottom falls away from me. God helps me think. I remind myself I have a safety net. I lose my sense of danger and can go on with the next step in my life. Leaning on a Higher Power and nothing else, I can stay on an even keel.

The backstory to all of this involves a lot of food and dieting. I remember first feeling fat when I was in the sixth grade. I'm a gay man, but for whatever reason, I fell in love with a girl and wanted to be her boyfriend. Suddenly I became aware of my big tummy and my fat butt, and I approached my mom for help. She started me on my first diet.

Dieting was a big part of our family life. My mom and dad both struggled with weight, though neither of them was big. They were meticulous people, so 5 or 10 extra pounds—or more—caused them concern. We talked about weight often, and I remember thinking that obesity was in my future. My mom would say, "Be careful what you eat, there's obesity in your father's family." My dad would warn me similarly about my mother's family. I was always fighting chubbiness. Exercise, dieting, overeating, exercise, dieting, overeating. That was my cycle.

So much confused me. All four of my grandparents were born in Greece, and I was raised in a religious household. My mom and dad stayed together, so our family was stable, but we were on a financial roller coaster. At one point, we worried about having enough money to put food on our table. Later, there were times when I was among the most well-to-do at school.

I struggled especially with relationships. I know now that I am highly sensitive and care deeply when others seem to feel upset with me or disapprove of me in any way. Today, I use the Serenity Prayer to help me see what I should do, but when I was growing up, I turned to flour and sugar every time I experienced discomfort.

I also developed stomachaches when I was a child. I spent a good portion of my second grade out of school with horrible stomach pains. I remember the doctor telling my mother that if I weren't so young, he would swear I had ulcers. By the time I was fifteen, I did end up in the hospital with bleeding ulcers. I remember thinking then that I was not going to make it to twenty-one.

Throughout my life, my roller coaster feelings have been manifested in my body. I'd show up in the doctor's office doubled over in agony. What was going on in my head? What was I worried about? What did I feel? Therapists would ask me, and I'd have no idea. I couldn't say "fear" or "envy." I had no vocabulary for my emotions. All I knew was that my body was in excruciating pain and that I was struggling with food.

Part of my problem was simply what I ate. Sometime in my late teens, I went to a physician who examined me and talked to me about my eating. "You really need to give up chili," he said. He leaned close and looked right into my eyes. "You have to understand that when you eat food like that, it's like eating glass. You can't eat it. It tears you up inside." I comprehended what he said, but I don't think I went more than two weeks before I was back to eating chili and beans. They were drugs for me. Candy, sweets, chili and beans, I had to have them.

Despite all my struggles with illness and eating, I graduated from high school, and after a couple of starts finished college. Law school followed, which was terrible. I ballooned from about 175 to 220 pounds within the first quarter. After I dropped out, my addictions bloomed in full force. I ate addictively, and I also abused alcohol, marijuana, and cigarettes.

When my health deteriorated, my mom let me move home. Shortly thereafter, at twenty-seven years old, I had stomach surgery. I was told that my stomach and duodenum had ulcerated so many times that the scar tissue prevented me from digesting my food. Doctors removed my duodenum and 40 percent of my stomach, and I've done fairly well ever since.

The U.S. economy was in bad shape then, and after I recovered from surgery I had difficulty finding a job. Though I didn't want to become a professor, it occurred to me that I might be able to work at a college or university in some other capacity. Further training led me to several good positions. I also married a beautiful woman from my church.

I was fairly trim during the time I was married. I am five feet, ten and a half inches tall, and I weighed about 170 pounds. My weight was down, but I worked constantly at controlling it. I was driven to entertain because I wanted to cook special foods. My wife and I would invite a couple over, and I'd make enough manicotti for eight people, an additional entrée, and two desserts that I'd found in a Julia Childs cookbook. During the entire dinner, just one thought lit up my brain: leftovers. I didn't want anyone to disapprove of my eating, so I took only moderate amounts at the dinner table. The highlight for me came after everyone left.

When I was thirty-eight, I developed a head-over-heels crush on a man at work. I talked with my therapist and my wife. Part of my coming out also involved a conversation with the priest of my church. At the time, I was head of the church's fundraising campaign and on the parish council, and I wanted the priest to know why my wife and I had decided to divorce. I said I was gay and hoped he wouldn't disapprove. He said, "Of course I don't disapprove. How could any of us disapprove of you when God made you this way? However, you wouldn't want to act on any of those impulses."

I let go of God at that point. I stopped going to church, finished the fundraising project as best I could, and resigned from the council. I also moved away, having found a job in another part of the state. From the day I came out, I stopped believing that I was held or cared about by God. I thought I was a bad person. I was somehow outside of God's family.

Significantly, that began another period of weight gain for me, and I reached 220 pounds again. *You're fat, and you're going to stay fat,* I told myself. I'd lost the ability to diet and was abusing alcohol, but how could anyone possibly get fatter than 220 pounds? Impossible. Deluding myself, I gave up struggling.

When I went in for my next annual physical, I weighed 245 pounds. Dismayed, I hired a personal trainer and began working with a nutritionist who was well credentialed and smart. Neither of them was able to help me stop eating. As a consequence, I was fired from two jobs. When I eat, I don't pay attention to the needs and wishes of other people, including colleagues, superiors, and the clients I am supposed to serve.

Once I lost my last job, I had trouble making the monthly payments on my condominium, so I rented it out and moved into a flat with two roommates. Both were overweight. One was in Weight Watchers, and the other had newly joined FA. I decided to try FA and set off for my first meeting, full of fear and with a superior attitude. I heard people there talking about food addiction and the impossibility of a food addict sanely eating flour, sugar, or unlimited quantities, but I thought they were crazy. How can a person be addicted to quantities of food?

Naturally enough, I am particularly addicted to quantities. I hated measuring my food. I also rebelled at the thought of writing down a plan for my meals the day before I was going to eat them. I wanted to eat just what I wanted to eat when I wanted to eat it. Still, I was desperate enough that I was willing to give FA a try. Someone asked, "Can you just do this for ninety days?" and I said, "I think I can do anything for ninety days."

I found a sponsor at my first meeting, but I struggled throughout my first weeks in FA. In other situations, they give you a room with rubber walls when you're an addict in withdrawal, but I didn't have that, and from September 20 to November 14, I kept breaking my abstinence. This was never intentional. I never said to myself, *I can't stand this anymore* or *Forget it! I'm going to eat an extra meal.* Rather, I would eat something that was not abstinent and suddenly think, *Oh, my God, what did*

I do?! One time someone told me my breath smelled terrible and gave me a breath mint. I popped the mint into my mouth before I could think, and that was the end of that period of abstinence.

Nothing spectacular happened on November 14, but two things had changed. I had gotten a new sponsor. He used to say to me, "If you need to talk, you can call me any time, day or night." One night, I woke up at about three o'clock and found myself on my way to the kitchen, headed toward the refrigerator. I was frightened to discover myself sleepwalking, so I called my sponsor. We talked, and then I got back into bed and went to sleep. I haven't broken my abstinence since that night.

My sponsor was helpful, but I believe that my release from addictive eating most fundamentally involved a change in my attitude toward a Higher Power. When I first came to an FA meeting, I was told I'd have to find such a Power to help me. Because of my experience coming out, I found this difficult, so people told me to act as if there was a caring Higher Power. They said, "Pray to God even if you don't believe He's listening or even if you don't think He's there. Pray anyway. Get on your knees anyway. Take quiet meditation time anyway." After a couple of months of doing those actions, I came to believe that a Power greater than myself could restore me to sanity, and I trusted. Whatever had driven me to eat before I could think or make a different choice came to a halt. My heart started to open, and I actually let God in. I've been abstinent for the eleven and a half years since.

As I've lived abstinently, slowly but surely, much that had been torn away from my life was restored to me. I got jobs back. Friendships that I'd neglected or trampled upon were renewed, or new friends were given to me. FA service became a key component in my recovery. My hyperactive mind and fidgety fingers quieted themselves when I reached out to help others. It's still transformative for me to staple and collate copies of meeting directories or to call a newcomer.

I gain far more from doing service than I ever receive in return. My analyst used to talk with me about my self-centeredness. He mentioned my inability to relate to others and to be aware of their needs. While I was grateful to him and all my other therapists, I didn't have the tools to help me take advantage of such observations. Service now accomplishes what could never occur before. As I talk with someone else about his or her concerns and as I share my own experience of recovery, I am freed from my self-centered fears. I'm given a sense of peace and gratitude.

I have a good life today, with a wonderful new job and a beautiful home. Fellow members of FA know and trust and like me, and I feel the same way about them. My relationship with my mother is another gift of recovery. I'd had a terrible time with my mom. I was convinced that every problem we'd ever had was her fault, but as I was doing the Twelve Steps in an AWOL, my sponsor asked me if there hadn't been at least one speck of a thing that might have been my fault. If so, she suggested, I needed to go to my mom and clean my side of the street.

I hadn't seen or spoken with my mom in three years, but when we finished the Ninth Step, I decided to go to her to apologize. I thought she would quickly acknowledge all of the awful things she'd done. Instead, she just said, "It's about time." At one point, we were gritting our teeth and having a tense conversation when there was a lull. To my amazement, she came to me, enveloped me in her arms, and told me that I was special in her life. My anger melted, and I was able to say how much I loved her. She's ninety-three now, and we are very close.

Today I'm well. I made a personal, individual choice to stop taking antidepressants and anti-anxiety medications, in part because I was afraid of the possibility of future side effects. I worked closely with my doctor to slowly cut back until I could stop taking them. A doctor's care was essential.

About four or five years into the program, I started taking supplements, and all those are gone now, too. I was on forty or fifty pills a day trying to improve my joints and body functions and overall health. Now I take little beyond an occasional antihistamine. If something seems awry physically, I ask myself if I've had enough water or if I need more rest, and I consult one health care practitioner who encourages this simple, gentle approach. My weight stays stable at 152 pounds.

The disease of food addiction wracks the body, spirit, and mind. It turns everything upside down. I'm in recovery now, though, and life doesn't feel hard or cruel. My heart's softened. Each time I let go of my own will, I'm a little more able to open up to God, to life, to beauty—to being present.

Recovery First

✧ ✧ ✧

T HERE ARE TWO THINGS I was made to be: I was made to be a pastor, and I was made to be a mother. I thank God for FA, so that I can now be both, as I was meant to be.

I believe I have been a food addict since birth. Obviously, when I was growing up and dealing with my addiction, I didn't know the term, but as I look back through the lens of what I have come to understand through FA, I see the patterns from very early on.

At one of my first FA meetings, someone said that food addiction is a disease of fear, doubt, and insecurity. That struck a chord in me, because I remember being afraid from a young age. I was painfully shy, which I now understand to be a fear of people. I didn't learn how to ride a bicycle until I was about fourteen because I was afraid of falling. I never learned how to rollerskate or skateboard. I was afraid of water, swimming, heights, bugs, and anything that moved fast. My life was limited and circumscribed by my fears.

Looking back, I've also realized that food had an unnatural place in my life. As I now watch my oldest son grow up, I see that he and other children can eat half a cookie and leave it because they want to go outside to play. I was never like that. I always wanted to eat something more. I never asked my parents for a toy or a doll. I asked them for money to buy snacks—the sweeter and greasier, the better.

My home was chaotic. My father was a violent alcoholic during a good part of my childhood and adolescence. My mother struggled with mental illness and other issues. There was a lot of screaming, fighting, and tension in our house, which added to my fear. I used food and reading as a way to escape, crawling into bed with a book and something sweet. By eating, reading, and fantasizing, I left the situation I was in.

My life was typical for a food addict. Food addiction is a progressive disease that always gets worse. Over time, I ate larger quantities and found ways to eat more often. As I got older and had more access to food, I used excessive exercise to keep my weight low.

One summer when I was a teenager, my routine began with a morning jog and weight lifting. I then walked miles to a swimming lesson, where I stood for an hour and fearfully refused to put my head in the water. Next, I headed for the tennis courts. I grew up in one of the southern states, where the temperature sometimes reached one hundred degrees, but I played tennis all day long. I exposed myself to the point where I developed blistering sunburns, even though I'm African American and my dark skin usually would not burn. Once I even burned the whites of my eyes.

After my day of tennis, I went home, drank a lot of fluids, and then left for my karate lesson. Classes lasted an hour and a half, and I convinced my instructor to let me do two of them, back to back. Between classes, I had to have someone go outside with me so we could wring the sweat out of my uniform. After the three hours of karate, I went home to do sit-ups and lift weights.

My weight stayed low to normal during my teenage years because of the exercise and the starving I did in between my binges. I took some laxatives, and I threw up on occasion, only because I got uncomfortably full. I also drank shots of Benedictine and brandy, because my father once told me that they would burn up food in the stomach. I'd binge, drink the alcohol, and then eat some more. I thought all of this worked fairly well, since I was five feet, four inches tall and weighed between 112 and 115 pounds.

I was a strong student in high school, but I developed such severe anxiety about math that my brain stopped. My father screamed at me and banged his fist on the table when he tried to help me with my homework. Sometimes all I managed on my math exams was to write my name.

The summer after I graduated, I entered a preparatory program for minority students who had been accepted by Ivy League schools. The math faculty were incredible. I did fairly well for a little while, but fear took me again, and I was unwilling to return to my calculus class. Addicts don't take feedback well, so I ignored the suggestion that I get some counseling. Instead, as soon as I entered the university in the fall, I walked straight into a calculus class and flunked it.

It took five years of struggle before I finished college. I gained weight, because I stayed in dormitories where I had access to an unlimited food plan and to nearby late-night cafes. I spent a lot of time eating alone in my room. The more I ate, the more depressed and isolated I became.

Right after my senior year, my mother had a psychotic break, and the doctors diagnosed her as a paranoid schizophrenic. I put on more pounds that summer and even more the following year when I began my first job. This was followed by a series of moves as I found other jobs and new places to live. I kept thinking that something outside me would make me happy. I was miserable. I hated my weight and my body, but I could never diet successfully.

In the early 1990s, my spiritual life began to change. I'd begun searching, looking here and there, and attending various churches. I finally joined one, but I was bereft. I had always believed that I would be happy if only: if only I had the right job, the right boyfriend, lived in the right place, had the right boss. At that point, I'd returned to the area where I wanted to live and had found a great job. I had a boyfriend and a wonderful apartment.

All was well, but I was eating like I had never eaten before. I went to see various therapists to find out why I was so unhappy and couldn't stop eating. One counselor told me that my inner parent was being too hard on my inner child and was beating her up by not letting her eat as she wished. I should indulge, she said, and then I wouldn't feel deprived. I was supposed to eat five M&Ms every morning, but those five inevitably led me to five more, which took me, as a start, to a whole bag of the candy.

I also went to see a nutritionist. She had plastic models of food in her desk, and she'd whip one out and say, "This is what four ounces of steak looks like." She tried to convince me that I could eat things made from flour and sugar. "Just eat in moderation," she would say. "Just have one." I was supposed to write down everything I had eaten, but I never told the truth. It didn't seem an option to write down all the food I ate, considering breakfast alone. On my way to work, I would stop by a bakery for breakfast. After I got to my office, I'd go to two of the four cafeterias and have two more breakfasts. Then at ten o'clock, I'd walk across the street to get a little something to have with my coffee.

As unhappy as I was, I started to have some epiphanies. At one point, I began to realize that I was just like my father. I had a great deal of resentment toward my father because of the havoc in our family caused by his alcoholism. I swore that I would never be like him, yet I started to see that I did with food what he did with alcohol.

I also began to understand that I did not have a weight problem. I had a food problem. I'd always said that I was unhappy because I was fat, that I just needed to find the right diet and to exercise more often. Suddenly I started thinking that there was something wrong with the *way* I ate. Normal people don't eat food that is stale or that has fallen on the floor. They don't eat until they burn their mouths with things that are too hot.

I'd started going back to church, so I began to pray.

When I was young, before we ate a special meal, we'd been taught to say, "God bless this food that we are about to receive for the nourishment of our bodies." For some reason, the thought popped into my head that I should say this prayer over everything that I ate—every candy bar, cookie, bag of sweets, box of crackers—every pound of all the junk that I put in my mouth. Each time I said the prayer, my flesh crawled, because it became very clear to me that God had nothing to do with what I was doing to my body with food. This was not God's will for me.

One moment always stands out in my memory. I had a Queen Anne dining room table that seated eight people. One day, I asked myself what I wanted, and I had a fantasy. I wanted the entire table covered with every delicacy I could imagine. I wanted to eat until everything was gone and more food magically appeared. I wanted to eat endlessly, without getting sick or fat. Then came the epiphany. How absolutely sad, I thought, that my dream for my life was to have an unending supply of food that I could eat by myself, without consequences.

As I felt more and more unhappy, I continued to go to church, and one Sunday, I stood up at the altar call. Ordinarily, people might go to the altar to ask for prayers if they had cancer or someone they loved had died, but that day, I walked to the front of the whole congregation and said, "I need help. I can't stop eating." The minister who was visiting made a joke about "spare tires" and how hard it is to push ourselves away from the table. I wanted to sink into the floor, but my pastor stood up and took the mike from him. "She's talking about addiction," he said, and with that, he prayed for me.

After the service, a woman approached me. She said she was a food addict in a twelve-step program for compulsive overeaters and asked if I wanted help. I said yes, and she suggested I buy a scale. She also discussed a shopping list and gave me a time to call her in the morning.

I started to get somewhat involved, but in the beginning, I attended just one meeting a week. We sat in a circle there, and I told everyone that they needed to go to therapy and get in touch with their inner child. I had a couple of different sponsors. One of them explained that she didn't feel she could help me after I told her I thought I could eat whole wheat bread. I was different, I said. I only had a problem with white flour.

Who needs a sponsor? I could sponsor myself, I decided. As my own sponsor, I felt free to eat bread as long as it wasn't white. My vegetables were varied: corn chips, potatoes, other snack chips. I used huge amounts of sweetener, ate peanut butter as a protein, and enjoyed all-fruit jelly as my fruit. In six months, I did lose a little weight, but I struggled constantly with food cravings.

Finally, I came to another surrender. I found a real sponsor, who happened to be in FA. The next morning, following her guidance, I ate my first abstinent breakfast. I cried while I ate. For me, becoming abstinent—avoiding foods made with sugar and flour and refraining from having unmeasured quantities—was like having my leg cut off without anesthesia. It was the hardest thing I have ever done. I still remember, though, that on day four of my abstinence, I had another epiphany. After a lifetime of lying about my eating, I finally had integrity. I felt clean! About two and a half months later, I was walking home from work when I realized that for the first time in my life, I had a moment when I felt no physical craving for any food and no wish to eat. A new world opened up before me.

I'd gotten engaged six months before I became abstinent, and I was just six months into my abstinence when I married. As I planned the wedding, all I could think about was the wedding cake. How could I get married without eating some? Was that fair or right?! If you had been inside my head, you'd have thought that the whole point of the wedding was the cake.

Fortunately, I stayed abstinent. I was told to remain in the day instead of worrying about the time ahead, and I discovered that when I am abstinent and in the present, I become a different person by the time I reach the future. On the day I actually got married, I was hardly aware of the cake because I was thinking instead about my husband and our two families. The cake was no longer important to me.

As a newcomer, I found FA in the area where the program first developed, and I was surrounded by people with strong recovery. I complained a lot about my sponsor and all I had to do. I realized later that I'd been complacent, because before we married, my husband got a job in another state, and we had to move.

In my new home, I had no access to FA meetings. People in the meetings I found were overweight, unhappy, and struggling with food. They demanded that I not talk about how much weight I'd lost or how long I'd been abstinent. They said I mustn't mention that I weighed and measured my food and avoided flour and sugar. Someone called me at home and kept hanging up the phone. When several people asked me to sponsor them and we organized FA meetings, others appeared at the meetings to object. When I began leading an AWOL, two women obstructed discussions from the front of the room.

I sat through all the words of opposition and prayed the Serenity Prayer. I made many phone calls to FA members with long-term abstinence and spent a lot of time on my knees. I had always isolated myself and never asked for help, so it was a blessing that I was finally able to reach out. Older, more experienced members gave me good guidance and specific suggestions. Above all, they reminded me that our program is based on attraction, not promotion. "Be a quiet witness," they said. "Show up at your meetings consistently, as you are, thin and attractive. This will resolve itself."

The older members were right. I didn't back down, and I didn't stop talking. As we continued our FA meetings despite the opposition and anger, new people saw our recovery and wanted it. I was able to share the FA program that was helping me. *Alcoholics Anonymous* describes the joy of watching a fellowship of recovery grow around us. I knew that joy.

I was happy where I was, but after two and a half years, my husband had to change jobs. I was approaching the end of the AWOL I was leading, and I had to tell him I couldn't move until it was finished. We can't know what will happen until we ask! My husband went to his supervisor, and in the end, everyone else was transferred quickly to another state. We followed four months later when my AWOL ended.

After our move, as I grew stronger in my abstinence, food no longer blocked me, and I started becoming the person God wanted me to be. I didn't understand it at the time, but as part of that process, I decided to go to seminary. FA taught me to depend on a Higher Power, but my time in seminary reinforced that lesson. There I faced my fears, and, instead of struggling and barely getting by, I developed a love of learning. Above all, my faith grew.

In seminary, I saw over and over again that when I put my recovery first and asked God for help, everything else fell into place. Despite my long commute and heavy load of homework, I never skipped an FA meeting. I continued to cook and to measure my meals during final exams. I got enough sleep. I stayed in touch with other FA members by phone. With recovery as my top priority, I didn't have enough time to thoroughly prepare for school, no matter how hard I tried. The night before one midterm exam, I attended my usual FA meeting. When I walked into class the next day, I'd completed only two-thirds of the required reading, but the test paper covered nothing beyond the materials I'd studied.

Test after test was like that exam. I asked God for help and received the help I needed. My work was always enough. Today, I absolutely trust that God will help me. No matter how pressured my schedule, I still take care of my recovery first. I don't skip meetings. Regarding my responsibilities, I ask myself, *Are you procrastinating? Are you doing the best that you can?* When I can honestly say,

I've kept recovery as my top priority, and I am doing the best that I can, I know all will be well. I trust God absolutely.

While I was in seminary, I became pregnant and lost the child. I walked through my sorrow abstinently, learning how to grieve without running to food for comfort. In active addiction, I'd suffered from clinical depression, but in recovery I discovered that sadness and depression are as different as night and day.

A year later, I got pregnant again. Throughout my nine months of morning sickness, people repeatedly urged me to eat crackers. Instead, I had three weighed and measured meals without flour or sugar and found other ways to manage my nausea. I saw morning sickness as a minor inconvenience that would eventually pass. Food addiction would kill me. I was very clear on the distinction, because I had seen the deadliness of relapse.

The birth of my child was one of the most spiritual experiences of my life. I looked at him and knew that I was meant to be a mother. I went through all the ups and downs of learning how to care for him, and in this, and in all my other relationships, the program helped me.

I became a completely different person than I was before FA. The program taught me how to be in relationships. I was able to make peace with my father before he died. I learned to speak honestly with someone instead of withdrawing when I felt hurt or angry. I set appropriate boundaries and said no when I needed to say no. My painful shyness lifted.

After seminary, I entered the ministry. Today, I know that the most important things I do as a pastor are to weigh and measure my food and to live my program of recovery.

My weight has been normal for years, but my need for abstinence goes far beyond weight. My job is to serve as a vehicle for God's presence. If I were eating addictively, that would be impossible. Instead, I keep my recovery first and do the best I can. My Higher Power then does the rest for me. I may be nervous, but I can speak in front of huge groups. If people can see my hands tremble a little while I'm officiating at a ceremony, so be it.

My addiction will never go away, so I need to keep my disease at bay. As an FA member, I am not called to reinvent the wheel. By doing a few simple things that have been laid out for me by the people who have gone before me, I have the wonderful gift of my life as it is. Food is in its proper place. I still have the same Queen Anne dining room table that seats eight. My family sits around that table, including my two little sons, whom I adore. Friends and parishioners and members of the fellowship of FA come to that table. I never dream of sitting there alone.

The Unbearable Obsession

✧ ✧ ✧

THE GREATEST OBSESSION of all my life was my weight. I can see now that all the other drugs I used—coffee, cigarettes, alcohol, marijuana—were part and parcel of my food addiction. They were always there, but food ran as a thread through all of them.

I've heard people share at meetings who had put on 100 pounds or felt afraid they'd gain so much weight they'd have to be craned out of the window of their house once they died. The disease is not as obvious as that in me. I don't directly relate to stories of 200-pound people sitting at home in a chair eating. I relate to people who talk about a constant obsession with the way they look and the feeling that if they were fat, they were bad. For me, being fat meant I was worthless and useless. Being skinny meant the opposite.

I'm an Australian and one of seven children, six of whom became alcoholics. We grew up in a nice area of Sydney in a loving environment. We were enrolled in Catholic schools. My mother and father were good parents who worked hard. My dad was an alcoholic and, I believe, a food addict, and my grandfather was also a food addict.

My grandfather went to AA in the mid-1950s. When I was two, in the 1960s, my mum issued my father the ultimatum: AA or else. So my dad and grandfather went to AA, and for a while my mum went to Al-Anon. My mum didn't stick with it, but she loved the prayers from *Alcoholics Anonymous*. I grew up seeing them all around our house, especially the Serenity Prayer. My mum wrote it on a tile in her own hand and had it put in a prominent place in our kitchen.

At home, there seemed to be some kind of stigma associated with alcoholism and AA, in that my dad and grandfather never spoke of the program. I can imagine maybe my dad was ashamed, but he died about ten months after I got into recovery and I never had a chance to talk with him about it. The program and the Serenity Prayer didn't mean much to me when I was growing up, but the prayer was etched into my brain, and when I came into AA at twenty-eight, I felt like I'd come home.

As is obvious, I had addiction in my genes. I became alcoholic, but food was always important to me. I stole money from my dad's change drawer to buy sweets. I got in big trouble with a boy from my class when I was eight or nine. He suggested I steal a bottle of soft drink from the school canteen so we could drink it on the way home. I took one, and when we didn't have a bottle opener, we were so determined to have some that we smashed the top and tried to drink through the jagged glass. I felt a profound shame when we were caught. You might think that would have been enough for me, but I kept stealing—more from the canteen, sweets from the school staff room, and food and alcohol from stores. The consequences of my actions never deterred me.

Our family focused a lot on food. My mum cooked for us every night—meat and three vegetables. "Three square meals," my parents said, but my mum often imposed diets on us girls. She'd say, "The girls won't have dessert tonight. The girls are on a diet." All of my sisters and I had trouble with our weight, and she was often trying to control us, but there was such a pull to the sweets. I remember my grandfather coming around to take us on "delicious walks," as he called them, so he could buy us ice creams and treats. I loved those walks.

I first went to a commercial weight loss program when I was thirteen. I had only 10 pounds to lose, and I lost them because I was a good girl on that diet. I went on a cruise, which had been the main reason for the diet and was the end of it, as well. On that cruise, I discovered cigarettes and alcohol and other substances that could help me control my weight.

I had a great desire to eat what I wanted to eat and yet stay healthy and slim. I could never work out how to accomplish both. I was constantly exercising, or smoking cigarettes and drinking gallons of coffee. When I discovered speed later in life, I used that to try to control my weight.

Alcohol eventually took me to a terrible bottom, and when I joined AA, I thought it would solve all my problems, including my struggles with my weight. Of course, that didn't happen. AA focused us all on not drinking, which was good, but I took full advantage of the encouragement to have sweets, Cokes, coffee, and such. Cigarettes were also considered okay. I was very grateful to AA, and over time, I stayed sober and slowly changed, but my troubles with my weight didn't change.

Having been fat for most of my life, I was very hard on myself. When I was thirteen, I was maybe 10 pounds overweight, but over the years, I kept gaining. By the time I finally came into FA, when I was forty-one, I needed to lose 30 or 40 pounds. I could see the progression. I knew what was ahead—50 pounds, then 60 pounds. Still, I never thought I had a food problem. Instead, I kept struggling hard against what I thought was a weight problem.

There was no dreadful, terrible experience that made me hit a rock bottom with food, but I got so that I couldn't bear my obsession. Will I? Won't I? Can I? Can't I? How much? How little? When do I eat? What do I eat? How much should I eat? On and on and on. I thought that if I could get thin, I'd have a boyfriend. I would attract good people into my life. Somehow, miraculously, my problems would disappear.

Eventually, I got into a twelve-step program for compulsive overeaters. I joined with an older sister. We sustained each other. Over a period of time, we would lose weight and then gain it back. "How's it going with the food?" one of us would ask. Generally, the answer was, "Not that great," or maybe, "It's okay at the moment."

I was involved for about thirteen years. I attended relapse and recovery workshops, I sponsored lots of people, I went on retreats, but my weight kept going up.

Finally, I pretty much stopped going, and by the time I heard about FA, I'd faced the reality that neither the food program nor the Twelve Steps of AA were going to solve my problem. I was obsessed with food. I couldn't stop thinking about it all day long, and I knew that my eating was becoming crazier. I'm five feet, one inch tall, and I weighed 145 pounds at the time.

One day, my sister said she'd met a woman from New York who had come to Australia and spoken at an AA meeting. The woman said that she was a food addict and that she was looking for other food addicts. My sister passed along the message and said that the woman was "thin and sane." She said, "There's something about her . . ."

I asked for the woman's number. When I called her, we spoke for about twenty minutes, and I found out that she had a story similar to mine. She'd been to AA first, but then she had joined FA. For the first time, I heard someone say that we are alcoholics with food—that we use food the way alcoholics use alcohol. I had never heard anyone speak so clearly. I understood the language of addiction when applied to alcohol, but I'd never linked addiction and food.

As I listened to the FA member speak, I realized that I was living in a wishy-washy world. I was clear with alcohol, but I wasn't clear with food. Sobriety in AA was simple: We didn't drink. I never said, "I can drink beer, but I can't drink wine." My food "abstinence," though, was different. It wasn't black and white. In the program for compulsive overeaters, abstinence was something we each defined for ourselves. My abstinence could evolve over time, or I could change it overnight. Sugar might be a problem, but not flour—or white flour might be a problem, but not brown flour.

All of a sudden the pieces of the puzzle fit into place. I saw that I was not treating food as a drug. I hadn't understood that the mental obsession I had with food and my weight was being driven by what I was putting into my mouth. Just as I had an allergy to alcohol that made me unable to stop drinking, I had an allergy to flour and sugar that made it impossible to stop eating.

This led me to a huge revelation. If I had an addiction related to food—an allergy combined with a mental obsession, as *Alcoholics Anonymous* describes it—I needed to treat food as I treated alcohol. I needed to *completely* abstain from the substances that I was powerless over, so that my eating wouldn't trigger my mental obsession.

My husband is a member of AA, and when I spoke with him later, I told him that I'd heard of a program where people weighed and measured their food. I had tried weighing and measuring my food before and had long since quit. "I don't know if I can do it again," I said. He simply replied, "Why don't you pray about it? Ask God. Just pray and see."

I had *Twenty-Four Hours a Day*, the meditation book we use in FA, but I hadn't read it for years. I took it to my bed and opened it up without choosing where. I remember well that the book opened to the page for September 27, which is about spiritual experiences. The text said, "What often takes place in a few months could seldom have been accomplished by years of self-discipline."

I thought, *Oh, my God, all these years I've been trying*

to deal with my problem through self-discipline, but I need a spiritual experience. I didn't need just a spiritual solution. I needed the actual spiritual experience. I needed God to remove my obsession and compulsion. I wasn't going to be able to remove my obsession and compulsion by any means that I was using by myself.

That night, I rang America and called the sponsor of the American woman who'd spoken with me. I told her the story of what I had just learned, and she asked if I wanted a sponsor. I said yes, and she told me what to do. I bought a scale the next day and started phoning her daily.

The huge difference, the enormous change between FA and any other program I'd done before, was the single, clear definition of abstinence in FA and my new understanding that I had to turn to God for help to remove the dreadful obsession that was driving me. My spiritual experience did not come in a flash of light. I had the educational variety described in *Alcoholics Anonymous.* Years of struggle had kept landing me back in the same place: Can I, can't I, will I, won't I eat? It was a horrible way to live. I'd had enough. My openness, my willingness to do something different, was a spiritual experience in itself. I was teachable.

After fourteen years of sobriety in AA and thirteen years in the twelve-step program for compulsive overeaters, I had to be willing to do things differently in FA. The big revelation was that honesty began with the food. I started by writing down what I was going to eat, committing it to my sponsor, and then actually eating it. In the past, I'd had a food plan, but if I decided by lunchtime that something else looked better, I changed what I ate. I don't know if I ever carefully weighed and measured what I ate, either. In FA, my measurements were spot on.

To use the tool of sponsorship, I had to be honest with my sponsor. In the other program, I loved to sponsor people and give away my "wisdom," but I don't think I liked being sponsored. In FA, as a sponsee, I had to be vulnerable and talk about what I was really feeling. I spoke more personally about my family relationships, my friendships, and things happening with my work. I appreciated the ways my sponsor encouraged me and guided me.

Even our FA meetings were different, once we opened them in Sydney. We'd always sat in circles before, but the American FA member who'd come to Australia put the chairs in rows, theatre style. I noticed that this made me focus on the person speaking, instead of looking at all the other listeners and their reactions. We started meetings right on time and used the break to greet newcomers. Once I had ninety days of abstinence, I raised my hand to share at every meeting.

FA began in my city with the involvement of two members—the American woman and me. A third member came a month or so later. We held our first FA meeting in September 2003, with seven of us attending. Soon three of us had ninety days of abstinence. About five months later, another American FA member came for a holiday, and we held an information session. That drew two new members. Our fellowship grew as we held other information sessions and attracted the interest of members of AA.

I traveled to America to do my Fifth Step when I was six months abstinent. At last, I was able to talk with my sponsor face to face and tell her everything I knew about myself that had gotten me into trouble. She met my family, and everyone in my family got acquainted with her. That trip was a turning point for me. Before then, I kept doubting a little, wondering, *What have I gotten myself into here?*

Back in Australia, my commitment to FA gradually changed. I was never told that I had to move away from AA, but I think I knew in my heart that I could not work two programs at one time. I tried. I looked at myself as an alcoholic and a food addict. Through a long, slow, gentle process, FA helped me see myself differently—as an addict. FA helped me address addiction, so I could work on all my issues in one place.

I was secure and happy in AA for many years. When people have been as closely associated with that program as I was, it's difficult to let go of the AA past. You feel like you're letting go of the program, but as I see it today, I didn't really do that. I'm working a stronger twelve-step program than ever before, but I am doing it in FA. This has given me relief and a huge freedom. I am grounded in one fellowship, without the confusion I used to feel when I went back and forth between AA and FA meetings.

I love what I receive through FA. My relationships have improved because of what I learn here. For me, "First things first" means that in any situation, I need to look at myself first. This gives me the ability to realize that even if someone else has problems that make him or her difficult, my own fear, doubt, and insecurity may be looming large. I can easily see the negativity in others, but where am I full of it myself? Unless I look inside first, I have no chance of helping anyone else.

I was startled to see my own blind spots in my relationship with my husband. After I'd been in FA for about two years, I asked him what he thought of the program. I expected he wouldn't say much, if anything, but instead, he replied, "Before you started FA, I didn't think we were going to make it." I was shocked. I had thought we were all right. Instead, I discovered that my self-centeredness had been a major problem. I'd had no idea how he felt, because from my point of view, life was all about me.

FA has given me the gift of clarity. It makes me think. I may stop eating addictively, but that does not mean that I'll be free from self-centeredness or other defects of character, as we call them. I value my relationship with my husband, so I have to ask myself, *How am I doing today? Am I still self-centered? Is my husband still thinking, "Are we going to make it?"* I'm grateful that we can be honest with each other and that our relationship is much better now.

I'm not cured or perfect. I know I've got a long way to go, but I'm learning how to live my life. FA completely takes care of my obsession. I weigh myself once a week, so I don't have any uncertainty or anxiety about my size. During my first six months in the program, I lost my extra weight, and I've been abstinent and in a normal-size body ever since.

FA's gifts are enormous. I'm eight years abstinent and understand my priorities now: recovery first, family second, job third. My husband and I can be honest with each other. At work, I don't put myself in situations that are complicated and emotionally charged or filled with confrontations. My life is much simpler and happier than it used to be.

Because of FA, I've had a spiritual experience and received a spiritual solution. I've been given what I most wanted—peace of mind. I'm so grateful, but I don't ever feel that I've arrived. I know I need to keep moving forward, so every morning, I still get on my knees and ask God to give me the grace to stay surrendered, to remain humble and willing.

I Came Back to FA

◇ ◇ ◇

I WAS BORN IN MEXICO. My dad came to the United States to work in the fields here, so I saw him only when the season was over and he and all the other men returned to Mexico in the wintertime. My father was an angry drunk, God bless him. I was afraid of him. How drunk was he going to be when he came home? Was he going to hit my mom? Was he going to yell, or was he going to go straight to sleep?

My mom was seventeen when she had me. By the time she was twenty-two, she had four little girls. She didn't know what to do with us, didn't know how to cope. She has never shown any of us affection. I believe she was a food addict, though she would never admit it.

I was the chubbiest child in our extended family. I always wanted food. My cousins played outside, but I tried to stay behind with my grandmother in her kitchen. I couldn't run as fast as my cousins could, and they teased me. "Look at you! You're so fat!" People in Mexico are honest with you. They'll tell you, "You're fat." That's it.

Back then, if you were fat, you were considered healthy. Wherever our family went, people made comments about us. They'd look at us girls and say, "Oh, look at this one! Her eyes are so beautiful. And this one has such a cute little mouth." Then they'd get to me, and they'd say, "She's so chubby."

When I turned four, my dad asked my mom to come to the U.S. to see if she'd be willing to live here. He didn't want us to come. She was supposed to try it first. We were left with my grandmother and aunt, but I was the one who'd always taken care of the rest of the kids. I was the oldest of the sisters. I was the strong one.

The night my mom left, I received the only kiss I ever remember getting from her. I pretended to be asleep because I knew it was hard for her to leave us, and I didn't want to make it harder by crying in front of her. She leaned over and kissed me on the forehead very lightly, and I just lay still.

The few months my mom was gone, I felt like an abandoned orphan. Food was my only comfort. My mom came back to Mexico, but then it was decided that our whole family would move to the U.S. I had to leave my grandparents, who were the only people who had ever shown me love. Oh, how I missed them! In the United States, I'd go out at night and look at the sky for the three stars all in a row. When I was at home with my grandmother, she'd pointed out those stars to me and said, "No matter where you are, just go outside and look up at the sky. When you see those three stars, you'll know I'm watching you. I'm taking care of you."

We came to the U.S. in March, and by June I was fluent in English. I could read, write, and speak it. I remember my teacher came to our house to show my parents how impressed she was. She was amazed I'd learned so quickly, but I was terribly insecure.

My eating got much worse in the U.S. In Mexico, we had only a few television channels and hardly any packaged snacks. We mostly played outside. Here, I had many more options. My mom often worked the night shift in the cannery, and she let us do anything we wanted. We opened boxes of cereal and Hostess cakes and Twinkies. I went crazy. The TV and food—that was it for me.

I had a tough time. I was always afraid. My dad's drinking got worse, and he didn't allow me to see much of my friends. I was locked out if I was ever away from home past 10:00 at night. College didn't work out. I wanted to go so badly, but when I failed an algebra class, I felt I was stupid and gave up completely. I never thought I was worth anything or that I could follow my dreams.

I met my husband right after I graduated from high school and married him when I was nineteen. That's when my troubles really began. My husband drank too much. He was jealous and verbally abusive, often accusing me of flirting with other men. I was never interested in anyone else, but he treated me terribly. I ate because it was the only comfort I had. I couldn't tell my mom. I didn't have a single person to confide in. All I could do was eat.

I got pregnant right away. The hope of having the baby and taking care of her was all that kept me going. My daughter was born in the winter, just before my twenty-first birthday. I spent that New Year's Eve alone with her because my husband was out drinking.

I am five feet, three inches tall. When my first daughter was born, I weighed about 184 pounds. The second time I got pregnant, I hit 204. I remember sitting on the bed and looking at myself in the mirror. I felt hopeless, but I continued to eat. What else could I do? I did think once that if I stopped eating sweets and bread, I might lose some weight. *Couldn't someone tell me what to eat?!* I wondered. But who would tell me? Who? There seemed to be no way out, and each time I got pregnant and gave birth, I gained another 20 pounds. I got on a scale only once a year, when I went in for my annual physical exam, which was awful. By the time I had my third daughter, I weighed 224 pounds.

At that point, I was so afraid of gaining more weight that I took it upon myself to get my tubes tied. I spoke to my husband just as he was going out the door to work. "By the way," I told him, "I'm getting my tubes tied tomorrow." My doctor didn't want to do it. "You've always wanted to have four children," he said. "Why don't you have the fourth child, and then I'll tie your tubes." I insisted on having the procedure done because I didn't see what I could do if I gained another 20 pounds.

For at least a year after I got my tubes tied, I dreamed of a baby. I had nightmares, actually, dreaming of the baby I didn't have—the baby I should have had, that I wanted to have and could have had. I couldn't deal with my guilt, and I was having a hard time with my husband's verbal abuse, so I just kept turning to the food.

Often, I supported our family. My mother and mother-in-law took care of my babies. Every day, I went to a bakery in the morning. I ate a lot of food at work, and then on the way home, I stopped at another bakery and bought three entire cakes. At home, I stood at the counter in my kitchen and slivered away at one of them until it was gone. I ate most of the second and the third ones after the girls had gone to bed and in the morning before they got up. I remember thinking, *I don't have to die to go to hell. I'm in it. I'm living it.*

One year, I weighed 228 pounds when I went in for my pap smear. The nurse looked at my chart and told me I was a walking time bomb. She said that if I didn't get some weight off, I'd die soon. Then she asked me if I'd ever heard of one of the twelve-step programs for people with food problems. I had heard of it, but I knew people there used the AA Big Book and the Serenity Prayer. As far as I was concerned, I wasn't an alcoholic. There was nothing wrong with me!

I didn't let the nurse see it, but I was furious, and I did nothing. Four years from that day, FA found me. I'd gone to a back-to-school night and saw the mother of my daughter's friend. My jaw dropped. I watched her all evening and stayed late to find out how she'd lost her weight. She took me to my first meeting and guided me to a sponsor.

I started FA at 237 pounds. During the first month, I lost 23 pounds. My husband was glad, but he thought my involvement was temporary. The weight kept coming off me, fast, and after a while, he began to get upset with me. He hated the fact that on Saturday mornings, his special time with me, I went to an FA meeting instead. He resented that I attended three meetings a week and spent time on the phone with my sponsor. He felt the program was taking me away from him.

Meanwhile, as I kept losing weight, I felt good. *I've got this down,* I thought to myself. I began to believe I was different from everyone else in the program. The rules didn't apply to me. I didn't have to get on my knees to ask for my abstinence, or take half an hour of quiet time, or read *Alcoholics Anonymous. My husband should read that book*, I thought. *My dad should read it. Not me.* I found my husband's copy of the book when I was cleaning the garage one day, and I threw it away. He'd gone to AA for a while, ordered by the court after he was caught driving under the influence. He liked *Alcoholics Anonymous*, but he started drinking again as soon as he fulfilled the judge's order and could quit AA.

To this day, I'm not exactly clear what happened to me in FA, but I know that I started to become dishonest with food. I'd weigh out protein and eat 4.1 instead of 4.0 ounces. I'd make a food plan and then change the fruit or vegetable I ate just because I felt like it. This was no big deal in my eyes, so I never mentioned the changes to my sponsor.

Before long, I decided I would leave the program. My husband hated my going to FA, and we were about to take a vacation in Mexico. I wouldn't be able to go to meetings while we were there, so I thought it would be a good time to wean myself away from FA.

I still remember my first bite of non-abstinent food. While my husband was asleep one day, I took a mouthful of a sandwich I'd made him. The bread was already in my mouth when I changed my mind. I didn't want to eat it, but I'd already swallowed half the bite. It was too late. I ate the rest, feeling that I was falling into a hole where there was no light and no way out.

My vacation in Mexico was the worst in my life. I couldn't stop eating, but I had to pretend in front of my husband that I was in complete control. Each day I hid my eating at the same time that I was trying to get more food. I was supposed to be on a diet.

Before the vacation ended, while we were at the airport, I realized that I could not leave FA. I didn't want to leave. I'd experienced two weeks of desperate bingeing, and that was enough. As we were waiting for our plane, I said to my husband, "Okay. I guess everything goes back to normal tomorrow." I meant that I was going to go back to my FA meetings and my program. By the look on his face, I knew he understood me. He was bitterly disappointed.

Despite my intention to be abstinent, when we got back, nothing returned to normal. I wanted to be abstinent, but I couldn't stop eating and lying. I'd abstain for a day, eat the next day, and never talk about it. I was still losing weight, but that was no comfort. One day, at my sister-in-law's wedding, I put two pieces of fruit in my mouth while I was helping to clean up. The next morning, I started by placing one slice of cake on a plate and eating it with a fork in the kitchen, where no one could see me. By the end of the day, there was no fork, and no plate, and no hiding, and I didn't care who saw me. I got on the scale the following day, nauseated and sick, and found that I'd gained 7 pounds from one day of eating.

My sponsor was in the hospital at that point. She was in intensive care for a month, in danger of dying. She lived five minutes away from me, and when she got home from the hospital, she needed my help, but I was so deep into eating, I couldn't reach out. I couldn't show up when she needed me most. And the lies! I pretended to my temporary sponsor that I was abstinent. "I'm fine," I'd say. I was always fine.

While I was struggling with abstinence, my husband was constantly confronting me, wanting me to leave the program. Finally, one day, he asked for a divorce. I was devastated. I called lots of women. One of them said, "Let him go. You do what you need to do for yourself. Take care of yourself. Work your program. Weigh and measure your food. Let him do whatever he wants to do." I listened to her, thank God, and I stayed in FA.

No one incident happened that made me abstinent, but I was going to many meetings, and I kept hearing one person speak. I'll call her Mary. She always talked about her own dishonesty, saying that honesty was what kept her abstinent. She'd get up to speak, and I'd think, *Oh, no! There goes Honesty Mary again,* but after hearing about honesty over and over, I finally got honest myself. I was back working with my regular sponsor. We had an understanding about which day was the first day of my abstinence—supposedly. I finally admitted that I wasn't abstinent that day, and I talked about every other lie I'd told her. One day at a time, ever since that conversation, I've been honestly abstinent.

Amazingly, too, my husband didn't leave. He started to respect the program and to respect me. He did a complete turnaround. After I'd been abstinent for about a year, he said to me one day, "Have you noticed that I haven't been drinking?" I hadn't noticed. "It's been three months since I've had a drink," he said. I'm eleven and a half years abstinent now, and he's just a few months behind me in his sobriety.

My father also hasn't had a drink since I've been abstinent. My father and husband don't go to AA, but it's as though my recovery carries the three of us. This is a huge miracle that I can't explain. They see my recovery, and it must help them. I did absolutely nothing to try to save them, not that I could have. I never told them to quit drinking.

I'm full of gratitude now. My husband and I are happy together. My health is good. I used to suffer from sleep apnea. I'd wake up in the middle of the night choking, feeling certain I was going to die from it one day. I haven't had an episode of apnea since I stopped eating flour and sugar. I can also walk up a flight of stairs without feeling as if my heart is about to burst out of my chest. These changes still amaze me, but I've experienced an even more powerful gift.

One night, a few years ago, I was awakened by a phone call. When I answered, I heard one of my daughters crying, telling me that her sister had been attacked and beaten. I was stunned. For a mother, there can be nothing worse than learning that her child has been hurt. I was sobbing. My first thought was to get on my knees. I knelt and I prayed with all my heart, "Please, God, please help me to stay away from food. Please, I don't want to turn to food." I thought my husband was standing behind me. I felt him there, but when I turned around, I saw no one. I got up from my knees, and I was lifted.

My daughter and our family faced hard days afterward. My sponsor comforted me and helped me see more clearly than I could see on my own. I didn't walk through that time. God and the Twelve Steps carried me through.

In FA, we're told to make recovery our first priority, our families second, our jobs third. I finally understand this. I used to feel bad each time I missed an event in my daughters' lives. No matter how much I wanted to, sometimes I couldn't see them off to their winter balls or other activities because I had to go to my committed FA meetings. Now I understand that "recovery first" means me first and God first. My recovery from food addiction is God's will for me today, so I have to weigh and measure my food, do my quiet time, go to my meetings. My recovery carries me through today and into tomorrow, and it makes it possible for me to be available to my husband and my daughters.

I often remember the time when I came back from Mexico and was eating and bingeing against my own will. I talked with someone who had been in the program for years, and she put it to me plainly. "Which do you choose?" she asked. "Do you want recovery or do you want misery?"

Each day when we wake up, all of us food addicts face that question. I know now, my life depends on my choice. I thought I was going to die at forty-four, but forty-four came and went. I'm alive today only because of my abstinence and FA.

The Last Five Percent

✧ ✧ ✧

IN THE FOURTEEN YEARS I've been abstinent, my weight has not fluctuated more than 5 pounds. I am five feet, ten inches tall, and I weigh between 160 and 165 pounds. I am happy in a wonderful, stable marriage and am free from any compulsion or obsession regarding eating or exercise.

These facts about me are miracles, because I coped with my feelings of fear by hiding and eating from the time I was young. I grew up in a home of love and instability. My parents had a volatile relationship, though they were supportive of me. My dad was soft spoken and caring. He suffered from mental illness and was in and out of psychiatric hospitals perhaps a dozen times in my life. I was always on guard with my mother, though her anger was directed at my father, not me. I was never sure when she was going to fly into a rage. There's a history of anger on my mother's side of the family. It's said that her father once killed a horse with a cane, and a close relative of hers was imprisoned for murder.

As a preschooler, I felt terribly afraid and alone, and from an early age, I turned to food. I think I was at first able to maintain a normal weight because of my high metabolism. I was a nervous wreck. We were members of a strong religious community, and whenever I entered our church, I saw a sign on the bottom of the pulpit that said, "Be therefore perfect." I looked at those words every Sunday for three hours. I concluded that if I could be perfect, I could escape my anxiety, but my striving for perfection just increased my tension.

I began to become conscious of my body around the time I turned fourteen or fifteen. I felt horrible about myself, and I soon began to get heavier. I don't look fat in my old photos, so I guess that I probably gained only about 5 pounds, but those few pounds felt like 100. I wanted control over my weight and finally found the perfect solution in running, which satisfied all my needs at once. Racing and training allowed me to be alone, maintain my low weight, and enjoy a runner's endorphin high.

I began a pattern of anesthetizing my tension and fear by exercising excessively and bingeing at night. Inevitably, I pushed too hard and injured myself, which forced me to stop exercising temporarily. I then got caught in a repeating cycle of running, losing 5 pounds, injuring myself, and gaining the weight back each time I got hurt.

I was a high achiever in high school. Once I got to college, I excelled in my classes and made the dean's list. I was also accepted on the highly competitive track team. As a walk-on, not a recruit, I nonetheless benefited from its world-class coach, and I pretended that I was an athlete of Olympic caliber.

In college, my illness progressed. I was running up to one hundred miles a week, but instead of facing a 5-pound cycle, I gained and lost 10 or 15 pounds. Whenever I injured myself and then returned to the team, I had to face my running buddies. Working out with people who are of Olympic caliber, you can't have an inch of fat on your body. They'd jab me about my weight, I'd train hard to lose it, and I'd injure myself again.

The pattern of exercise, bingeing, and injury continued after I graduated. I used running to help me control my weight and cope with my life, but I also turned to relationships. Moving from one relationship to another, I exited whenever there was any kind of problem. I'd left my family religion and wanted to do whatever I felt like doing.

I was thirty years old when my dad died, and I went into a severe depression. After lying on my couch for days, I walked out to the highway behind the house where I lived and hesitated before the one step that would take me into the path of a black Kenworth truck. Ironically, I was trained as a family therapist, and at the time, I was counseling as many as forty-two families a week in my private practice. I was also running between fifty and one hundred miles each week, depending on my injuries.

Right now, I feel I'm describing someone else because I'm so far from the person I used to be. Everyone who knew me then thought I was fine, but I badly needed help. I knew I didn't want to die, but I didn't want to live, either, so I made an appointment with a psychiatrist. He told me I had my father's illness and diagnosed me as being manic depressive, saying that the disease was progressive and that I'd be on lithium for the rest of my life.

After our session, I sat in front of a drugstore and tore up the prescription for the medication. I remember thinking, *I'm not going to be like my dad. I can lick this. I can overcome it.* I was determined. So I went for a run and then got myself into counseling. I worked with a therapist who was three hours north of me because I was too proud to go to anyone in my own community.

My one long therapy session each month helped me start looking at my life. I gained a degree of stability, though I ate on the way to therapy and on the way home. I had no idea how to deal with the insights that came up. I kept returning to food and exercise, trying to escape the pressure I felt to be perfect, but within a couple of years, I met and married my wife. The love I found in our relationship and the acceptance I felt from her helped me, and my disease went into remission for three or four years.

Two years after our marriage, when my wife got pregnant, I gained 50 pounds. We joked about it at the time, but I realize now that I was hanging on to her. When our baby was born and she transferred her attention from me to our child, I felt rejected and turned again to food. My bingeing then lasted four or five hours and ended only when I felt so sick I couldn't move. I was never full; I was painfully stuffed. This led me to purging. I didn't intend to become a bulimic. I first put my fingers down my throat simply to handle the pain of my jammed stomach. I got a hit from it, too, though, because I thought it would help me control my weight.

After the first time, I didn't purge again for four or five months, but before long, the purging came every four or five weeks. Over the course of two years, I progressed to the point where I was throwing up every week. I was obsessed with the scale and sometimes weighed myself as many as ten times a day. My weight swings had increased to 30 or 40 pounds a year in my thirties, and I was 50 pounds up and down when I was forty. Looking back, I see no difference between myself and an alcoholic. I remember sitting on a park bench, cradling a brown bag of food at 2:00 in the morning when my wife was home struggling alone with a colicky baby.

I gave up my private practice and was fifteen years into a consulting business when I faced the fact that my eating was affecting my ability to function professionally. My wife tried to hold our family, and me, together, but my mental illness and addiction were getting bigger than either of us could handle. I was still trying to manage my life without lithium and, at that point, without counseling, but I knew I needed help, so I decided to get some coaching from a man who could address my problem: an issue in my business, I thought.

My coach spent considerable time getting to know me, and as we were walking around his neighborhood and talking one day, I told him how unstable I'd become. I never mentioned food, but he opened up about his recovery in Alcoholics Anonymous. He'd been in AA and sober for ten years, and when I heard his story, I broke down. "That's my story!" I said, and for the first time in my life, my feeling of aloneness lifted. I'd never had a problem with alcohol, but my issues with food were no different than his with booze.

My new friend took me to an open AA meeting. I will never forget it. I cried through the whole meeting, because I finally felt at home. He introduced me to someone in a twelve-step program for compulsive overeaters, and I joined a group, where I found support, understanding, and some relief.

During my first year in the twelve-step program, my primary motive was to lose weight so that I could run more marathons. I did lose 60 pounds, but I called my sponsor only once a week, and I continued bingeing. I'd have to say that I was around that program, not in it, because I was never completely open and honest with anyone there. I remember ending one binge at 7:20, just before a meeting began, and sharing at the meeting as though I had ten years, not ten minutes, of abstinence. I wasn't willing to stop eating addictively, but something kept drawing me back. I didn't understand it then, but I needed the Twelve Steps.

One night, I met two women from Boston who were in FA. One had lost 80 pounds and the other 120. Both had kept their weight off for eight years or so. They spoke at a meeting, and as I listened, I was struck by far more than the pounds they'd lost. I was stunned when one of them said she was free from food cravings. She called this "neutrality."

In all my life, I had never experienced neutrality with food. I could stay on a diet for months, but I was always tense from the war in my head and the effort of exerting my will. Should I eat or should I not? I was owned by the constant urge to eat and the struggle not to break my diet. Inevitably, I'd pick up some food. I'd tell myself I'd begin the diet again the next day, and I'd be off into a binge. I could never master my cravings.

After the meeting, we went out for supper with our visitors. I listened carefully to their descriptions of what they did and watched what they ate. *I can do this,* I thought. Two weeks later, on New Year's Eve, I was in our bathroom, leaning over the toilet and purging the food I had bought at a health food store. Between bouts of throwing up, I lay on the floor, pounding it with my fists in frustration.

I never want to forget that last binge. When I got up off my knees, I picked up the phone and called the woman in Boston who'd said she had neutrality with food. I was weeping. "I'm completely defeated," I said. "I can't go on this way. Would you sponsor me?" I assumed that she was too important to have time for me, but she agreed, and I've been working with her ever since.

The first month with my new sponsor, I was motivated by my wish to run the Boston Marathon. I knew I'd have no problem qualifying to compete, but I wanted to place among the top ten in my age bracket. When my sponsor innocently urged me to come to Boston sometime, I mentioned my plan. She remained oddly silent.

When we want to get well, we often find ourselves willing to do 95 percent of the program, but I now believe that recovery lies in the surrender and doing of the 5 percent we resist. I offered my new sponsor no argument about any of the food suggestions she made, but there was no way that I wanted to adjust the level of my exercise. When she asked me how much I was exercising, I just said, "Every day." She suggested that I cut back to three times a week. "Okay," I said. On average, I was exercising two or three hours a day—running, lifting weights, and cross training—so I adjusted to six hours of exercise three days a week. I began at a healthy weight, but within a month, I'd lost 20 pounds. I was on top of the world! I knew I could run a near world-class marathon with my weight that low and my newfound energy.

One day, my sponsor asked me how much I weighed. "Around 145," I said. "Why don't you send me a picture?" she asked. We couldn't send photos over the Internet in those days, so, as she requested, I took a picture of myself in a bathing suit and mailed it to her. The minute she got it, she called me. "What are you doing?!" she asked, and I knew at that moment that if I was going to get well, I'd have to give up exercise. That was the biggest surrender of my life. I knew that I had to let it go.

I'd made mistakes with food during my first month in the program, and I had to become honest about them, but I don't think my recovery really started until I became honest about exercise. Sure enough, my sponsor asked me to stop for a while. When I asked how long, she replied, "As long as it takes—until you don't *need* to exercise. Get to the point where you want to exercise but don't need to, and then you'll be ready to begin again in a weighed and measured way."

For six months, I did not exercise. Although this was one of the hardest surrenders of my life, it was also the most freeing. "Put as much effort into your quiet time as you've put into exercising," my sponsor suggested. I had the will power and discipline to achieve six-minute miles in a marathon, but I couldn't sit quietly for even five minutes. I'd start my meditation time and find myself looking at my watch repeatedly. *When is this going to be over?!* I'd think, noticing my feet restlessly pushing at the floor.

At first, I was able to sit still for a full thirty minutes only by the force of my will. In the early days, I called my sponsor at 5:15 a.m., and I began my quiet time at 5:30. I told myself that my call to God was just fifteen minutes after my call to my sponsor. My sponsor helped by reminding me that sometimes I would feel quiet and sometimes not. "Just show up. Sit with your rear end on the seat and learn how to be still," she said. "Practice."

By practicing every day without fail, I did learn to be still. I took a big turn toward recovery, and I never looked back. Today, I don't use exercise to manage my weight or my moods. I do it because it's good for me. I gave up running and took up hiking and yoga. I don't race and run my way through my life anymore. I don't turn to food. I look for help from a Higher Power, instead.

I know from my own experience that if I ask for help, God can keep me from eating addictively. Once, when I was nine days abstinent, my wife brought some bags of groceries into the kitchen and set them on the table. I wanted to eat everything I saw there. I knew I had to leave, so I went to my bedroom and got on my knees. I said the first three Steps and then kept talking. I felt like I was addressing the air, but I asked for help so I wouldn't give in to what felt like an overwhelming and uncontrollable craving. Immediately the thought came to me as clearly as a voice in the room: *Pick up the phone.*

I picked up the telephone and called my sponsor, who happened to have ten or fifteen long-time FA members at her house for a party. My sponsor talked with me quickly and then said she had to leave, but she called out, "I've got a newcomer on the phone. Anyone want to talk to a newcomer?" I was on the west coast of Canada and they were on the east coast of the United States, but her FA friends passed the phone from one to another and bridged more than three thousand miles as they talked with me. After an hour, when I finally hung up, I no longer wanted to eat. I wasn't willing my way into not eating. The desire had been removed from me, and for the first time in my life, I had the experience of freedom. Neutrality.

At that moment, I recognized God's power, and I began to understand the core of the program. FA teaches me tools and disciplines that bring me to the experience of God working in my life. Meetings, phone calls, and the other tools don't keep me abstinent. I must do them, but it's God who keeps me abstinent.

I built on that experience, using my quiet time to feel the Higher Power in me, my body, and my life. I needed access to a Power, not an intellectual concept, so feeling was far more important than thinking. I also made a point of going to Boston every year. Everyone at the party who had come to the phone was friendly. "Hey, come down here and pay us a visit. You can stay at my place," they each said. Until then, I had always reserved rooms in hotels because I wanted to be alone and in complete control of my environment, but I took them up on their offers.

I always encourage people who are, as I was, far from others in the FA program, to travel to an area with strong meetings and stay there for a while. I suggest that they live with the people there. We can learn a lot from what members say at meetings, but we gain even more by seeing how they live in recovery.

My recovery has required mindfulness and effort. I believe that mental illness still lives in me, just as food addiction does. If working the FA program didn't keep my moods from swinging between extremes, I wouldn't hesitate to take medication, but that would be a tool of last resort, and I have never needed it. Weighed and measured food, a weighed and measured life, and a relationship with a Higher Power keep me abstinent and stable. If I find myself overworking, I cut back. If I feel a little lonely, as I have recently, I bring more of myself into my relationships instead of falling into self-centeredness and waiting for people to tend to my needs. If I have a moment of success or great happiness at home and I start to become too excited, I transfer the feeling into gratitude. I can never be too grateful, but too much excitement can tip me into serious trouble. As a result, my moods have stabilized.

In all this, of course, I'm just sharing my own experience, and I give no advice to anyone else. I've had forty years of living in tension and addiction, and many fewer years in recovery. I'm still learning, but one day at a time, I show up as a father, a husband, and an FA member. God is doing the rest.

They Finally Had to Admit Defeat

✧ ✧ ✧

Fierce will power helped these members to achieve some success in their battles with weight, work, and life, but in the end, they were never able to conquer their addiction. They found recovery through FA.

So I Tried Surgery

✧ ✧ ✧

I HAVE BEEN MORBIDLY OBESE, but as miserable as I was in my body, my mental state during the time of my active food addiction was even worse. Once, at three o'clock in the morning, when I couldn't stop eating, I was lying on the floor of my bedroom holding my stomach. I felt something was ripping inside me. I'd never felt such pain and was debating with myself about calling for an ambulance. Then I saw a road. I was on one end of it and God was far away on the other. Between us there was a huge pile of food. That was hell on earth, being blocked from God, and it was food that stood between us.

I have early memories of the pleasure and comfort of eating. My grandmother mailed us care packages every month. She packed most of the box with candy. My parents thought they hid the sweets, but I found them and snacked on them all day. The highlight of my week came when we went out for dinner on Friday and Saturday nights and Sunday after church. Both of my parents came from poor families, but they succeeded in their careers and provided a nice home for my sister and me. Having plenty of food and being able to go out to dinner were important in my family.

Growing up, I felt like the odd person out. When I look back at early photos of myself, I see that I was a little chunky, but I felt huge. My twin sister was thin. I got lots of comments about my weight at home, and when my sister and I were apart, people always tried to distinguish us. "Are you the fat one or the skinny one?" they'd ask. I was the fat one.

I said three prayers every day during all of my childhood and into the time I was in high school. "God," I prayed, "take my acne away, make my hair grow longer, and somehow get me thin." Nothing changed. I stayed overweight, and I was uncomfortable in my own skin.

When I tell my story, I keep coming back to the word "uncomfortable." My parents kept us involved in church and Girl Scouts, the soccer team, and an organization for African American families in my area. I took leadership positions in all of the groups and had wonderful friends, but I didn't feel like I belonged. My high school was primarily white, so I felt like an outsider there, too. Everywhere I went, I worried about what other people thought of me.

I was physically miserable for years. I felt that my skin was crawling on my upper body and legs. My body shook, and sometimes I had terrible headaches, probably because my blood sugar was out of whack. Once I started my period in junior high school, I had to take mega-doses of painkillers—eight at once, three times a day. For two or three days a month, I struggled to keep from throwing up. My mind raced, though I tried to soothe myself by twisting my neck or tracing the corners of windows with my eyes.

When it was time for college, I wanted to get lost in a big school. Turning down scholarships from two small places, I chose a school with 22,000 students, only 900 of whom were black. Again, I was socially and physically uncomfortable, and I began drinking. I remember having ten or eleven rum and cokes in a bar and then spending the rest of the night eating in my room. Whenever I had cash, I told my friends I'd treat, and I made them feel bad until they agreed to go out to eat with me. Really, I was begging for their time and attention.

I got heavier in college, though I struggled against gaining the weight. I sometimes starved myself and ran five miles a day, but I also became bulimic. At one point, every girl at the end of the hall where I lived was throwing up. My roommate shared her techniques with me. We stayed up late drinking and eating bags of chips and cookies. Soon I was smoking, running, eating, drinking, and throwing up.

Senior year, I gained about 50 pounds, despite my bulimia and a pack of cigarettes a day. It seemed I was either eating to change how I felt or smoking to keep myself from eating. By the time I graduated, I weighed almost 200 pounds. I felt some self-esteem because I applied for eight jobs and received eight offers, but I had no sense of who I was. I'd always adapted myself to my friends or to whatever man I was dating.

After graduation, I took a job as a counselor and lost weight by starving myself for about a year. Eating five hundred calories and running ten miles a day, I got down to 150 pounds. My bulimia stopped, and I felt high from being in a right-sized body, but I couldn't stay stable. Before I knew it, I'd gained 60 pounds. I was stealing desserts from the bags of food my agency bought for clients and purging as many as twenty-five times a day. A psychiatrist diagnosed me with bulimia and manic depression and prescribed medication for anxiety. I took the medicine and went for a while to a twelve-step program for compulsive overeaters, too.

Over the next years, I starved myself, exercised excessively, binged, and purged. I did a lot of drinking to alleviate my migraines and insomnia, and I ate night and day. After almost thirty years of struggle, with a lifetime membership in a gym and a record of failure in every commercial weight loss program I'd tried, I reached 340 pounds.

Bypass surgery began to look like a magic bullet to me. Having seen patients interviewed on a television show, I was aware of the possible consequences of the operation. Clearly, surgery alone wasn't a perfect answer, but I didn't hear what I didn't want to hear, and I didn't see what I didn't want to see, even after a six-week class, half a year in a support group, and a lengthy individual consultation with a doctor.

I'm sure that bypass surgery works for some people, but it did not work for me. Blatantly in denial, I thought the operation would change my body and allow me to eat whatever I wanted. Ultimately, I lost only 70 of my 340 pounds. After six months, when my weight loss completely stopped, I went back to my doctor, who infuriated me. "We told you in the beginning, the surgery is a tool. You still have to change the way you're eating," he said. What could I do? I didn't know how to alter my eating!

I had a terrible time after my surgery, which had failed me. I'd wanted an immediate, no-effort solution. I expected someone else to fix me and denied the evidence that the operation might not work for me—none of the post-operative members of my support group had lost all their weight. I also refused to acknowledge that surgery couldn't fix some of my problems. How could surgery address the deadness I felt inside, the constant pain of migraines, and my daily nausea and dizziness?

In some ways, I regret my surgery because it didn't work, yet I am also grateful for it. I don't know that I would ever have gotten abstinent if my life hadn't gotten even worse. After my operation, I married a man who was morbidly obese. Before we divorced, I drove us into debt. I moved from job to job or didn't work at all. I wasn't actively suicidal, but I didn't want to live, and I was afraid I couldn't keep myself safe.

Eventually, I found FA, but all my failures, including the bypass surgery, hadn't taught me that I was a food addict. Still not believing that I was completely out of control, I spent five years eating addictively after I first came to FA. I was, as we say, "around the program, not in it." I probably had twenty or twenty-five sponsors. One time I was abstinent for eighty days, but other than that, I gained and lost, gained and lost. Toward the end, I was bingeing on about eight thousand calories every night. I couldn't throw up because the bypass surgery took away my ability to be bulimic. I distanced myself from my friends and fought with my family. I was in hell, eating on my couch and separated from God.

One day at an FA meeting, a speaker said that although she'd been crazy before, she was getting better in FA. Seeing that she could talk coherently, had a husband and child, and was able to hold a job and get out of debt, I asked her to be my sponsor. My life got a little better working with her, but after I broke my abstinence two or three times, she told me she couldn't sponsor me if I didn't stay abstinent.

For the first time then, I finally understood that I had to quit turning to food. I didn't know how to stop, but I was able to hear people say, "Work the program!" so that's what I did. I started phoning FA members when I had feelings—bad or good. I'd seen my pattern of eating after wonderful experiences and hard ones. I needed to call, no matter what, just to talk things through.

I was able to be abstinent from the time I began to participate fully in FA, but my path wasn't a straight one. I had various problems, and my sponsor kept referring me to other twelve-step groups to address them. My program of recovery got huge; I was committed to going to many different kinds of meetings.

I was grateful to my sponsor, but after some time, I changed and began working with someone else, who had eighteen years of abstinence. She helped me simplify. It was much easier for me to look to FA for all of my answers. She also led me to my first experience of surrendering my own will—letting go of something that I wanted.

I'd always scheduled my life around church, and I was leading a Bible study class when I was newly abstinent. Because I hadn't been abstinent long, the weekly potlucks were hard for me, and, even though I wanted to teach, I was emotionally overwhelmed. I didn't know what to do. It didn't seem right to leave. Peace finally came one day when I saw that I needed to stop teaching for a while. I felt comfortable and right inside when I acknowledged my addiction and my need to take care of my recovery first.

I've been a Christian my whole life, but I'd never had any clarity about God's will and how to discern it. FA has taught me a lot about decision making. I ask God for help and talk with people in the program when I'm uncertain. I get many good suggestions, particularly about letting go. "Every surrender brings us closer to God," I've been told. That was true about the church class I stopped teaching, and these days my eyes are opening to other ways I might be holding on to my own will. If I'd just let go, I might feel better, not worse. Making the decision to let go is hard. Following through is the easy part.

I've had to be willing to change. I began dating a man when I'd been abstinent only six months. Within three weeks of meeting, we made plans to begin premarital counseling at my church. As the relationship continued, I became obsessed with him, and I started waking up at night feeling the old, horrible sensation of my skin crawling. I realized that if my feelings didn't go away, I'd eat.

I knew that another surrender was coming, but in the end, my boyfriend broke off with me. When we had the conversation, I felt a little bit of sadness, but a lot more lightness and relief. The feeling of my skin crawling went away, and something inside me shifted. I'd always stayed in relationships that weren't right for me because I was afraid there would never be anything better. When my boyfriend and I broke up, I realized I was learning different ways of thinking in FA and finding different answers.

I wanted more from my program, so I started asking questions and trying to really understand what I was hearing in meetings and on the phone. My sponsor kept directing me toward a positive view of any situation. I'd complain about my job, and she'd remind me that I was fortunate to have a job. She helped me see God's presence in my life, and I began to realize that I'd brought my childhood attitudes into adulthood. I'd asked for what I wanted—no acne, long hair, a thin body—and when that didn't happen, I thought that God didn't make it happen. I made lists for God and then jumped in and took action myself. I never left room for God to help me. I never stepped back and waited.

In FA, I am developing a relationship with a Higher Power. When I first got abstinent, I tested God. I asked for help and waited to see if I'd get it. I'd be up at night because of worries about work, and I'd ask God for a peaceful sleep. Before I knew it, I was waking up well rested in the morning. I was told to thank God for my one day of abstinence and to ask for another day, every day. I did that, and after five years of being around FA, I finally became abstinent and stayed abstinent. That made my faith grow. God was real to me.

It's hard to say I didn't have faith before, but I guess I didn't. I didn't understand faith. Today, I really believe that God knows what I need and that He'll provide it. He always has. Even in my addiction, when I was broke and buried in debt, I never went hungry. I was never homeless. My story is that God always took care of me. One way or another, whether we get what we want or not, I believe God takes care of each of us.

Today, I'm at a normal weight. I am slender! There are some consequences from my past obesity. I have wrinkly skin on my stomach and upper thighs, but that doesn't bother me. My body is what it is. I've also had trouble with my blood sugar as a result of my surgery. A gastric bypass leaves some people with reactive hypoglycemia. Two hours after eating certain foods, the blood sugar crashes. Working with information I got from my doctor, my sponsor solved the issue by adapting my food plan.

I had to have my gallbladder taken out this past summer—another consequence of the bypass—but I'm fine now. I don't have migraines and therefore don't have to take anti-seizure medication anymore. My skin doesn't crawl. I don't have acne. My hair has grown. I'm abstinent, and there's no food blocking the road between me and God.

The Kid from Canada

✧ ✧ ✧

I GREW UP IN CANADA, but when I was in my early twenties, soon after I had graduated from university and worked a little bit, I got offered a new job in New York City. This was during the big "dot.com" bubble, when Internet and technology companies were booming.

I'd struggled with my weight for years. I'm six feet tall and have been as high as 260 pounds, but I managed to get down to 185 before my move to New York. I remember partly feeling I'd be fine—sometimes I thought it would be a great opportunity. Mostly, though, I anticipated a disaster. After all, no matter how much weight I'd ever lost in the past, I'd always gotten fat again.

The job in New York was as I expected—crazy hours, a big expense account, weekend parties, and lots of free food that was delivered right to the office. Hard work, hard play—everything in excess. I was a mess inside, but I was very successful at work. The company was exploding. My bosses promoted me immediately and made me general manager of real estate for all of New York City—

me, this little kid from Canada. I was twenty-six, and some of the people working under me were grandmothers in their late fifties.

After my first six months, the company put me on a team of the top five producers in the country. We created all of the company training programs. They then asked me to facilitate the training sessions. They were hiring waves of people, and I was supposed to teach all of them to be like me: an overnight success. I probably put on 15 or 20 pounds that year, and I was devastated by the weight. I was stressed, and eating, and getting fatter and fatter and fatter.

One day, on stage in the middle of a presentation, I froze. My world crashed in on me. I stood like a deer in the headlights. Fear, anxiety, doubt, frustration—I don't know what caused it, but in front of everyone, I had to sit down. I couldn't talk, so someone else had to take over. I was humiliated.

From then on, I was in a fog. I went through the motions of life, but I'm sure I looked dazed. By day, I was a show-off, a big boss trying to hit his sales numbers and teaching people how to sell. Sitting on my couch alone late at night, I'd wonder how I'd gotten myself into such a mess. I wanted to throw in the towel and go live in my mom's basement at home.

Food played a huge role in what happened to me in New York and in everything that came before that. I'd struggled with my weight since I was a child. I grew up in the midst of a large extended family, and every Friday night, we got together for Shabbat dinners, alternating between relatives from my father's and my mother's side. We were about fifteen people, but we had enough food to feed an army. Each of the four mothers brought enough for twenty. Way back then, I distinctly remember that I had no gauge for stopping, even when I was physically full. I kept eating as long as the platters were passed.

My mom tried to get us to eat healthily, but at five or six years old, I was already stealing money from my dad's shoebox to buy my own food. There was no particular reason I ate. I ate for every reason—when I was happy, sad, bored, mad. I know now that I was lonely and didn't feel that I fit in. Food was my friend. I didn't have to worry about food not liking me. It kept me company, filled a void.

At school, as at work later, I did well, but I was a challenging, troubled boy. I was a big kid, so other kids made fun of me. I hated it and tried to be nice, tried to make friends with everyone, but at home I teased my sister and made my parents' lives difficult. When they took me to therapy, I thought every problem was their fault. Later on, as far as I could see, I was never the cause of any bad thing that ever happened. I could be alone in a house and break a glass. My immediate reaction? *This is not my fault. Whose fault is it? Let's figure that out.* I don't know how my parents and siblings survived living with me.

I kept losing and gaining weight. I went to Weight Watchers when I was ten. At thirteen, when I was about five feet, two or three inches tall, and weighed 213 pounds, I went to Weight Watchers Camp. I managed to get thin in high school, but I lost control in university and never got it back. I started drinking and blacking out, and whenever I got drunk, I ate everything that I wouldn't let myself have when I was sober. By my third year, I reached 260 pounds, and a doctor told me I was "morbidly obese."

I was terrified, but I'd been to weight loss camps and had done many diets, so I figured I knew what to do next. I had a strict regime—submarine sandwiches without meat, Diet Coke, no beer, and forty-five minutes daily on the exercise machine. For three months, I never missed a workout. As long as I kept to my routine, I was fine, but in the back of my mind I knew that the day I missed even one part of it, I would be in trouble.

That's exactly what happened. On the ninetieth day, I said to myself, *Three months! I've lost 70 pounds.* Life was great. People complimented me. I was a big man on campus. So I stopped my diet and vowed to start eating "in moderation." This was a problem only because I can't handle moderation. I don't know why, but by myself, without spiritual help and the support of a sponsor, I can't stick to moderate eating.

Slowly and painfully, over the next two and a half years, I gained back the weight I'd lost in ninety days. I'd known I was going to fail, so, as always, I'd kept all sizes of my clothes in bags at the side of my closet. By the time I was well into my first job, I was a mess again. I was working eighty or ninety hours a week and partying on weekends, waking up feeling sick and full from the night before. I'd try to go for a walk, but I'd end up at a brunch place, where I'd eat more.

By the time I reached my second job—the one in New York—I'd spent twenty years eating, struggling to lose weight, and gaining back everything I'd lost. Fortunately, I learned of FA in New York. My parents had met a woman who was in the program, and they gave me her number. I'll call her Eliza. I avoided phoning her for two months. The day I finally picked up the phone was one of the best in my life.

I didn't reach Eliza on my first try, so I left her a message. She called me back at noon and asked if I was awake. Of course I said yes, though I'd been sound asleep. When she suggested that I get myself up and call her later, at six o'clock in the evening, I thought it strange. I guess she knew I was in no shape for a conversation and wanted to be sure I was wide awake and coherent when we talked.

That afternoon, I went for a long walk in Central Park. Midway, I sat down on a bench. For years, I'd known that something was missing, something was wrong. I'd tried meditation and tried to pray. In the end, I had started believing in God in a helpless kind of way, but that day, I really prayed. I remember saying, "God, I've tried this before and I turned away from you, but I'm going to use you now. Can you please help me? Please, please help me." Then I went out for a big restaurant meal and returned home. I called Eliza at six o'clock.

During our call, Eliza told me about FA. She said that flour and sugar could be causing a lot of my problems. I didn't know much about AA, but she explained that for alcoholics, alcohol is a drug, and for people like us, flour and sugar are. This made some sense to me. She also said that she'd found faith because of FA. I had an open mind, but the major attraction for me was that FA was free. I'd spent thousands of dollars on gym memberships, strange doctors, and fad diets. Everything I had tried cost money. If FA worked and it was free, I wanted it.

Eliza had been in FA for two or three years, which seemed like eons to me. I was completely impressed, and when she told me to buy a scale and throw away the sweets and breads I'd been bingeing on, I did as she suggested. She also gave me the names and numbers of five FA members she wanted me to call and asked me to go to an FA meeting as soon as I could.

Eliza became my FA sponsor. I spoke with her every morning by phone, for fifteen minutes, and I began to plan and measure all my meals. My new FA life was overwhelming, but it was also fun. My clothes fit more loosely, and I started feeling better. I didn't know what to do with myself on weekends because I couldn't go out drinking like I used to, so I called other members of FA. When I was growing up, I never believed that anyone really wanted to be my friend, but when I made FA calls, I got the sense that people were happy to hear from me. They seemed to understand me, and our conversations were comfortable and easy.

I felt like I was in a different universe during my first few months in the program. I found myself leaving work at five or five-thirty to go to an FA meeting. By every prior definition in my life, this was insane. I used to keep the people who were working for me hostage until nine o'clock at night. Suddenly, I, the boss, was leaving early, not just once but twice a week. This would have been unimaginable before.

It was tough to stop eating flour and sugar, but I look back at my first months in the program fondly. My staff people were happy because they could go home and see their families. I became less of a micromanager at work, and I had a newfound feeling of peace.

I directly faced a question of faith for the first time when my 38-, 42-, and 44-inch pants no longer fit. My sponsor suggested that I take them to a consignment shop or give them away. I first refused, because I never threw my pants away. Number one, I was cheap. Number two, it would be crazy to throw away clothes that I'd have to buy again when I gained weight. I had a section of my closet for every size I ever wore, big to small.

I gained more faith when I finally got rid of my big clothes, initially trusting my sponsor while I was slowly learning to trust a Higher Power. My closet got emptier until finally I had nothing to wear. I'd never reached a size 33 before. It was time to start shopping.

My faith grew incrementally. I wouldn't say I was cynical, but I required proof that FA would work and God would take care of me. Every time I had to trust my Higher Power, I acted on blind faith. I didn't really feel trust until I had proof, based on a series of things that had happened when I acted *as if* I had faith. I began to see that when I trusted God, nothing happened as I planned, but in fact, things seemed to turn out even better than I'd planned.

After nine months in the program, for instance, I was laid off. I had enough money to cover two months of rent, and that was it. I told my sponsor I'd have to move back to Canada because I had no job and couldn't afford my expenses. She suggested that I stay put, continue my AWOL, and take whatever seemed to be the next right action each day, trusting that in the end everything would work out.

I'd been applying to business schools, with the help and support of people in FA, and the week I submitted my final application, I got an unexpected phone call from a man I'd worked with in Canada. He happened to need people for a New Jersey office, a twenty-minute drive from my house. I had no car, but not long afterward, one of my buddies offered me the use of his. Suddenly I had a job and the means to get there.

I have had many experiences like that one. I am not inherently a person who prays. I start with logic. I test things. They either work or they don't. Over time, I found that faith worked. Each time I hit a rough spot or a period of uncertainty—when I had to decide on a business school or was first getting to know the amazing, beautiful woman I married—I was told, "Ask for God's will, not your will." As I kept making the choice to ask for God's will, I learned from my experience that if I'm not in charge, my life turns out a lot better than it would otherwise.

Of course, I had to let go of my will so I could look for and do God's will, instead. One of my earliest experiences of this kind of surrender was the first meal that I planned and measured in FA—my first abstinent meal. I looked at my plate of food and felt sure it was not enough. I didn't think I could make it from that meal to the next, but the next meal came, and the one after that, and then I went to bed, having made it through one day abstinently.

I've been abstinent and at a healthy weight of 165 to 170 pounds for a little over eleven years now, and I feel truly neutral around food. In other areas of my life, I've sometimes still had an urge to make choices that don't support my abstinence, but I've always tried to keep my priorities straight: recovery, family, and then job.

The program has taught me to take care of myself. On an FA meeting night, although I may want to stay home to tuck my daughters into bed, I know that I can't. FA meetings, phone calls, and quiet time are among the disciplines, or tools, that make it possible for me to stay abstinent. Without abstinence, I can't take care of my family or do my job. So I plan my life first around my disciplines, and then, when I do put my girls to sleep, I am entirely focused on them, not on the food in the kitchen.

I give FA a lot of credit for teaching me the importance of family. After business school, when I was sitting on a beach in Spain trying to decide where to go next, I saw everyone else who graduated moving to Manhattan, London, Hong Kong, Tokyo, or other big centers of commerce. I wanted to be with my family, so I returned to Canada.

As I thought about where to live, FA also taught me to look first at my needs for my program. I knew I needed FA people around me. Though there were no meetings in the city where I grew up, something inside told me that if I came back, I could help build an FA fellowship.

Establishing FA meetings was a daunting task I couldn't accomplish on my own. In the beginning, one other person and I started a meeting. We closed it within a year after she moved away, and I went to AA for the next two years. Finally, another person got six months of abstinence, and we started another meeting together.

Over the course of the four years it's taken for FA to grow in my community, I've had a lot of frustration and doubt. During the many months I had no fellowship here, my sponsor kept telling me to take action and to trust. Now we have nine meetings a week. Sixty people come to the Saturday meeting. In my city, there are hundreds of abstinent people committed to the FA program of recovery. I'm amazed, and I'm grateful for the Twelve Traditions, which guide our relationships and service. When there have been bumps along the way, the Traditions have always helped guide us.

I went through many trials before I came to believe, but today my faith is rock solid. I'm not in charge. There is something bigger than me taking care of me, always. I'm still trying to do better at maintaining constant contact with God, but that conscious contact is the bottom line of my life.

Freedom

✧ ✧ ✧

I GREW UP IN THE SUBURBS in a normal home: mother, father, and seven children. We were a little out of the ordinary, being such a big family. One of my brothers had cerebral palsy, which was also unusual. I admire my parents for their dedication to him. Our trips to the hospital with my brother meant that I saw little children with no arms and no legs. This made me grateful for what I had, and yet I grew up feeling lost in the midst of the nine of us. I didn't know you could go to someone and say, "I'm hurt" or "I don't know what to do." We were raised with the belief that children were to be seen and not heard. The attitude was "Behave and get along, and you'll be fine."

My earliest memories are of a time when I did exactly what I wanted to do. At three, I followed some other children up the street and my brother had to come get me. Sometime between ages six and nine, I ran away again when I got mad at my mother for some reason. My little sister came with me, and we walked all the way to my grandparents' house on the other side of town. That started a pattern for me: If you don't like something, run—escape!

I was rebellious. In my teenage years I ran away for a whole week. I swore my friends to secrecy so they wouldn't tell anyone where I was. I know I worried my parents to death. In recovery, it was painful for me to realize the pain I'd caused them. Thank God, I got to make amends to them before they died.

I have early memories of food. I was probably in second grade when I went to a birthday party and ate so much cake that I threw up when I got home. Sugar became an important part of my life. I loved sweets and carbohydrates—bread, gravy, jars of Marshmallow Fluff. I'd give up candy for Lent and then eat it like crazy on Sundays when we were allowed a reprieve.

We didn't have a lot of food around our house. I'd come home from school and take one sliver after another of whatever sweet thing my mother had on hand. She'd be furious, but none of the seven of us would own up to taking it. I was the only heavy one in the family, so I was the most logical suspect. I was always sneaking, until I started working. All of my jobs involved food. Waitressing was perfect. I can remember bringing home a whole pie to eat by myself.

I first started dieting when I was thirteen. By the time I was about fifteen, I'd been introduced to a doctor who prescribed powerful diet pills for me, Black Beauties. I wasn't very heavy as a teenager, perhaps 10 or 15 pounds more than my friends, but I felt awful about myself—shy and inadequate and ugly and unable to communicate. I couldn't accept myself as I was, where I was. It seemed everyone else knew how to talk. Why didn't I have their script? I didn't want to be in my family. I wanted to be in another family. And I wasn't "normal" with food. I watched my friends and tried to copy them. They had one drink and one snack, so I'd decide to have the same. The trouble was that one snack for my friends ended with one snack, but one snack for me led to four or five more.

My parents stood by me when I got pregnant at nineteen. They gave me a little lecture about what happens when you stay out all hours of the night and hang around with boys, and then they asked me what I wanted to do. I said I wanted to get married. My husband was Protestant, I was Catholic, and I was pregnant, but we had a regular Catholic wedding, which was unthinkable then.

I was going for a secretarial degree at a community college at the time. I was grateful that I was married, but I was embarrassed to walk the halls at school, pregnant as could be. My eating got much worse. I'd have breakfast, which was necessary for my health, of course, and then I would pack a lunch. I'd eat the lunch in the morning on the way to school and have a snack once I got there, around ten o'clock. Then I would have another lunch, another snack in the afternoon, a stop on my way home for one more snack, and then have dinner at home with my husband. I wasn't a binge eater. I just ate all the time, all day long. I remember being aghast when I got on the scale before I delivered my son. I'd gained 60 pounds and weighed 199, at five feet, five inches tall. I had no idea that later in my life I'd reach 210.

Being married, having a baby, needing to be responsible—I had a hard time with all of that. I woke up after the delivery of my son and thought, *What are you going to do?!* I kept asking myself that question. My husband and I had partied all the time before we were married. He had his six-pack of beer, I had my brownies, and we were all set! We were happy. I hadn't realized that he was alcoholic and I was a food addict. I wasn't ready for married life.

We had a few good years in our early marriage, and then I got pregnant again, which gave me a pivotal lesson. When I went into labor, the maternity floor was busy and I was put on a gurney in the hallway. I'd had a cup of coffee that morning, which prevented them from giving me anything for my pain. As they wheeled me into the delivery room, I was grabbing at the walls screaming, "Knock me out! Knock me out! You're forgetting to knock me out!" I ended up in natural childbirth without any anesthesia, and it was wonderful. It taught me that something I fear as painful can end up being one of the most rewarding experiences of my life.

My relationship with my husband didn't get any better, and his drinking increased. We were moving from town to town, which was hard for me, and in the midst of one of our frequent moves, he beat me up for the second time. In the end, I stayed married for thirteen years, though my husband beat me three times. I never told a soul because of my embarrassment. Many people say that if someone hit them once, they would leave, but that instinct inside me was broken, and I was afraid to try to raise my children alone.

I tried to commit suicide once. I thought that I was the reason for my husband's drinking and that everyone would be better off without me. I remember feeling furious that I stayed alive, but the suicide attempt was the beginning of my recovery. I was sent to the mental ward of a hospital and had to go into group therapy. I marveled that the doctors and teachers in our group had problems, too, and I felt a little better, realizing that I wasn't the worst of the worst. Against medical advice, I checked out of the hospital, but I did take the suggestion that I find a way to continue group therapy. That began the process of looking at myself, as I moved into Al-Anon and then into FA.

The recovery programs brought me face to face with myself and my addiction, though I didn't call it addiction at the time. I was a massive people pleaser. I always knew what my friends liked and didn't like, the movies they preferred, the clothes they liked to wear, the food they enjoyed, but I didn't have a clue what I liked. I had no insides. I was an empty shell. I went along with whatever anyone else thought. I never felt anger. It just seemed important that I be nice.

As time went on, my approach became *Don't think, don't feel, just be good.* I remember being shocked when someone told me she had trouble making friends. Learn what other people like and do everything they want you to do, and it's simple to have friends. To this day, I still struggle sometimes with the old feeling that I have no value. I have to practice being true to myself by asking, *What do you like? What do you want? What do you believe?*

Food calmed me and soothed all my upsets. I ate if I was lonely, if I was happy, if I was sad, and if I had a minute to spare. I ate especially when I didn't know where to turn or when I had the uncomfortable feeling of not knowing who I was. I had wonderful friends, and yet I couldn't talk with them as I needed to. I don't think I could have even identified what I wanted to say.

I didn't take FA seriously for many years, though I saw the truth a few times early on. I remember sitting next to a pretty woman and feeling amazed that she talked with me during the break. When I told her I'd been coming to the program for a while, she said, "What are you waiting for?" That hit me hard. Another time, speaking with someone else, I had a strong feeling that I was home. The people at the meetings understood my experiences with food, and they liked to talk deep. I wanted so badly to be like them, but I didn't know how. No one close to me talked seriously about how they truly felt if their feelings were hurt, or brought up problems they were having, or spoke about God. In our family, we went to church every week, but we never mentioned God.

My first year, I got a good sponsor. She tried to teach me the ropes, but I had just started a softball league with the beautiful people in a town nearby. They were rich and fun, and they loved excitement. The parties after the games were the highlight for all of us. I'd joined an AWOL, and one night the AWOL meeting conflicted with one of our parties. It was my turn to host, but I wouldn't talk with my sponsor about my dilemma—not me. I just skipped the AWOL, made all the food for the party, and couldn't wait for everyone to leave so I could eat the way I wanted to eat. The paradox of my life was that I wanted recovery, but I didn't want it badly enough to give up my old way of life. I was sitting on the fence wondering if being with the beautiful people was going to make me happy or if doing the program was going to make me happy. Trying to do both didn't work.

For twelve years, I stayed at the outskirts of the program. I dropped in and out of FA, always fighting what was offered there. I must have had fifteen or twenty different sponsors. I was scared of the complete surrender required by the program—the need to give up my life the way it was. I spent a lot of time at non-FA meetings, where much less was expected.

It took all of twelve years for God to humble and prune me. I'd get a sponsor who was strongly committed to FA and not listen to her suggestions, or I'd choose someone who broke her abstinence and then disappeared. I switched sponsors for no reason at all or for bad reasons. Someone wouldn't give me a food plan that included milk for breakfast, and I'd leave her for someone who'd give me that milk. I wanted to do this part of the program but not that part. I didn't see the need for *all* the tools, which were for other sick people, not me.

Through all those twelve years, I went in and out of addictive eating, struggling unsuccessfully to be abstinent. I got a year of abstinence once, and even two or three years, but I always ate addictively again. Entrenched in the world and still attracted to the beautiful people, I was going away on weekends and involved in a Brownie troop and my children's sports teams. I couldn't imagine making my recovery a higher priority than my children's activities. I didn't understand that it was impossible for me to be sane and present for my children when I was eating addictively.

I remember I joined an early AWOL with a couple of hundred other people. The night before one of the AWOL meetings, I went to a Brownie troop sleepout and was up all night. I had only a little crumb of a brownie, so I thought I had done well, but I must have felt guilty, because at the end of the AWOL, I approached one of the leaders to see if I could continue. With everyone else, I'd taken a commitment to remain abstinent, so the AWOL leader said, "You're out," like an umpire would say to a player sliding into first base. After that, I went to meetings where a lot of people were eating addictively so I could bad-mouth the people who were successfully abstinent.

The only thing I did right during my twelve years of addictive eating was that I kept coming to meetings. I never left the program. I'd gotten my weight down, and it stayed down. Most of the time, I had only about 15 extra pounds on me. The issue went way beyond weight, though. I saw peace and joy in abstinent people, but I couldn't find it myself. I had a big, black hole inside me.

People who are struggling often ask what made me finally surrender. I can't say that it was a horrible binge or any one big incident. All I know is that I finally couldn't stand the pain. One weekend, I finally had enough. The weekend began with corn chips. My children were grown, and I was driving to Canada with some other people to see my son's college hockey game. I ate corn chips all afternoon, rationalizing that the chips were my lunchtime grain portion. At dinner, as we rushed to get to the game, I realized that the protein I'd ordered was breaded. I rationalized eating that, too, thinking that there wasn't time to order another meal and I didn't want to embarrass myself in front of everyone by sending my plate back. I figured I was forced to eat the breaded food. I told myself I had no other choice.

The dinner in Canada was the last straw. I could not deny anymore that I wasn't able to get abstinent on my own. I couldn't maintain the facade that I was all right. When I got home, I went to one of the strongest meetings I knew and asked one of the most committed people there to sponsor me. I was so out of touch that I wondered aloud to her if I was abstinent. I never mentioned the afternoon I spent eating corn chips or the breaded meat, but she suggested that I start at the beginning, on a first day of abstinence. It was only after I began with her that I finally got honest about everything I'd eaten and done.

I grew up in the sixties, and it had always seemed cool to rebel. Working with my new sponsor, though, I reached the point where I gave up. If she had asked me to eat shoe leather, I'd have eaten shoe leather. Because of her, I went to FA meetings in the city instead of staying in the suburbs. Nothing had been consistent there, especially me. I'd dropped in and out of various meetings there for years, arriving late, leaving early, spending a lot of time in the hallway talking with people I knew.

Recovery for me happened when it was supposed to happen—when I was ready. I finally wanted freedom from the bondage of food. I was willing to open up, and I found out that I could talk to my sponsor about *any-*

thing I needed to. She didn't bite my head off or laugh at me. If I hadn't been able to ask questions, I probably would have gotten angry and quit working with her, as I had with all the sponsors I'd had before. Instead, as I started to understand why we do what we do, I began to change. I was willing to commit to meetings where people were focused on recovery, and I made a lot of phone calls to other FA members every day.

I'd never been part of the FA fellowship before. I had never seen myself as a person inside the bus with everyone else. I put myself under the bus or on top of it. For the first time, I was willing to be inside the bus. My old approach had been "I don't know about me. Let's talk about you." I had to stop isolating, stop living in my old, people-pleasing world, so I made the phone calls and really talked about what was going on for me. After I'd been abstinent ninety days, I faced a big moment in my recovery. I saw that I had hope to share. I could speak from the front of the room and greet the newcomers.

Sponsors help us through the situations that used to drive us to eat. My new sponsor was patient and loving. I'd had a hard time with my mother my whole life, but my sponsor walked me through the last ten years of my mother's life and taught me how to love her. My sponsor was there at the tail end of my divorce from my first husband, when I had to go back to court. Above all, she taught me how to go to God. I'd want an answer from her, and she'd say, "Why don't you take some quiet time? Meditate and think about that."

I hated *Twenty-Four Hours a Day*, our meditation book. It seemed way too religious for me. Still, I read it every morning, as my sponsor suggested—just the one book and not the eleven other daily devotionals I had been reading each day. After I read the day's passage from *Twenty-Four Hours a Day*, I sat still for my quiet time. In the beginning, I could only sit for a minute or two, but I worked myself up to half an hour.

My spiritual awakening was the slow, educational type. Starting with *Twenty-Four Hours a Day* and quiet time in the morning, I began to have a relationship with a Higher Power. I'd been waiting for a big, bellowing voice from God. I expected to be told, "Go do this wonderful thing!" Instead, every morning I heard a little voice say, "Get up, get dressed, and go to work." Throughout the day, when I faced a difficult situation or had a craving to eat addictively, I would say the Serenity Prayer over and over, or I'd take a little phrase from the reading in the morning and repeat it.

God was working in my life. After my divorce, I married again, and about a year and a half into my abstinence, my husband had to move to another state for his work. I commuted to see him each month and then finally decided to move. I was like a scared little kid when I left, but the next few years were amazing. I've always been a strong believer in service, and I found people hungry for recovery in my new community. They'd never heard of the disciplines and tools and hope of our recovery. I didn't have a job, so I sponsored as many people as I could. I had basically the same schedule I have today. I got up early in the morning and talked with one sponsee after another.

I loved my new life. I'd lost 85 pounds and was comfortable and stable in my abstinence. Before I knew it, I was co-leading an AWOL. I didn't always know what to say, but God worked through my sponsor to help me find my voice. As I led the AWOL, my conviction about FA really took hold, because I saw people get abstinent, stay abstinent, and have an experience of God working in their own lives. Whenever there was a problem, I'd think, *I can't wait to see how God is going to work this one out!* I was exhilarated.

Today I feel happy and secure, and I'm in awe of the fellowship that's developed through FA. My sponsees have stayed abstinent, and when some of them have had to move away, they've taken the program with them and started fellowships in other areas. I sometimes see people leaving FA to "do more research," as we say, and I am grateful, grateful, grateful that I know so clearly now what works for me and what does not work for me.

When my children were younger, I felt terrible leaving them to go to a meeting, but the other day my daughter said that the best thing that ever happened to her was my coming into FA. That meant the world to me. I am nineteen years abstinent now, and my weight never changes, year to year. Basic, simple food is fine with me. I am done with research. I'm done with looking for loopholes. I'm done with struggling. I'm grateful, and I'm free.

The Runner

✧ ✧ ✧

As far back as I can remember, I felt different from everyone else. I think that's a feeling that's common to addicts. I longed to belong, but at the same time, part of me wanted to be different and better than other people. I made myself separate from them.

Fear kept me separate, too. I could name the fear sometimes—fear of going to kindergarten, fear of boys or teachers, fear of not knowing the answers in school—but even when the particular fears went away, they were replaced by fears of something else. I did excellently academically, but I was always afraid of tests. Every time I took one, I was terrified I'd fail. I was sure that if I failed, *I* was a failure.

Everything in life became a test for me. What college could I get into? It had to be the best. What place could I win in a race? I had to be number one. I became an endurance athlete and a cutthroat competitor, even with my friends. After I got into recovery, I told a friend from college how lonely I'd been, how closed off and afraid. She was surprised I'd felt so alone. "You had so many friends," she said. "We all voted you track captain. You were connected with so many people." I couldn't, or wouldn't, ever admit that I felt worried or inadequate; I could never be as open as other people.

When I think of my competitiveness and loneliness, I also think of sugar. There were four children in my family. My dad was an engineer, and my mom was a nurse. We didn't have a lot of money or material things. My mom didn't buy or believe in having a lot of junk food around the house, but I can remember, without a doubt, that I liked sugar. I didn't have access to sweet snacks and desserts, so I was drawn to things like ketchup, baked beans, and canned fruits. When I was a child, my friends and I would walk to McDonald's and they would laugh because I would ask for twelve packets of ketchup. Sometimes I'd go back and ask for more.

By the time I was in fifth or sixth grade, the only time I ever felt comforted was when I was putting food in my mouth. Chewing and swallowing gave me peace from my worry and fear. I didn't have to have sugar or flour. Dinner would do. When I was eating, the world went away.

Eventually, I wanted to feel at all times like I felt when I was eating. I needed something in my mouth. Physiologically, a person can't eat all day long, so as my disease progressed, I found substitutes. I sucked on sugar-free candy from morning to night, or chewed gum, or ate bags of carrots. I got so that I could drink ten or twelve Diet Cokes a day, or that much coffee, and I could still sleep at night.

Somewhere around freshman year in high school, my friends convinced me to go out for track, and I started running. I did very well, but my body was developing and I was gaining weight, so I began dieting. From then on, I was either strictly on a diet or I couldn't stop eating. I wasn't fat. I'm five feet, two and a half inches tall, and I probably weighed about 125 pounds.

I had a sweet relationship with a boy from another school in those days. There were no cell phones, so I waited by the phone for his call every night. One night, he didn't call. He didn't phone the next night, either, or the next. Girls weren't supposed to call boys then, so I only found out through a friend that he'd broken up with me. I was devastated.

I never told anyone how terrible I felt. Instead, one evening after I cleared the dishes, I eyed a cake my sister had baked, which was sitting on our table. I was dieting, of course, but I had a craving for just a little something sweet, so I stuck my fork into the cake and took one bite. After that, the fork had a life of its own. Inside my head, my brain said, "Stop, stop, stop. Don't eat." I kept hearing, "I don't want to get fat," but another part of my brain was controlling my fork, and it wouldn't stop my hand from moving to my mouth.

Finally, with a massive effort, I was able to put the fork down. I was wearing tight designer jeans, and I felt awful, so I went to the bathroom. When I leaned over to flush the toilet, everything came back up. I remember feeling high after that happened, because I'd found an answer. I suddenly had a secret. I had a perfect solution. I had control. I could button up my pants and feel thin.

I thought, *I am never going to do this again. I'm not going to overeat, but on the other hand, if I do overeat, I have a way out.* Thus began a journey into bulimia that I never intended or planned. I was hooked.

In the beginning, I would throw up only if I had terribly overeaten. Because I felt that I was making a choice to purge, it was fairly easy to talk with some of my friends about it. Then I began to rationalize. Purging was not pleasant, so I'd think, *I've eaten one dessert— I might as well eat all that I want before I have to make myself throw up.*

I could hold unbelievable amounts of food in my stomach without getting full, whether because of food addiction or as a result of a quirk in my individual physiology. Eventually, I was eating an entire cake or two boxes of cookies and a half gallon of chocolate milk. As my disease progressed, I realized I'd totally lost control. I had no choice over the bingeing or the purging, though I didn't want to do either one, and I stopped talking about it with anyone.

Life got more difficult as I continued high school. I was obsessed with food and was competing at high levels in academics, dance, and track. To get relief from the constant pressure and stress, I sometimes cried for hours, lying in bed by myself at night.

When I got into an Ivy League college, I resolved never to throw up again. For a while, I kept my weight under control through exercise, but I binged and threw up just once, and then I was back in the cycle, finding food and bathrooms all over the campus. Every experience I had in college was colored by my bingeing and purging.

I worked with two different therapists. I quit track because of the pressure to be thin and then couldn't bear my loneliness when I lost the only friends I had. I rejoined the team, but the antidepressants I began taking made me gain weight and slowed my running. Winning and being better than everyone else had been the glue that held me together, and when that was gone, I fell apart.

In the end, I had to take a medical leave of absence. Back home, with two jobs, I was running at five in the morning or riding an exercise bike for hours. When I overdosed on antidepressants one night, the therapist I was working with pushed me into treatment. He'd realized that his patients with so-called eating disorders had the same personality traits as the drug and alcohol addicts he was treating, and he'd found a twelve-step treatment center that addressed food.

Sitting in the airplane as I flew south for treatment, I remember wanting desperately to believe that the center would cure me. Inside, I think I knew that there was no way a mental condition like mine could evaporate, but I hoped that treatment would be just like surgery. Someone would remove my problem from me.

I thought I was going to a kind of spa. I packed leotards for aerobics and expected to write in a journal and swim, but I was in for a surprise. After we landed and I got to the treatment center, my luggage was searched for sharp objects and the doors were locked behind me.

During treatment, we were required to go to twelve-step meetings for compulsive overeaters three times a week, sometimes outside the ward. A kind AA man who was trying to help me, a fellow addict, picked me up and drove me there. I couldn't understand what I was hearing and hated going. "How long do I have to go to these things?!" I'd complain. He'd say, "Honey, you only have to keep going to meetings until you want to go to them."

I spent three months in the locked ward. My last day, the psychiatrist looked me in the eyes and said, "When you get out of here, you're going to fall flat on your face, but I believe that in the end you're going to make it." I had a big ego, and that made me mad, but I did exactly as she said. The night I got out, I drank, binged, and purged.

For a number of years after that I kept trying. I went to meetings and talked to other food addicts, so life was better, but I still resorted to using food when I felt stressed or afraid. Full relapse came after I graduated from college. I'd gained a spot on a prestigious running team and moved to a nearby city to work with its well-known coach. My food addiction was then even more painful than before. I was running like a maniac and starving myself, and I had never felt so hopeless. One day, crying, I got on my knees in my apartment. Palms up, I said, "God, show me what to do. I will do *anything.*" Shortly after that, the phone rang, and someone suggested that I try an FA meeting. I'd heard of the program but knew nothing about it.

The phone call that afternoon led me to a turning point. I went to the FA meeting and got a sponsor. My sponsor had been hopeless about her inability to stop eating, but she had an answer now. I wanted her answer—I wanted to be abstinent—so when she told me to go to four meetings a week, I went to four meetings a week; when she asked me to pray for help to abstain from addictive eating, I prayed. I didn't have rebellious feelings about anything she suggested, because I didn't see that I had any choices left. What did I have to lose?

I ended up going to five meetings a week and getting involved in FA service. After four or five months, my sponsor broke her abstinence, and I had to work with someone else. I was grateful for the experience. Because I'd been following my first sponsor's suggestion that I make at least three phone calls a day to other FA members, I was fully part of the fellowship and was quickly able to find a different sponsor.

I weighed about 101 pounds when I began working with my new sponsor, and to my horror, she told me that I needed to gain weight. This was a huge, hard surrender for me. Everything I had eaten before had been nonfat or low fat. I didn't want to binge or purge or to eat flour or sugar, but there was no way I wanted to eat full-fat foods or to gain 10 pounds.

My sponsor and other members of FA helped me specifically with my undereating and bulimia. Our food plan usually includes plenty of salad and vegetables. Most people feel full and contented after our meals, but I was terrified by the feeling of fullness, which immediately triggered my impulse to throw up. My sponsor adjusted my plan so I had the necessary calories but less bulk. I learned to sit quietly and pray before each meal. I ate very slowly because eating quickly also triggered my wish to purge.

Meetings were usually very helpful, but sometimes I had to work on my attitude there. Understandably, many people talked about how happy they felt as they lost weight and gained back their lives. In contrast, I had come into the program and been confronted with the need to gain weight: something I *didn't* want to do. I had to aim for a result that I'd tried all my life to avoid. I sometimes felt angry, but, like all FA members, I was there because I needed to learn to accept life on life's terms. If we are too heavy, we need to lose weight. If we are too thin, we need to gain.

I struggled, too, with setting limits beyond the boundaries of my food plan. My cup of life was overflowing when I came into FA. Part of my disease was a pattern of doing too much. I'd always thought of myself as a superwoman. I was an overachiever in every area of my life, and I was super thin. I didn't like the stress required for me to achieve at the highest levels and maintain my thinness, but I liked being told I was incredible. I always remember an FA member saying, "You've got to eat crazy to live crazy." She meant that when you have a life that's insanely busy, you have to eat in insane ways to fuel and maintain it.

Sometimes I felt rebellious and angry, but I knew inside that she was right. I had to let go of my thinness and my frantic pace. In my first AWOL, one of the leaders said, "Practice being average. Practice being satisfied." She seemed to be talking directly to me. I had to let go of my hyperactivity and punishing thinness. Instead of focusing on myself, I needed to try to help someone else.

She often told us that God solved all her problems while she was busy thinking about others.

I didn't find it easy to think about others, but FA helped me change my attitude and my life. After five years of abstinence, I got pregnant for the first time. I talked openly about my addiction with my doctors and nurses. They understood how hard it was for me to be weighed, and we worked out a way to make that less stressful. When they prescribed a glucose test, they measured my blood sugar levels before and after I ate an abstinent meal, avoiding any need for me to eat sugar.

I had a difficult pregnancy. I prayed my way through it. After years of making myself throw up, I was frightened by an intense nausea that sometimes forced me into bouts of vomiting I couldn't stop. Four times, I had to go to the hospital for dehydration. Worried that I was losing weight, the doctors and nurses would give me license to eat. "Have anything you want!" they'd say. "Have some cookies." I'm grateful for the strength and resilience I was given through FA. I knew that sugar, flour, and extra food were all poison for me.

My first baby was born healthy, and I have since had two more children. In a few months, God willing, I will have been abstinent twenty years. Today I'm forty-four, and I steadily maintain a slender weight of 116 to 120 pounds. I actually bought a bikini this year, which is a miracle, since I spent my life hating my body, even when I looked good. I'm an endurance athlete, and I swim, run, and bike, but I don't do any of it to lose weight. I do it now for pure pleasure. I enjoy my body.

My daughters and son have known me only in my recovery. I'm not a supermom, who bakes or cooks fantastic meals. I prepare simple, basic foods, and my husband and I spend hours with our children outside. I used to feel special when I won awards and I was thin, but I don't need to struggle to achieve any of that now. One day in my quiet time, I felt a warmth spread through my whole body. Then and ever since, I've known that I am loved. I am special to my Higher Power, just as I am.

Fat Pants

✧ ✧ ✧

I WAS EATING *when I didn't want to be eating.* The phrase came into my head in a small, clear voice one day while I was sitting in my morning meditation. I had already been in recovery for three years, but in all that time, I hadn't been able to see myself as a food addict. That morning, I suddenly understood.

I always had some justification for the way I ate. *I eat a lot because . . .* , I would say to myself, and then I would fill in the blank. I chose from a list. *I am a tall girl. I have a fast metabolism. I am bored. I am hung over. I have low blood sugar. I am high. I am Jewish. I am HUNGRY!*

My childhood proves that you do not need to come from trauma to become an addict. Nothing horrible happened to me when I was young. I grew up in a loving, supportive, two-parent household with my older brother. My parents both had professional careers, and they did well. I was trying to describe my house to someone the other day, and she said, "It sounds like a mansion." I didn't think of it that way, but our house was on three acres of land, and it was so big that sometimes you couldn't find anybody in it.

I was privileged as a child. I excelled in music and dance, and I had all kinds of lessons and went to the best private schools. I have loving parents who never pressured us, but, as I've heard so often from other people in FA, I never felt that I was enough or that I fit in. My brother was extraordinarily gifted. He became a professional opera singer. I felt far less talented. I wanted to be skinny, with long, blond, straight hair. I wanted to be called Tiffany or Ashley or Kelly, but I was Jewish. I wanted a boyfriend. I never had one. I wanted to wear a size two, like my friends, but I was gawky and my stomach stuck out.

In high school, the academic competition was fierce, and I was constantly afraid. I studied for hours, but never without food. I remember chewing gum on one side of my mouth, chewing food on the other side of my mouth, and drinking Diet Coke in the middle. I also began having health problems related to my autoimmune system, thyroid, and blood sugar levels, none of which were diagnosed.

My first year at college, I began bingeing on alcohol. I had never cared about alcohol, but I felt uncomfortable socially. My friends drank, so I did, too. I drank to get drunk. In the middle of the year, the doctors diagnosed me with thyroid cancer. After surgery, I was in and out of the hospital. My weight went up until they were able to regulate my thyroid, and then it went down. I was obsessed with my weight. Food became more and more of a problem. My response was an attempt to control what

I ate. I wrote down everything I took in. I had whole bags of carrots or fat-free popcorn, but I never touched the cakes and candies.

I have been blessed to inherit money a couple of times, and because of it, I was not in reality. After college, I moved to Seattle, where I went from one job to another, blowing through my money. I was lost. Eventually, I ended up in Cambodia, where I fell in love with a Cambodian man and almost immediately decided to live with him. He was Buddhist, and because he'd grown up in an isolated village, he didn't speak English. I didn't know a word of Khmer. We managed to communicate only because both of us happened to know a little French. Neither of us was fluent, which made the relationship difficult.

In Cambodia, my eating took off. I had a strange delusion. *I'm in Cambodia,* I told myself, *this eating doesn't count.* Before, I'd always clamped down tightly. I had big meals and lots of snacks, but I held on to control. In Cambodia, I felt I had carte blanche. A banana off a tree? That was Mother Nature. So healthy. The fish? That fish was swimming in the water that very morning. Wonderful fish. Someone told me that Cokes kill parasites, so I drank four Cokes a day. I did that for the parasites. I wore sarongs daily because they were adjustable. No one said anything about my weight going up.

When I got back to the U.S., I found I didn't fit into my Western clothes. I moved to Seattle again for a few months and hated it, so I moved to Chicago. I hated Chicago, too. I lived in a tenement apartment and actually got a job, but the gloves had come off in Cambodia, and I couldn't put them on again. I ate like I had never eaten before—greasy, sugary, fatty foods. I didn't recognize myself. I lost a lot of my ability to function. I'd always been a very high-functioning addict, but I almost got fired from my job. I had to quit before they let me go.

I was in therapy at that point, and I felt suicidal. I remember saying to my therapist, "I want to talk about my past lives. That's why I'm messed up right now." She said, "Really? Why don't we talk about this life?" I wouldn't have it. I needed a past-life regression, I was sure. I had no idea I had a food problem. Not a clue. In addition, the chiropractor I was seeing at that time had told me I was not fat. He said, "You just have candida in your stomach." I believed him. To be honest, it might have been possible. I've since learned that I do have a lot of food allergies. I probably did have some bloating, but not 30 pounds worth. You don't bloat 30 pounds.

This started my two-year quest. I explored acupuncture and past-life regression and my inner child and blue-green algae and psychiatry and therapy and *The Writer's Way* to try to deal with my problem, which I knew was that I was anxious and bloated.

All the while, I had two girlfriends in FA. I loved what they were doing. They were thin and happy. I wasn't, but I didn't think I was a food addict. To be a food addict you have to eat a whole pizza. You have to take food out of the garbage can. I never did any of that. If you're a food addict, you can't stop eating. I could stop eating. As I told them, I could stop at one granola bar. Of course, an hour later, I'd have a piece of fruit, and an hour after that I'd dig into a huge bowl of cereal. An hour after that I'd find something else to put into my mouth, but I ate healthy food. Grapes, for example. Grapes aren't bad for you. Who cares if I just ate a whole bag of grapes? Besides, I said, "I'm Jewish." (Jewish people naturally eat a lot.) Besides I had low blood sugar. And besides that, I had candida in my stomach.

Then I really lost it. I had a boyfriend in Chicago. He broke up with me, right after four people happened to ask me if I was pregnant because my stomach stuck out so far. I looked like a little beanpole with a basketball in front of it. I was twenty-seven, and all of my girlfriends were getting engaged and married. I felt like I was going to die if I didn't get married.

I was brought to my knees. I called my friend in the program and said, "I know I really need God. I think the Twelve Steps would be great. But I'm not a food addict, and I don't know what to do." She began asking me questions. "When you see a skinny woman on the street, what do you think? When you eat, do you ever feel guilty, as if you ate too much?" I told her the truth: "I hate skinny women. And I feel guilty every time I eat." Then she asked me how much I weighed. I told her that I was five feet, seven inches and that I weighed 148 pounds. She asked a few more questions, but I kept saying, "I really don't think I'm a food addict." I had another idea. How about Emotions Anonymous? She didn't see how one could abstain from emotions, but she encouraged me to check into other twelve-step programs. I went online and looked at one after another. None of them was right for me. I knew in the back of my mind that I had a problem with food, but I was terrified to look. Food was my balm. I couldn't let go of it.

My friend continued to encourage me. "Jump in," she said. "Do this program for ninety days. If you get better, then keep on keeping on. If not, you can do something else. What you're doing now is not working." I knew she was right, and that gave me the courage to try.

So I came in to FA and got a sponsor. I was absolutely terrified. I actually had a medical problem, and my first years in the program were really hard because my food plan needed adjustment. Still, I clung to FA because (a) the weight started flying off my body and (b) I was shown a way to get through all the terror that used to drive me to eat. Once I got abstinent and gained some perspective, I was shocked by the hold that food used to have on me.

My sponsor laid out the foundation of the program, reminding me that I was giving up flour and sugar and unmeasured quantities just one day at a time. We spoke every morning on the phone. I imagine for her it must have been like standing in front of an open fire hydrant. I spewed rage, jealousy, fear, and resentments. She kept telling me to ask God for help and to not break my abstinence, no matter how I felt or what happened. I thought, *This is impossible. God is not going to keep me from eating. God isn't going to get me from meal to meal without my struggling every moment between.*

One night, about two months into my recovery, the urge to eat outside of my food plan and meal time overwhelmed me. I was in a rigorous graduate program and had a paper due the next day. It was midnight. I had procrastinated on doing the work, and I panicked. It was too late to call anyone in FA for help with my anxiety, but somehow I got the idea to wear my "fat pants." Those were pants I had put in a bag full of clothes for the Salvation Army. They were size twelve, and I was a size six. They were falling off me. Somehow, I knew that I needed to feel exactly what I felt when I was so big and hated myself every waking minute of the day.

I put on my fat pants and knelt down. I was crying. I prayed, "God, I don't know who you are or how this thing works, but I want to eat so badly right now, and I desperately want to stay abstinent. Please, God, remove this desire to eat. Please help me now." Something told me, *Don't get up until the feeling of wanting to eat passes.* I prayed more, and then the feeling passed. A peace came over me. I couldn't believe it. I had never been able to resist the desire to eat before. Grateful and abstinent, I finished my paper and went to bed.

My experience that night gave me the foundation for a newfound faith in a Power greater than myself. Before, I had turned to God only in times of crisis, like when my grandmother died, or on a High Holy Day when I tried to repent for my wrongdoings. This was entirely different. This God was close, personal, effective, and there to restore me to sanity.

The next time something scary happened and I wanted to eat, I said to myself, *Remember that time you put on those fat pants and hit your knees, and you asked your Higher Power for help? You didn't eat and the feeling passed, remember? Okay! If that could happen then, it can happen again.* Then I'd pray, "God, can you help me?" It worked every time, and each time I didn't eat addictively, my faith grew deeper. I kept turning to a Higher Power, and I got a stronger and stronger sense that all was well, that I was not going to fall apart, and that the earth was not going to shatter.

I never turned back once I came into the program. My life changed. I walked through breaking up with two boyfriends, one of whom I'd thought I would marry, and I did not break my abstinence. I finished two graduate programs. I changed careers. I went on countless blind dates. I attended the weddings of scores of dear friends. I underwent grueling medical procedures and cancer treatments. I wrote papers, got traffic tickets, babysat despite my longing for my own baby, and studied for licensing exams; plus, I have lived with chronic daily headaches for years—headaches that have stumped every doctor I've seen. All of this, and I have not eaten.

FA also unexpectedly brought me back to Judaism. I have a new relationship with the religion of my childhood. I'm drawn to the prayers, which are thousands of years old. "Who is like You, God, working miraculous wonders. Who is like you?"

Truly, who is like God? God has kept me from eating. God has kept me from killing myself. God has kept me from sleeping with random men. I've been given a second chance. Our Higher Power is not just an idea, a concept. I think that when we walk through a hard time as addicts, when we face a difficulty and don't run away, God, our Higher Power, is the foundation of our strength.

Sane and Happy Usefulness

✧ ✧ ✧

I WAS BORN IN ENGLAND at the end of World War II, when goods were rationed and there wasn't much available. My mother baked lots of pastries and breads to make the food we had go as far as possible. Some of my best memories are of being with my mother when we ate or she prepared our meal. Food was a tie to her.

As I grew up, my body was a bit jiggly. I tended to be overweight, probably because I loved to eat my mother's pastries. I remember sneaking things out of the fridge when she wasn't looking, but I also know that after our meals, when I was sent to take the bones to the dogs, I used to pick them clean before the animals ever got them. I felt a lot of shame about my behavior. No one else ate that way.

I don't have a lot of happy memories from childhood. My mother suffered from depression and rage. She went from being way up high and talking to God and the vacuum cleaner, to not being able to get out of bed. I loved her and she loved me, but it hurt me that I could never fix her unhappiness. She had a total breakdown when I was sixteen. By that time, though I wasn't fat, I felt fat. I got the message when I was quite young: My sister was the pretty one; I was the ugly one. I wasn't good enough. I needed to be thin.

Sometimes I tried not to eat, and other days I ate a lot, but I never really dieted until I got engaged. Then I starved myself. My husband is a shorter, small man, and I was afraid that I'd stand next to him at our wedding a huge, fat woman. I wore a mini-dress that day, and though I was thin, I remember looking at my knees in our photographs and thinking, as ever, that I was fat. After the ceremony, when my husband carried me over the threshold, all I could do was pray that he would make it.

After we married, I found a job in London, but I discovered I didn't know how to be married and work. I couldn't figure out how to juggle housework and my job. When I got pregnant, I decided to give up on trying to do both and just stay home.

I put on 64 pounds with my first child. I wasn't a pregnant woman with a little bump in front. I was fat all the way around, twenty-one years old, and not prepared to be a mother. When my daughter was a newborn, some friends of mine once came to take me out for the afternoon. I remember looking at my reflection in the window, still with all my extra weight, thinking, *Oh, my God, you have a baby at home! What have you done?! What are you going to do?* I was terrified.

After my daughter's birth, I started to avoid people. I withdrew because of my weight, too ashamed to let people see how I looked. We received a wedding invitation from my husband's cousin, and I never even sent a reply. Years later they spoke of how we'd missed their wedding. I missed my husband's grandfather's funeral for the same reason.

Over time, I managed to lose all my extra weight except the last 20 pounds, but when I had my second child two years later, I put on another 64 pounds. After my daughter's birth, I took a panicked trip to a doctor. He offered to weigh me once a week. I hated it, but I must have wanted help, because I was honest with him. I told him that I couldn't stop eating baby formula. I piled it into my mouth throughout the day, mostly the dry powder. "Of course that makes you gain weight," he said, but that was it.

My husband and I had everything that you would think would make someone happy: a brand-new house built for us, two children, a car, my parents around the corner. I appreciated none of it. Sometimes I binged, and sometimes I restricted what I ate. Much of my eating was completely unconscious. I'd go to the fridge, help myself to some pie, one slice at a time, and shut my eyes. I complained about my unmet wants and needs, then and throughout our marriage. Just as *I* was never enough when I was a child, my life was never enough when I was an adult, and I gave my husband the message that he was not a good provider.

After a while, I decided I'd be able to handle life better if we lived abroad. I'd be thin there, I thought. When a job opportunity opened up in the Middle East, without a second thought, we decided to move. My husband left England first, and before the children and I joined him, I starved myself, really starved myself. Once I got to the Middle East, I became anorexic. I'm five feet, six inches tall, and I think I weighed about 90 pounds. I couldn't be thin enough. I smoked pot and cigarettes, took diet pills, and looked at myself in the mirror ninety-five times a day. I wouldn't go to the supermarket alone because I was afraid of losing control of my spending, as I had back home. I violated my own values sexually, and I guess I'd say that I starved myself into a state of paranoia. Some years later, when we moved elsewhere in the Middle East, I broke down completely. I was put on antipsychotic medication, and for five days I was in a medically induced coma. I was supposed to feel better when I woke up.

Eventually, we returned to England, and I went back to my old ways—eating and not eating, eating and not eating. I was afraid to leave the house and used to have to call my mother to talk about my anxiety before I'd have the strength to walk out my front door. When my husband later decided to go to the United States, I didn't want to leave, and I made it as hard on him as I could. I spent lots of money to punish him.

We moved to the U.S., where I didn't know a soul, and I've never been as lonely as I was then. Eating numbed me against my rage and loneliness, and the bad feelings I had about my body. I never felt like I was enough. At one point, I tried to throw myself out of a moving car and was admitted to the hospital in a straitjacket. Doctors prescribed antipsychotics and put me in a locked ward for a week. They diagnosed me with schizoid psychosis.

Once I got out of the hospital, I mostly stayed home, watching soap operas and gobbling food. I first learned of a twelve-step program for compulsive overeaters from a television show. I heard about people turning to God on that program, and when I tried out one of their meetings and heard such talk again, I started praying. Somehow, I ate only three times a day, though I had no food plan. Before each meal, I stood in front of the refrigerator and asked God to show me what to eat. I lost 40 pounds and thought, *This works!* Then my sister came to visit from Australia, and we took her out to dinner. That started me on a six-year binge. Though always trying to control myself, I was in and out of addictive eating, and I reached 200 pounds.

During that time, I stopped asking God what I should eat and didn't go to meetings, but I did begin to look for a spiritual solution to my problem, and I found my way to a church. Worshipping and meditating faithfully, I was still so depressed it was hard for me to move. One day, someone at church talked about a different twelve-step program for food—there are several—and I decided to try one of those meetings. There I found a more structured program. I followed every suggestion—got a sponsor, bought a scale, weighed and measured my food. I was willing because I was gaining weight in 50-pound increments and didn't have any other solution.

By following the second twelve-step program closely, I was able to stop eating foods with flour and sugar for four years of abstinence, and I got off my medications, but then I fell into complacency and grandiosity. Having lost the humility of a newcomer, I attended only one meeting a week and didn't stay in touch with other members. I went back on antidepressants. Slowly I fell into relapse, until I ended up eating four pounds of chocolate while I was in Heathrow Airport, waiting for the plane after my father died.

My relapse lasted four or five years, until one day, in anguish, I wrote a prayer in my journal. "Please, God," I wrote, "I need an AA-like program for my food. I need to feel like a newcomer. I don't know how to stop eating. Please, please help me." I was humbled. Within three months, I got a phone call from a friend who said she wanted to tell me about a program called FA. She said FA worked, and when she invited me to a meeting that night, I told her I'd go. It was God's answer to my prayer.

At my first FA meeting, I got a sponsor. I was determined not to leave without one. My sponsor gave me a food plan, and when I wrote down what I planned to eat the next day, all the voices in my head immediately went away. For years my head had been filled with noise: *I want to eat; I should eat; I shouldn't eat; I can't eat this; I want to eat that; if I eat this I won't eat that . . .* Finally, my head became quiet. I gave up. I admitted I couldn't handle food by myself. Then I had hope. The next day I knelt in the morning to ask for abstinence, said the first three Steps, and got peace.

I remember my first day in FA, the very first day of my abstinence. I talked about faith to my sponsor. She asked, "Have you been abstinent so far today?" I said yes. "Were you abstinent yesterday?" I told her no. She said, "That's your first little germ of faith right there. You know that you did not get yourself abstinent. Abstinence is your first miracle. Go with that, don't forget it, and you just watch how your faith will grow. You'll see another miracle and another. You'll find that you can get to an FA meeting and feel that you belong, and you can phone me on time, and you can call other people in FA. You'll be able to show up for your recovery and your life. Pay attention to the miracles, and that's how you'll build your faith, one little seed at a time." I did what my sponsor suggested, paying attention, and I saw the miracles in my life.

After I got into FA, my relationship with my husband changed. He'd hated the other twelve-step programs I'd been in because when I was there, I used to identify my problem as being him. At meetings, we'd all whine and complain about our husbands. I couldn't do that in FA. I had to take responsibility for my own behavior. My husband saw the difference in me, and about four years later, he decided that he wanted to join FA, too.

So there we were, both in FA, and the miracles piled up. After years of isolation and bouts of being unable to leave my house, I found I *wanted* to be of service and to be connected within a community. I was able to fly to Canada to speak at an FA information meeting, trusting that the FA people hosting me would take care of whatever I needed to eat. I lose things easily, but I didn't worry about misplacing my passport or ticket. I didn't feel afraid that I would binge on the plane. My purpose and priority were to do service for my Higher Power, and I didn't have a moment of anxiety.

FA has given me a new way to live my life. I've learned to ask my Higher Power for help with everything that is hard for me. The economy is bad now, and my husband

and I have had to adjust. We sold our house, a miracle in itself. I needed a job, and real estate presented itself, but I had to pass a difficult exam to get a license. I am not a disciplined person, never have been, and I did not want to study. The materials overwhelmed me. I never missed an FA meeting and I made lots of phone calls to program members, but each afternoon, I also took practice tests. Tests. Tests. Tests. Before I began, I always got on my knees and asked God to help me stay focused and not give up. Sometimes I felt totally discouraged, but eventually I worked my way up from scores of about 38 percent to scores in the 90s.

The day of the actual exam, I asked God for help with math especially, and I prayed for clarity. I felt my Higher Power sitting in the seat next to me. I was given only one math question, which is unheard of, and I remembered the answer to the question from the crash course I'd taken the previous day. I did the three-hour exam in an hour and a quarter, and I passed it.

I've had many such experiences of God's help, so my trust keeps deepening. I asked God to relieve my fear when one of my children entered a field of work that required her to carry a gun. I knew she might have to shoot it, or someone might use one on her. I asked God to help me pay our bills when each one felt like a sign of my incompetence and I was afraid we might not have the money to cover them all. And I've asked God to give me the right words or to keep my mouth closed, so I am more patient, kind, and tolerant with my husband. Sometimes I say the same prayer every day for more than a year, but God helps me every time.

Today, my life isn't perfect. I'm confused about what direction to take in my work. I don't always know what to do in my relationships with my daughters, whom I dearly love, or how I can best help my grandchildren. No matter the situation, though, my relationship with my Higher Power sustains me. All I need do is to ask God for guidance, and then I feel that I can get through anything.

FA has been the greatest gift in my life. Because of the program, my weight is and has been normal. I eat simply, but I do not take my freedom for granted. My grandiosity is gone. I have been sloppy and complacent before, and I know the consequences. I weigh and measure the food I eat 100 percent accurately and honestly, and I don't put anything fancy on it. I aim to be, and to stay, a grateful newcomer.

I've had years of psychiatry, two suicide attempts, hospitalizations, and many tries to normalize with medications. I've weighed 90 pounds, and I've weighed 200. I never want to presume to give advice to anyone else, but I do want to share my hope. Thanks to FA and to the way of life I've been given, I am medication free and emotionally stable. I've been abstinent since I entered the program thirteen years ago, and I have the life of "sane and happy usefulness" that *Alcoholics Anonymous* promises.

Failing at Success

✧ ✧ ✧

A S EARLY AS KINDERGARTEN, I had an overdeveloped sense of responsibility. Each day, our kindergarten teacher used to ask a student to lead all the children down to the bathroom in the basement. One morning, it was my turn to lead the crowd, and I walked everyone down. The job was done at that point, but later, as the teacher tried to line us up to go back upstairs, I clearly remember calling out from the back, "Miss Silverstein, don't you worry. I've got the line from back here." At five, I was already trying to take charge as a member of the command team.

From early on, I thought my role in life was to be strong and responsible. Viewing myself that way, it seemed acceptable and logical that I needed a lot of food. I had a tough job to do, after all. When I was an adult, overwork and overeating ran together for me. On one job, I worked eleven hours a day and gained 40 or 50 pounds. This just seemed a necessary part of the significant role that I thought I had in the world. I didn't take care of myself because I had to take care of everyone else.

It always seems important for me to start my story with the point that I'm the oldest of seven children in an Irish Catholic family. I think that my personality got formed by my being the eldest daughter. The children came quickly in my family. Every couple of years my mother had another baby. With each baby, I had to be more independent. I needed to take care of myself and help with my siblings.

As the oldest sister and the biggest sibling of the bunch, I felt entitled to lots of food. When I was no more than four or five, I was stealing brownies from the breadbox early in the morning and sneaking gravy straight out of the serving bowl at dinnertime. The early onset of my drive to eat flour and sugar makes me think that I was suffering from a biological and physiological condition, not a psychological one. My body craved those foods. My behaviors were those of an incipient addict: Once I ate a little, I always had to eat more.

I was large in my adolescence, and by the time I entered college, at five feet eight and 172 pounds, I saw myself as outsized and ungainly. I wanted social success above all, but I felt unattractive and negative about myself as a woman. Very quickly after first encountering alcohol, I began to drink addictively. I found that alcohol took away my social fears. My feelings of being fat and horsey, my insecurity about my femininity, all disappeared, and I was able to flirt and feel thin and attractive. I also continued to eat. Vending machines, microwaves, and the bread and cheese I stole from my job in the cafeteria form a big part of my college memories.

During my senior year, I got involved with a friend's boyfriend. We were drinking and eating buddies, and our relationship revolved around the beer and pizza we had in my dorm room. A year after I entered graduate school, he enrolled in the same school, and our relationship continued.

I did enough with the academics to get by, but I mainly focused on my relationship with my boyfriend and the beer and pizza. Because I had developed gall bladder disease, I had terrible bouts of pain and nausea every time I ate cheese. Seven trips to the emergency room did not stop me from ordering my pizza with "extra cheese." I was a typical addict, repeating one behavior and expecting a different result. As sick as I got, I could not stop myself, and gall bladder surgery finally provided the only solution I was able to see. I continued to eat addictively for another twenty-seven years.

I had a troubled relationship with my boyfriend, but after graduate school he wanted to get out of his mother's house. Suddenly, the notion of being a bride seemed like a good idea, so I decided to get married. I gave the matter little more thought than that. I am sure I had a beer in my hand at the time.

I know now that my decision to marry was connected with my food addiction. It was a direct consequence of feeling fat and unattractive, of my belief that I had no appeal to men. I married the first man who was interested in me, just because he was there. Alcohol also played a role, clouding my judgment.

I now recognize and accept that there have been consequences to my addictions. I squandered ten years of
my life in that marriage. We'd drink, he'd cry, I'd cry,
we'd get over it, and I would be emotionally manipu-
lated into putting the relationship back together again.
I was afraid of my husband, who was physically violent
with me, and I was unable to advocate for myself or express my anger.

I worked full-time, went to law school three nights a
week, and coped with an abusive marriage. Sugar gave
me the energy and stamina I needed to commute miles
to school and to function after a full day of work. Pasta,
crackers, and other flour products dulled my nerves and
calmed me down enough to bear the stress and loneliness
I felt. I did a lot of my grocery shopping in drug stores.
Dinner was easy: three candy bars or a big jar of nuts.

After about six years, it came clear to me that I needed
to get out of my marriage. Four years later, with the help
of my family, I finally escaped, but I reached 225 pounds
of repressed rage before I did. Despite all the times that I
joined diet programs or tried famous diets, I was unable
to control my eating. One of my last attempts to address
my weight was a medically supervised fast that allowed
me only a few ounces of protein a day. I fasted as long as
I could, perhaps two or three weeks at a time, and then
I'd start baking cookies.

I would not under any circumstances recommend it,
but the "fast" gave me a chance to experience the difference between eating flour and sugar and eating only
protein. I could see the direct contrast. Once I ate flour
and sugar, I could not stop. One bite was like putting a

match to gasoline. The eating that followed was a con-flagration. In contrast, if I could control myself long enough, sticking only to protein, my appetite fell off, the cravings passed, and I was able to fast for another ten days or so until the next time I lost control.

By cycling between bingeing and fasting, I managed to lose about 75 pounds in a year, but when I began to gain weight again and the fasting program went bank-rupt, I found my way into a twelve-step meeting for compulsive overeaters. I tried to get what they called ab-stinence, but there was no generally accepted definition of the term, and no one suggested a food plan. I never told anyone that I was still drinking.

The first part of my recovery began when I asked someone to sponsor me. I'd met a woman who, as we say, "had what I wanted"—she had a boyfriend. She was also a recovering alcoholic, and she was a straight shooter. Within two months of our working together, I could no longer continue drinking. I joined Alcoholics Anonymous, got sober, and gained some sense of what it means to do the Steps—the spiritual actions that lead to recovery. To the extent that I was able, I did some of the Steps and asked God to take from me what I perceived to be my compulsion to overeat. That was as far as I got.

I stayed in that twelve-step program for compulsive overeaters for thirteen years, without a food plan and be-lieving that if I asked God for help, He would somehow take the fork out of my hand. My clothes were getting tighter, but I honestly believed that the dry cleaner was shrinking them. I will never be critical of that program, but it gave me only moments of relief, not sustained recovery. How could I change when I was still depending on food? I needed a food plan, direction, and discipline.

I vividly remember a moment of clarity in a meeting I happened upon once, when people were discussing the formal creation of what became the organization of Food Addicts in Recovery Anonymous. I heard someone speak about the necessity that we abstain from "addictive eating" if we are to recover. That suddenly made sense to me, and for the first time in my life, I understood that I'd have to stop eating addictively *first,* if I wanted to get well and have a connection with a Higher Power. I'd been trying to do the process in reverse!

Not long afterward, I found my way to an FA meeting. During the break, the person sitting next to me asked me for my story. I said that I had thirteen years in a different food recovery program, ten years in AA, and that I was dabbling in FA. Of course, you can't "dabble" in FA. You're either doing it or you're not doing it. So she said, "Any time you want to jump into the pool, I can help you."

I thought about that for the rest of the meeting, and I thought about it some more. That's what I did in those days: I thought about things. I kept going to meetings, waiting for the perfect person to sponsor me. *What am I going to do? Am I going to wait for God Himself to come in here and sponsor me?* I said to myself. So I finally approached the woman and asked, "Will you help me?"

My request for help was a key moment in my recovery. My ego had to be deflated enough, I had to be defeated enough, that I could admit that I couldn't help myself. Today, based on my experience, I don't volunteer to sponsor people. I think it's essential that a person want help and ask for it. Then I am absolutely there, with my hand held out.

From the moment I began working with an FA sponsor, my life changed. The third day of my recovery in FA, I found myself explaining to my sponsor why my ideas for my food plan were better than her ideas for my food plan. Suddenly, I realized that I had forfeited my right to decide what I was going eat. My entire life I had been trying to find a diet that would permit me to eat whatever I wanted to eat and still be thin. I had never found that diet, and I was fifty years old. It occurred to me that for once in my life, I should stop talking and listen, so I quickly pulled in my guns and settled down. I surrendered.

Joining FA, I felt like I was grabbed by the scruff of my neck and put onto a bus going sixty miles an hour. Right away, I was chopping vegetables, making salads, and committing to attend several meetings a week. At first the program seemed a bit crazy, but I knew *I* was crazy and hardly one to judge. Within a month and a half, I heard through our family grapevine that my mother had described me as being happier than she'd ever seen me in my life.

This is not the end of my story, for despite my abstinence, I felt a lot of fear. For years, I had been tortured by food and weight and bingeing and fasting, trying to diet and breaking my diet. I could never sustain a diet for more than two or three weeks, and I didn't see why "abstinence" would be different. After a few weeks of not deviating from my committed food plan by one tomato seed, I was afraid I would break my abstinence and lose this wonderful gift that I had found. My sponsor told me that if I did today what I did yesterday, I need not fear. By daily following the simple actions suggested by our program, I would have another day of abstinence. Since then, I have done each day what I did the day before, and for the past eleven years, I've never had to worry about my abstinence again.

The urgency I felt to hold on to my abstinence and my recovery has caused me to go to God for help to stay abstinent and then for aid with the things that may seem to be more grave than what I eat. I write that with tongue in cheek, for, in fact, there is nothing more important than maintaining my abstinence. But I also turn to my Higher Power for help with all of my problems, starting with work.

I had changed fields before my divorce and had a successful career as a lawyer. The demands on my time had always been enormous, but FA transformed my response. I first took the hours I needed to ensure the safety of my own recovery from food addiction, and then I asked God for help with my professional responsibilities. The results were amazing: Depositions were canceled, trials were settled, and I began to experience some breathing room. During the day, when my anxiety spiked, the knots in my stomach dissolved whenever I repeated, "It's in your hands, God. It's in your hands." If I couldn't sleep because of my worries about work, I'd say, "You've got the night shift, God," and I would drop off. Today, any anxiety is my trigger to turn to God.

Four years into my abstinence, a surprising opportunity opened up, and I decided to apply. I knew that the new position would allow me much more control over my time and would strongly support my life in recovery. Throughout the application process, I took some quiet time before each of the numerous interviews and asked God for help: "If you want me to have this job, you've got to give me the words for the interview, because I can't do it on my own."

In the end, I was given the job—an appointment to a government commission requiring considerable judgment and discretion. Each day, I interact with people who are afraid and facing tragedy, poverty, or the loss of liberty. I would never have been selected for this position as an active addict, and I know that my effectiveness depends upon my abstinence. Because I am not eating addictively, I have an inner source of guidance that permits me to be sure footed in difficult situations. Any time I feel stress or uncertainty, I can turn to God and say, "Show me how you want me to handle this" or just "Help me here." At the very moment that I am functioning fully in a work setting, I am also receiving, silently and separately, the insight I need to make a suggestion or decision or respond to a question.

For over a decade, I have been a food addict in continuous recovery. The joys of having my own family have not been given to me, but I am blessed with a rewarding, fulfilling life. At work, I am in a position to do good for people and to leave them feeling that they have been treated with dignity and respect. I love my family and have wonderful friends. Each day, I live fully, following the course I believe my Higher Power has set for me. If I make mistakes, I take immediate action to remedy my errors. I have self-respect and insist on being respected. I am in a healthy body and feel good about myself.

My abstinence and peace of mind are paramount for me, and each day, I protect them. I may not have everything I thought I wanted, but I have everything I need. I feel joyful, contented, and enormously grateful.

Me? A Food Addict?

✧ ✧ ✧

MY STORY is a little different in that I had no weight to lose when I came into FA. I joined the program when my wife told me that she was going to join. I went to my first FA meeting because I was afraid to be left alone at home. I imagined myself in front of the television, sitting on the floor, legs under the coffee table, eating pizza by myself. The image was lonely and unappealing. My wife was somewhat of a Higher Power for me at that point. If she was in a good mood, I was in a good mood. If she was in a bad mood, I was scared and also in a bad mood. It seemed best to go along with her, since she'd already decided she'd be attending regularly.

My wife and I had a history of involvement with twelve-step programs. In fact, at one point I counted, and I discovered that I'd been to eight different programs. Not surprisingly perhaps, when I got to the FA meeting, I saw two men I'd known from other programs. I was immediately impressed by them. They looked trim and fit. Even more important, they had changed in ways that

I never saw them change in the other programs. I could tell that FA had fundamentally altered who they were. They were clear-eyed, right-sized, and when they spoke of a relationship with a Higher Power, I saw that they were sharing from actual experience. For me, a Higher Power was theoretical. I knew all the right words, I knew the Steps, I had memorized portions of the Big Book, but I hadn't really had a spiritual experience.

For years, I had used a variety of twelve-step programs for self-improvement. I started with Al-Anon because my father had been diagnosed as an alcoholic. Next came Emotions Anonymous. If I mastered the difficulties I had expressing my emotions, surely my problems would go away, I thought. After a while, I went to Narcotics Anonymous, not because I had a problem with drugs but because a friend was going and it looked interesting. Next came Sex Addicts Anonymous, followed by Sex and Love Addicts Anonymous. Both those programs helped, so I joined Debtors Anonymous. When I started earning money and took care of my debts, I moved on to Arts Anonymous. I needed support for my creativity. Alcoholics Anonymous drew me for a number of years. I took what I liked, left the rest, and kept moving.

In all the years I went to twelve-step programs, the core of my being never changed. Each time the externals of my life got better, I felt I'd licked my problems and moved on. I earned more money. I got better at expressing my emotions. I became less fearful about my creativity, less afraid of other people, more successful in relationships. I got married. I got more of everything I wanted, but for what? I had a self-centered approach to programs that were inherently about letting go of the self.

When the two men I knew talked about their experience in FA, I suddenly saw that I had never let go. I had a core of fear that had never changed. I didn't like myself. I felt I was unattractive, and I was insecure about my abilities. I wanted to please, I wanted to look good, I wanted people to like me, so I had no freedom. I couldn't speak spontaneously. I screened my words two or three times before I said anything, especially when I was in a group of people. I trusted no one. Despite the years I spent in twelve-step programs, I had only once asked someone to sponsor and help me. Most of the time, I sponsored myself. Clearly, I was the best candidate for the job! Who could know me better than me? I'd never sponsored anyone else, either. My time was valuable. I had important things to do.

Something about those men attracted me, however, and I realized I wanted to change. I remembered my craziness when I once tried to work on different Steps in the programs I was simultaneously attending. This time, I decided that I wanted to put one program on the table in front of me and do it.

I let go of all involvement in other twelve-step programs, but when I started FA, I was unsure that I was actually a food addict. People I met at meetings told me not to worry, suggesting that I do the program and see if my life got better. That made sense, so, typically, I began by sponsoring myself. In other words, I dieted, using the FA food plan. When I quickly lost too much weight, I became afraid. There weren't many sponsors available in our small fellowship, so I got one who was halfway across the country from me. When I called him, I told him I'd give the program thirty days. He said, "I'll take ninety." I agreed, and that's how I began.

I'm thankful I was willing to make a ninety-day commitment because I would have been out the door for good if I'd stayed for only thirty days. I had a hard withdrawal from flour and sugar. It took me at least six or eight weeks to get through it, but in some ways, I struggled as much with my mind as I did with food. I started FA in April, several months before cherries were available, but I was obsessed with the fruit. My sponsor suggested that I keep it simple and not eat cherries. I could not understand why I couldn't pay someone to pit the fruit or help me calculate the average weight of a pit so that I could account for all the pits when I weighed out my portion. That bothered me intensely. I also worried about the poor food addicts in Thailand. How could they ever do this program when their national cuisine heavily featured noodles? And what about all the misplaced commas in the *Twenty-Four Hours a Day* book? Couldn't someone fix them? I had lots of good ideas. It took weeks for some of them to subside.

I finally let go and "surrendered," as we say, a month after I joined the program. I had taken a trip out of town, and when I got back, I had a latte. I needed one, I'd decided. The next morning, my sponsor told me I'd broken my abstinence. I was livid. Later, I realized that I had wanted to do everything perfectly, and I was angry because I hated to fail. After a few days passed, I also had to acknowledge to myself that I'd broken an important, ongoing commitment I'd made regarding one of my other addictions. By facing both breaks, I was ready to accept my powerlessness and to see that I needed to begin again.

As I committed myself to abstinence and completely gave up eating flour and sugar, I finally realized that I had a problem with food. Like other food addicts, I'd used food as a means of coping with my feelings. When I was angry, frustrated, or bored, I'd felt I had to eat. I'd needed my chips. I'd needed my breath mints. I'd felt like I couldn't live without cereal. I'd rationalized that I ate because of a lack of energy and prided myself on my supposedly healthy habits, but once I started eating, I often couldn't stop.

In FA, I began to see myself differently. I remembered how, as a child, I could never save money because I spent all my allowance on candy. When I was a little older, I'd been driven to walk back and forth between the kitchen and the pantry, eating one food after another as I tried fruitlessly to satisfy myself. My perspective on my physical problems changed, too. I'd always thought that because of my genes, I had a spastic esophagus, like my father. Sometimes when I swallowed, food got caught, blocking my throat until I either forced it down or made myself throw up. In FA, I discovered that food got backed up because I shoveled it into my mouth too fast. I chewed and swallowed without pausing between bites, eating with a kind of desperation. Actually, I had no physical problem with my esophagus once I slowed down.

Throughout my life, I'd stayed thin, but in abstinence, I saw that I'd been obsessed with my weight. I'm six feet tall, and as an adult, I'd ranged from the high 130s to 165 pounds. Within that 25-pound range, I'd always felt afraid that I was too thin or worried that I'd gotten too fat. At 153, I vowed I'd give up all fats and sugar, but the next minute I told myself I'd better bulk up. I never had peace. At one point, I went to the gym religiously for two years. I remember that I finally reached 165 pounds, but in that moment of happiness, my first thought was *I can't wait to see what I'd look like at 175.* Right around then, I moved abroad, where I immediately lost 15 pounds. I cursed God for that weight loss, because I felt I'd earned the muscle.

I probably could have put on weight if I'd really worked at it, but I was thin boned and frenetic. I was a perpetual motion machine. No one ever described me as calm. They said I was hyperactive and too intense. They were right. In every way, I worked hard at my life. In FA, we say that we do 1 percent and God takes care of 99 percent of our recovery. My approach before the program was that I should do 99 percent and leave about a percent for God to accomplish. I was always trying to improve myself.

I've had good sponsors in FA. After my first sponsor broke his abstinence, I worked temporarily with a woman for about a week. She kept talking about God. "Ask God what you're supposed to do," she'd say. It drove me nuts. Why didn't she tell me what to do? "Just give me a rule book," I wanted to say. I didn't want God.

The woman suggested that I move on to a man who could sponsor me, and I'm grateful that I continue to work with the same sponsor today. It's been easy to talk with him, man to man. He understood my drive to try to control myself and my circumstances, and he has helped me learn how to let go. I never knew how to relax and have fun, to be present and loving.

AWOL played, and still plays, a huge role in my recovery. During my first AWOL, I wrote a seventy-five-page inventory of myself. I had resentments going back to preschool. I remembered a boy who took a toy that I wanted, and at age forty-two, I still wanted to kill him. I had issues. My sponsor sat with me for five and a half hours to hear all of them. I was stunned. Nothing that I shared made him run out of the room, and he never showed a trace of disgust at anything I revealed. I felt fully accepted. Afterward, for the first time in my life, I followed the instructions in *Alcoholics Anonymous* and sat still for an hour with myself and God.

Being with a presence greater than myself after my Fifth Step opened doors for me, but I remember the Eleventh Step most of all. As we talked about prayer and meditation in AWOL, my quiet time got a little quieter. I stopped spending the thirty minutes planning my future or dreaming about winning the lottery. I also completely changed the way that I faced uncertainties in my life.

When I started FA, my wife and I were in the midst of efforts to try to get pregnant. We had a couple of miscarriages, and then we decided to become foster parents. This forced me to rely on God, because being a foster parent with the ultimate goal of adopting is an inherently insecure proposition. You can never know the outcome. We learned that the hard way.

The state eventually placed a little boy and girl with us, a brother and sister. We thought the placement would be permanent, but it was not. The children were first moved to another foster family, then returned to us, one at a time. Ultimately, we were only able to adopt our son.

If I hadn't been in FA, I might well have run away from my marriage, and I certainly could not have endured foster parenting with any kind of equanimity. When I had faced problems before, I'd asked God to take care of them by dealing with the people who seemed to me to be in my way. I was viciously self-centered. I once had an employee I found difficult, and, to be honest, I prayed that she'd have a car accident. As an addict in recovery, though, I knew I could not pray for the children's parents to relapse into drug addiction so that my wife and I could adopt them. I realized that was barbaric. *I'd better pray for God's will to be done, whatever that may be,* I thought, and that's what I did.

I was angry and sad when we were told that we couldn't adopt both children. The decision made no sense to me. The only way I could come to terms with it was to surrender and pray, "Thy will, not mine, be done." Today, I still have to trust that God has a plan for my wife and me, as well as for our son and his sister. I use FA's Twelve Steps so that I won't be pulled into resentment and frustration, and from there back into food and addiction. I am very clear that I have to let go and let God.

Since I've joined the program, I've moved from belief to faith, but not all at once. I'm from a family of ministers, so I've always believed in God, but I never practiced that belief on a daily basis. When I first came into FA, I was told to get on my knees and ask for my abstinence every morning. I was supposed to kneel and say thank you at the end of each day. This made no sense to me when I started, but everyone told me to act as if I believed. The praying on my knees, my daily quiet time, the reading I did each day in *Twenty-Four Hours a Day* and *Alcoholics Anonymous* all had a cumulative effect, and after a while, I slowly began to sense the presence of a Power greater than myself.

Today, I know that I need to keep doing AWOLs and go deeper into trusting, deeper into willingness to ask God for help. Often, I do things myself and then check in with God afterward. Slowly, I'm learning to turn to God more frequently, to pause and listen, to be quiet and see what comes up. Left to my own devices, I'd still be a spinning top. I need spiritual guidance and discipline to do even the most basic things sometimes—to do one task instead of trying to take on three at once.

Like everyone, we have some bumps in our road. Our son has difficulties. He's very high on the boy scale. He gets anxious, and when he is fearful, he screams and cries and calls us names. We practice a lot of patience. My sponsor tells me my son is my spiritual teacher. God wants me to learn. What supports does my son need? What kind of loving? What do I need to do differently? Each day, I'm invited to step out of my comfort zone and ask God what I need to do to connect with my son on his terms. When he starts yelling and throwing things, I'm grateful I can pick up the phone and talk with people in this program who have faced difficult parenting challenges abstinently.

I've got a full life today. In addition to my son, we're parenting a little girl who is awake two and three times a night. She's a foster child, and it looks like we will be able to adopt her. I thank God for this program, because while there are no guarantees, I feel assured that I will be in the best shape possible as the children grow up. Food is neutral for me now. My weight is normal. It goes up and down a little, probably from lack of sleep and the rigors of parenting, but I don't worry. My sponsor adjusts my food plan as necessary. I try to work out with weights twice a week, not so that I can get bigger, but to make sure that my body is healthy and I can pick up my son without injuring myself. He's faced a lot of trauma, and he likes to be held.

The other day, I realized that if we can adopt our little girl, I will be seventy when she graduates from high school. The way I see it, I'm living my life backwards. I spent my twenties and thirties in active addiction, bouncing from relationship to relationship. I had no capacity for love. I married when I was almost forty. Now, instead of heading into retirement, I'm just coming into the fullness of my life as a food addict in recovery, one day at a time.

The Courage to Change

✧ ✧ ✧

I WEIGHED ONLY 3.5 POUNDS when I was born. I was thin for the first few years of my life, but when I was four or five, I was able to get some foods by myself. One night, my mother found me in front of the refrigerator eating plain, leftover noodles. That started one of the main struggles of my childhood. I wanted lots of sweet, starchy food, and my parents wanted to control my access to it. They were ashamed that their daughter was fat. I remember opening my lunch box at school one day and finding half a head of lettuce that my mother had packed for me.

My parents were amazing self-made people. My father was an orphan. He hadn't gone to school beyond the fifth grade, but he taught himself civil engineering through a correspondence course and eventually served as chief engineer on a nationally known project. My mother was a naturalist and teacher. They were thin, smart, older parents. I, their only child, was not only fat. I didn't perform well at school because of the pressure I felt. I didn't get the good grades my parents wished I'd get.

My parents tried to help me. We consulted a diet doctor in New York, who gave me a calorie counter, and my dad also started weighing me before I went to school each day. I remember vividly the morning I crossed the line marking 100 pounds. "Well," he said, "we'll never see the other side of that again."

I was shocked when I was taken to a psychiatrist. Believing that if they got the best doctor, something could be done, something could be gotten right, my mother took me to the head of a psychoanalytic institute when I was twelve. He'd spent every summer with Anna Freud. I went for sessions with him every day after school until I was in junior high.

Life was uncomfortable at home and at school. There were all kinds of unwritten rules defining how you had to behave in the 1950s, and I never came to any of them naturally. I literally studied other children, practically taking notes on how they carried their books, wore their socks, or tied their shoes. I always felt different.

At seventeen, when I left for art school, I looked good because I'd managed to diet down before I left. Again, not knowing how to be me, I took my cues from other people. There was never a time when I didn't want to eat, but in college I learned to do all the grown-up drugs. By using cigarettes, caffeine, marijuana, and alcohol, I kept my weight down. I was probably five feet six and my driver's license said I weighed 130 pounds. I wanted to be 125, but I was around 138 or 140. I felt bigger than a house. If you've been obsessed by weight all your life, when you gain an extra 15 pounds, in your own mind, you're fat.

Men were an issue. In my freshman year alone, I dated over seventy-five of them, several of them many times. I proudly made a list of all of them when I went home for the summer. I'd been awkward and had felt ugly for so long, I was amazed to be pretty and desirable. It went right to my head. Not until I got into FA and became abstinent did it ever occur to me that the word *promiscuous* might have applied to me. Of course, my life wasn't about sex, I'd have said. It was all about true love.

Between the men, the drugs, and my crazy lifestyle, my life became unmanageable. I ran away with a drummer, totaled my car, dropped out of college, and finally went back to my parents, because I had nowhere else to go. My poor mother and father! They were good people who came from a nice neighborhood, and I'd turned into someone they couldn't begin to relate to or understand. God bless them, they were supportive even when they hardly knew what to do with me. I lived with them and returned to a psychiatrist I'd worked with before. I'd draw all night, see him in the morning, and then go to bed. There were some hard times, but I did have a wonderful stint as an aqua belle in a sea theatre, swimming in a tank with dolphins.

When I finally decided I wanted more from life than swimming upside down in a water tank, I transferred to a university and completed a bachelor of fine arts degree. Over the next few years, I had boyfriend after boyfriend and pursued many a grand scheme. I taught for a year, then headed off to Europe. I moved from there to

California, where I lived with a man I'd met on a plane between Paris and London. Next came Arizona. I had a great commission for 350 paintings there, but I was in love with a married man, and that didn't work out, so after I finished the paintings, I went to New England, to an island off the coast.

After I moved again, still in New England, I found a career and a mentor, and I devoted myself with huge energy to a new field of work. During this period of my life, I used men and cigarettes to keep the food at bay, but whenever I was unhappy, I didn't want alcohol or marijuana. I wanted to eat. Food became a drug for me. I'd tell myself all kinds of things. *Tomorrow I'll lose weight. Tomorrow I'll go on a diet. Tomorrow I'll start running every day. Tomorrow I'll eat only bean sprouts.* But day after day, I'd be back to bingeing. As *Alcoholics Anonymous* would have asked, "Where was my high resolve?" I couldn't stop myself.

For the first three years of my work, I had excellent job reviews, but then one day, my mentor told me he could no longer count on me. He never knew when I'd come into the office, how late I'd be, or how to contact me. I was eating addictively and was an emotional mess, and I could no more look at myself and say I'd improve than I could fly to the moon. When anyone criticized me, I was gone. That time, as usual, I took offense and quit.

Though I succeeded in starting my own business and establishing myself after I left my mentor, I was terrified. I became afraid to leave my apartment. Sometimes I crawled into the back of my closet and hunkered down to hide behind my own coats and shoes. I lost weight at first, but when I quit smoking, I forfeited any control of what and how I ate. Even though I was in group and individual therapy then, my weight started rising. I'd been afraid of weighing 140 pounds my whole life. Suddenly I was in the 150s, and then I saw 165 on the scale. I knew I was going to reach 200 or 300 pounds, because I couldn't diet and I couldn't stop eating.

One day, my therapist left for a trip around the world and gave me an appointment to see her when she returned in a year. I'd done everything by then. I knew all about dieting and nutrition, I'd tried being a vegetarian, and I'd been in every kind of therapy for years. My insurance gave me a lifetime cap of $10,000 for therapy, and I had only about $200 left. I didn't know what to do. How did people live after they had no more therapy? What did they do?

Instead of trying to find another therapist, I decided to go to a twelve-step meeting for compulsive overeaters. This was not FA, but the book *Alcoholics Anonymous* was available there, and I bought a copy. Reading the book, I was impressed by the help that AA people gave each other. I had paid a fortune for psychoanalysis and therapy, but in AA and in that first twelve-step program I'd found for food, everything was free. There were meetings to go to and the phone numbers of people to call.

Eventually, someone took me to an Al-Anon meeting, and I started going to Al-Anon and then to AA. I was trying desperately to work a recovery program for food, too, because eating was my main problem, but I wasn't succeeding. I managed to get some kind of freedom from bingeing by eating three "moderate" meals a day, as was suggested. This only meant that I was digging into three mountains of food each day. I'm not calling that abstinent by a long shot, but I did get my weight down to a reasonable level, and in the context of that time and place, a lot of people thought I was magnificent. We sat in a circle at our meetings. I'd been crying for years in therapy, so I cried at the meetings, too. People seemed to think it was wonderful when I cried, and I agreed. I thought crying made me feel better.

When my therapist returned from her trip, I reached a turning point. It was time for me to go back to therapy. The prospect made me intensely afraid, because I recognized that therapy was a kind of addiction for me. I was hooked on it. I didn't need it anymore and didn't want to do it, but I felt unable to be myself and say so.

The night before my appointment, I was scared. I'd been to a meeting that night and had talked to program members on the phone. My sponsor had said I needed to get on my knees and talk to God. I'd listened to her, been to many meetings, read books and pamphlets, and asked people about God, but I was still left thinking, *God? I don't know.* Late at night, in fear, I finally got on my knees by my bed and put my head into my folded hands. "God," I said, "I don't know who you are, or what you are. I don't know anything, but I'm so scared. I don't know what to do. Please, help me." I felt funny asking for help from something I didn't know or understand, but I just went ahead and asked.

Soon a feeling of warmth started in my chest. It spread until I was filled with peace. Relaxed and happy, I was amazed. Something had come upon me, and it was real. Finally, I got the courage to move very carefully into bed—slowly because I was afraid of disturbing or interrupting whatever had come. I slept, and when I woke up, I was singing.

The next day, I wrote the slogan "Let go and let God" on the palm of my hand and went to my therapy appointment. I was able to say goodbye to my therapist and to thank her. We talked about the Twelve Steps and God, and I asked why, through therapy, I hadn't been able to get the recovery I was starting to find. She said, "I believe in your case, you lacked courage." I've often thought of that over the years. In the second line of the Serenity Prayer, we ask for the courage to change. I wish I'd known long ago what I was lacking and had been able to seek it somehow. I've found it now in FA and the Twelve Steps.

The night I knelt by my bed was my first spiritual experience. I never again doubted that there is a God. God is real. I wish I could say I never thought of food again, but that's not the case. I still hadn't found FA when my dad died. In my grief, I got an ulcer, and I also entered an abusive relationship with a man who superficially reminded me of my father. What with the man and the ulcer, which was eating a hole through my stomach, I started nibbling rice cakes and drinking milk between meals. I kept telling myself I was abstinent, until finally I was eating birthday cake and full-scale, syrupy breakfasts. All bets were off. I was gaining weight like mad, and I was crying and miserable.

One night, at an AA meeting, I saw a woman who had lost a lot of weight. She had clear eyes and looked good, and she told me she was going to meetings with people who weighed and measured their food. I couldn't get away from her fast enough, but I knew I was crazy, and I finally called her. She gave me the number of a woman who agreed to sponsor me, and that was how I was introduced to the FA program.

My new sponsor took me to a meeting the night that I called. She helped me plan what to eat for dinner and taught me how to weigh and measure my food. I was originally a night eater. When I'd used cigarettes to control myself, I starved all day and binged at night, but at that point my illness had progressed and I was eating around the clock. I carried food in my pockets and my briefcase, and I found food wherever I went.

I literally could not stop eating, so the night I got home from my first meeting, I got on my knees and prayed for help to be abstinent until I could call my sponsor in the morning. I vowed to do anything necessary to avoid eating. To my surprise, instead of having to distract myself with reading or television, I slept peacefully through the night. The next morning, my sponsor asked, "How are you?" I told her I was abstinent, and she said, "Thank you, God." Every day for a month, we started our conversation with those words.

My sponsor and I lived far from the Boston area, where the FA program had begun. GPS navigating systems had not yet been invented, so I bought maps, a magnifying glass, and a light for reading at night, and then I drove for miles to FA meetings. Sometimes I got lost, but it was worth it. People stood up and said, "I've lost 75 pounds." Then they added that that happened ten or fifteen or twenty years ago, and they were still stable at their maintenance weight. I was flabbergasted. They talked about keeping food simple, which was a revelation to me. I was putting my carrots into a blender and trying to make them interesting with cinnamon and other spices.

My sponsor taught me how to stay abstinent by using the principles and Steps of FA. She talked about committing to meetings and being rigorously honest when I measured my food. She encouraged me to make phone calls to other FA members every day so I could break my isolation and develop the connections that would help me when I hit a hard time.

Instead of giving me rules, she explained the logic of what we do. She also gave me an important perspective on the program. "We are food addicts," she said, "and we have a program perfectly designed for recovery from our particular addiction, so follow what's been given to you." I hold on to that and say it to my sponsees today. FA gives us exactly what we need. It's perfectly designed for recovery from food addiction, which is subtle, insidious, and different from other addictions. We can't quit using the drug that calls to us. We have to eat three times a day.

FA works. I lost all my extra weight and got down to 125 pounds. More important, through study of the Twelve Steps in AWOLs, I started to grow up and change. I gave up the crying, and I kept my commitments to my own recovery.

When I first came into the program, my sponsor suggested that I not date for a year. I'd never been married, but I'd been engaged five times, and, given my history of promiscuity, I was happy to be done with men for a while. I willingly focused intensely on my program. All went well for nine months, until I met a man who was at the top of my profession, a professor at a prestigious university. When he approached me, I couldn't believe that anyone would hold me to the commitment not to date for a year. This was too rare an opportunity, and, after all, I had completed all but three months of the promised twelve.

For a few days, I called various FA members, taking a poll, but someone who had been abstinent for years told me that she had never seen anyone begin a relationship with only nine months of recovery and maintain abstinence. She said, "When they start dating too soon, people always end up losing both their abstinence and their relationship. Then they're back in FA, sitting in the farthest corner of the room, unable to meet anyone's eyes. They gain their weight, and that's the end."

I knew in my core that she was right, and I became willing to tell the professor that I couldn't see or communicate with him for three months. It wasn't easy to explain, but I believed absolutely in the FA program. I knew that the FA people had something that was critically important to me. My parents had taken me to the best doctors in the biggest cities, but I heard the truth in a small, old church hall at FA meetings in Massachusetts.

I've found what is right for me, and I have never doubted or thought of leaving the program since. Hard though some of the FA suggestions have been, I've taken them all. When I came into the program, it was as though someone turned the lights on. My past made sense to me. I could see and understand why I'd been frightened and self-centered.

In FA, for the first time in my life, I had power. I could take action. Once I could admit that I was afraid, I could ask for the comfort to help me get over my fear, and then I had strength. Through the power I got from a Higher Power, change was possible. I could "lean on the everlasting arms," as the old hymn says.

My growth through FA has been amazing. I am calmer. I was a child before, with no tolerance for heat or cold, hunger, or discomfort of any kind. I was hypersensitive, particularly regarding any kind of criticism.

I've got a sense of humor now, and I can look at my own behavior. I try hard to be kind. I don't have to agree with everyone, and certainly I don't have to change my beliefs or my own program of recovery because of anyone else's opinions, but I try to be caring and compassionate. In any situation, I want to be part of the solution, not part of the problem.

My weight has been the same for eighteen years. Now that I'm older, I'm five feet, five inches tall, and I weigh 125, give or take a pound. Basically, my weight doesn't change. The food I eat is as simple as it's ever been. I don't have to have big fruits or special this or that. I don't worry about not having "enough." Before FA, I never felt I had enough of anything, but now I have a sense of satisfaction in my life. I'm content, so whatever food I eat is plenty.

I'm married now. My husband is not the famous professor, and I am happy. Today, there are three things that

I never question: One is God, the second is FA, and the third is that my husband is the perfect man for me. I never let doubt enter my mind regarding God, FA, or my marriage, so my life, my program, and my love get clearer and stronger, year by year.

Through Life's Transitions

✧ ✧ ✧

These members entered recovery when they were in their teens and early twenties. FA and the Twelve Steps enabled them to abstinently navigate the major transitions leading to full adulthood— dating, marriage, work, the birth of children, and the loss of beloved members of their families.

The Unending Urge to Eat

✧ ✧ ✧

I JOINED FA WHEN I was a senior in high school, and I've been abstinent from addictive eating ever since. I am thirty-two years old now. My husband and I just had a beautiful baby boy. It's a gift from my Higher Power that I was abstinent when I met my husband, stayed abstinent through our dating, wedding ceremony, and pregnancy, and I'm abstinent now.

I came into the world under interesting circumstances. My mother left home with a twenty-six-year-old man when she was sixteen. She came from a stable family, and when she had me a year later, she returned and settled us both in an apartment below my grandparents.

For a while, I was the center of the world for my mother, her sister, and my grandparents. I had a lot of love and felt comfortable at home. Only since I've been in FA have I realized that I was also fearful. I didn't like to leave home.

When I was six or seven, my fear increased. Suddenly, I was no longer the only child in the family. My aunt

337

had a baby, and my mom met someone who moved in with us. He was a loving man, but he was an alcoholic, and his daughter came to visit us on weekends.

Addiction runs in our family. I have many blood relatives who are obese and many others who are alcoholic. I always loved eating, and as I look back on my life, I realize that all of my early memories involve food. My mom kept one dish for butter and one for sugar on our table. Before I was five, I was using my hands to eat out of both. That was odd behavior and a sign of trouble. Who scoops butter out of a dish and puts it in her mouth with her hands?

As I grew older, I ate the way I wanted to eat, and the people in my family began to express concern. When we were leaving for a trip, for example, my aunt might buy a dozen doughnuts. I assumed that we would all keep eating the doughnuts until we wanted to stop— which would be when they were gone. Sugar made me feel calm, safe, comfortable, and warm. I never felt full, and I didn't understand why, if doughnuts were available, anyone would stop eating them.

By the time I entered first grade, I was self-conscious about my attachment to food and ashamed of my weight. I was in a city school, and girls began to have boyfriends, and their first kisses, when we were only in fourth grade. It seemed I was the only one without a boy to kiss me. I correlated this with being fat, and I began to obsess about my weight. I was 110 pounds and had to wear clothes for women when my friends weighed 60 pounds and were dressed like children. A commercial weight loss program I tried didn't help.

I had a terrible time in high school. By carefully observing what my friends ate and watching their weight, I saw that I couldn't be like them. I couldn't eat and be thin because I couldn't stop eating. I didn't want to stop.

As I gained more and more weight, I felt awful. I had acne and braces. When I went to the mall with friends to try on clothes for fun, I couldn't find things that fit. In every way, I struggled to belong. I started wearing men's jeans and oversized, rock-and-roll t-shirts, thinking that the boys would like me if I looked like they did. I pretended I'd done drugs and gone to parties when I'd actually been at home watching movies with a couple of friends. I tried out for the basketball team after only one day of practice with my uncle and auditioned for the chorus without being able to sing. I would have been happy taking art classes, but instead I joined the school band and futilely attempted to learn cheerleading.

As my food addiction progressed, I didn't recognize myself. I didn't know that I was enough—that my own skills and assets were fine. I felt like I was breaking. Thinking that a new high school would mean a new life, I changed schools. This did give me a new start for a little while. I had a cute dress and had a boyfriend for a couple of months, but I was just myself; pretty soon the boy broke up with me, and I was again eating during every free period at school.

One day, I sat down for lunch with a friend, as I always did. At that point, I was eating chips for breakfast and stopping at fast-food takeout windows over and over. I'd just seen my former boyfriend looking at a friend of mine, and I felt desperate. My friend was overweight like me, but her lunch that day included vegetables. Clearly, something was different. I asked her what she was doing, and she finally said something about the Twelve Steps. I feel now that everything in my life had prepared me for that moment.

I had already been exposed to the Twelve Steps when I was young because my mom's boyfriend had issues with alcohol and we had been to family counseling. I'd learned about AA there, and I started to put two and two together as I thought about my own life. I couldn't articulate my understanding, but for a long time, I'd known that I couldn't do anything about my weight. One time, when I told my stepfather he needed AA, he said, "Well, you need AA for food." I didn't feel that he was wrong. I was embarrassed, but he'd seen the truth— my own addictive behavior. I'd also had what I now know was a spiritual experience. *I'm not meant to be fat and unhappy*, I thought. *This isn't really who I am. I am on the wrong path.*

At lunch, when my friend mentioned the Twelve Steps, I was primed and ready. I wanted to know more, but I was about to go on vacation with my relatives. We left right away for California, and I spent the entire holiday unable to think of anything but my next meal. I dreaded the time between breakfast and lunch. At one point, I sat in front of a beautiful ocean in my big body and had my uncle take a picture of me, hoping he would see how bad I felt. He did say he was concerned about my eating, and that helped prepare me a little more for the FA program. I didn't know it, but my Higher Power was working in my life.

My aunt always dieted when she came home from a trip. Looking ahead, she told me about the melon diet she intended to do. She said the diet was simple: melons and more melons. In that instant, I recognized that I couldn't eat melons for the rest of my life. I needed a solution that wouldn't have an end. What would I do after I ate all the melons, even if I got thin for once? I told my aunt I was going to try something else.

I went to my first FA meeting after I got back from our vacation. I was eighteen, and the room was full of people who looked like parents and grandparents, but I still knew I was home. I was five feet, six inches and weighed 178 pounds. I felt like a lump of bread dough. When I heard a member tell her story, I understood that there was something in me that had to be reined in and to stay reined in. My Higher Power gave me a big gift by helping me understand that my urge to eat was never going to go away.

Later, after I'd gotten started in the program and had a question or complaint about my food plan, a member said, "Whatever you eat is just food." I was shocked. Food was never "just food" for me, but I knew that I wanted it to be. If only eating could be like sleeping or bathing—just one of many things I did in the day. I didn't want thoughts of food and weight to take up 80 percent of my brain.

The day I started FA, my life changed. Abstinence gave me freedom. I talked with my sponsor about an appropriate food plan, and with her help, I used that structure to decide what I would eat each day. I committed to my plan for one day, abstaining from eating one bite more or one bite less, and soon my obsession lifted. My weight didn't go down right away, but I immediately felt thinner. I looked classmates I'd feared right in their eyes. I smiled, and people smiled back. My real self began to come out.

Staying abstinent one day at a time, I lost all my extra weight by the time of my senior prom. I felt beautiful that night. My date stood me up, so I went with a freshman instead. I didn't care, because I felt so good about myself. I danced, headed to the senior breakfast, ate abstinent food there, and had fun. I'd waited my whole life for what I found in FA. The program encapsulated everything I'd searched for. I had always wanted to have a spiritual connection with a Higher Power, and I wanted contact with people.

After about a year of abstinence, I moved to another state for college. I spoke with someone in the kitchen right after I got there, explaining that I needed to weigh and measure what I ate. Most students who are in FA recovery start out by weighing and measuring their food right in the cafeteria, but the man I spoke with introduced me to the person who prepared food in the back. That man suggested that I keep my scale in his room, measure my food there, and then go back to the seating area. He started to teach me Creole every day, and he became my friend. My Higher Power made abstinence easily possible for me, even in a public cafeteria. I just needed to take the first step by asking for what I needed.

During my first year at school, the people in the kitchen got to know me, which felt nice, but eventually I started weighing my food in public. That was more convenient, and I'd become more comfortable with who I was. Whenever anyone questioned me, I explained that I needed to measure my food because of my health. If I felt I could be helpful, I shared openly and in depth about food addiction and FA. I was unsettled in the beginning, but it's easier to have a scale and walk around in a thin body—happy and healthy and cute—than it is to be fat and unhappy and have no scale. I thought, *Who cares?! I'm not embarrassed.* After a while, no one noticed.

In the middle of college, I switched schools and goals, but I stayed abstinent. I spent my entire twenties in recovery, dating and having fun, though I did make some mistakes. For a long time, I was attracted to addicts. I was still looking for the cool kids with the fast cars and motorcycles. I went to clubs with my friends. I didn't drink and didn't eat, but after a while I got tired of being the designated driver. By the time I met my husband, I had finally experienced some healthy relationships. I'd had roommates who were in FA and had made friends with my sponsor and other FA members.

When I met my husband, I thought I would never be attracted to him because he was so stable. There was nothing exciting or different about him. We became friends, though, and I began to appreciate his good qualities. He was kind and treated me well, and when he made a commitment, he kept it.

After a few months, we were talking each night before bed and spending every weekend together. One evening, because of my recovery, I was able to tell him how I felt about him. I trusted my Higher Power and did not try to hide myself or control the outcome. In an honest conversation, we decided we'd try dating. Eventually, we got married.

I have a great relationship with my husband because of my FA recovery. When I'm wrong, I promptly admit it. He does this, too, partly because of me, I think. He's a good person, so he's able to apologize, but if he were living with someone who never admitted she was wrong, it might be hard to admit it himself. Honesty is important to us. We're open with each other about everything.

My marriage is also good because when I met my husband, I liked who I was. Again, this was because of FA. We each felt we were nice additions to each other's lives. Even today, as much as I love him, I know I'd be all right without him. People die. They are imperfect. They get divorced. Relationships end. Despite how difficult life can sometimes be, I feel solid because I depend on my Higher Power. I have a God of my own understanding.

The FA program has given me the gift of myself. When I was a child, I used to love to run and play on the beach. I stopped when I gained weight because of the shame I felt about myself. I'm a normal weight now and have been for the past fourteen years. I am grateful to be a wife and a mother. Above all, I'm thankful that I am at last free from food and from any effort to be someone other than who I am.

No Middle Ground

◇ ◇ ◇

I HAVE NEVER BEEN FAT, but I know I am a food addict because I have spent years battling with food. When I think of the early signs of the disease of food addiction in my life, I go back to when I was three or four years old and my parents were in the process of a separation and divorce. I turned a corner then and changed from a normal, happy little boy to someone more introverted and withdrawn.

I don't think I was a food addict when I was that young boy, but the fear, doubt, and insecurity that drive addiction were already becoming part of my life. My childhood was hard. I wasn't good at getting my schoolwork done, and I was awkward socially. Fear made me isolate, and I spent hours alone in my room drawing and painting. Early on, I also developed scary levels of anger. I don't know when it started, but until I was about twelve or thirteen, I flew into rages when I didn't get my way. One day, when my mother told me

I couldn't have something I wanted, I tore my bedroom door off its hinges, threw it on the floor, and stomped on it.

Sometime in middle school, when I was twelve or thirteen, my violent anger went away and I took a turn for the worse. Instead of trying to handle school and behave correctly, I gave up. I skipped my classes and stopped doing homework because I felt I couldn't get my assignments done. I didn't realize that I was so afraid of failing, I was unwilling to try. In sixth grade, I had been an honors student. Within the next two years, I was twice forced to leave public school, and I ended up in a school for behaviorally challenging children.

I've heard that depression is anger turned inward, which I think describes what happened to me. I became suicidally depressed. My mother forced me to start seeing a therapist, and I was put on my first antidepressant the summer after I finished eighth grade. The medication didn't help.

My life got very hard. I have an extreme side to my personality, and on a ten-point scale of intensity, I lost the ability to find five. I was stuck at either zero or ten. I became fixated on becoming bigger and stronger. I followed punishing, intricate, workout regimens with iron discipline. Lifting weights and running led to more isolation. I also began to focus more on food. Health foods became a central part of my way of life, as I made a moral decision to become a vegetarian.

I know now that my emotional and mental trouble really stemmed from a spiritual need. I wanted something to take the edge off my awful feelings of isolation, and I had no Higher Power or any person I felt could help me. Big platefuls of food seemed to work at first.

In the next few years, I kept turning more corners, walking toward full-blown addiction, but the ways that food came to dominate me happened so subtly I hardly noticed. In the name of building muscle, I gave myself permission to eat the larger quantities I really wanted. I had only naturally sweetened this and whole flour that, but something changed. I was less and less able to reach the satisfied, comfortable feeling I'd gotten before. I made strange concoctions, blending vegetables and grains with molasses and olive oil, for example. I was always looking for exactly the right combination, but I could never find it.

I quit high school when I was sixteen and found a place with housemates. The quantities and ways that I ate got even more bizarre, but I decided that the source of my problems lay outside myself. I reasoned that I felt awful and alienated because our society as a whole was one of isolation and disconnection. I was sure that finding a community and a way back to nature would put me on track.

My life became more extreme. I moved to a nearby community of people who were living simply and sustainably on their land. That winter, I slept outside in the snow under a tarp, until it collapsed, and then in various open-air, unheated structures. After a year, I reached the same point of despair that had first brought me to the community. My addiction had progressed, and I was eating bowl after bowl of natural food concoctions, secretly and until I was sick.

I never want to forget where addiction took me in the next months of my life. My use of food as a drug and the feeling of desperation I had because of my eating drove me into self-imposed homelessness. I left the first community after a year for a more radical commune in Texas, which I quit after one month. Back on the road with only a backpack, I hopped freight trains, walked miles through sprawling cities and suburbs, and slept outdoors in the rain under my flimsy tarp. I remember sitting in the dark by myself at a freeway rest stop, eating and feeling cut off from any life that was normal or even tolerable.

In North Carolina, I stayed with the kind friends of an old friend. I was there two weeks, rifling through their kitchen whenever they left the house or went to bed. One night, I found something wrapped in tinfoil in their freezer. It looked kind of good, so I sawed a corner off. Piece by piece, I finished the whole thing. Later I found out that I had eaten the top to my hosts' wedding cake. It was old—they hadn't wanted it—and they laughed off the incident, but I felt humiliated and pained.

Late one night, I finally took the first step toward finding a solution for my food addiction. Desperately searching natural health books for a way to deal with my sugar craving and depression, I suddenly realized that something was wrong with me. I saw that I, Mr. Health Food, had a problem I couldn't manage alone. I needed help.

I looked in the phone book for an eating disorders clinic or a support group and found the phone number of a twelve-step program for compulsive overeaters. The next day, I went to a meeting in a little town in the hills of North Carolina. When I opened the door, I saw just two overweight women. I'd always been ashamed of my strange, secret eating, so their openness about when and how they ate had a powerful effect on me. They also mentioned the Twelve Steps and the tools we can use to help us stop eating. They gave me hope that there might be a way out, even though they were struggling.

Eventually, I ended up on the road again, headed east. I got as far as Maryland, but I woke up one morning in a field full of poison ivy, and that was all I could take. I hopped a bus. Before I made it all the way back, an elderly, black woman boarded and sat next to me. She was a long-time AA member, eager to share her recovery. It was as if an angel had been put in my path, yet, back in Massachusetts, I felt that nothing in me had changed. I remember walking down a little, two-lane highway shoving fistfuls of candy into my mouth with the same desperate, hopeless feelings I'd always had.

Still, something must have shifted, because a few days later, at a party, I was able to ask for help. Pulling one of my friends aside, I told him I needed to talk. "I don't know what to do about food. I'm out of control," I said. It turned out that my friend had been in AA for years, and he took out a book: *Alcoholics Anonymous*. He knew I was talking about addiction, even if I didn't, and before long, he introduced me to my first sponsor.

I joined the same twelve-step program I'd found in North Carolina, but I had a way to go yet before I reached any kind of recovery. I must have been making up my own food plan, because I remember eating dandelion greens with ground-up sunflower and flax seeds for breakfast. I was going to meetings, but I couldn't find a way to be abstinent. Every couple of days, I went off the deep end, back into bingeing. *Alcoholics Anonymous* bored me a little; I had no idea of its power.

My sponsor once asked me, "Do you think you are powerless over food?" I gave it some thought. At that point, I was secretly going through the cupboards in my supervisor's family kitchen and stealing large amounts of food from a conference center near where I worked. On reflection, though, it seemed to me that sometimes I could control what I ate and sometimes I couldn't. Since I wasn't out of control all of the time, I decided I wasn't totally out of control. Needless to say, I had to continue eating addictively for a while longer. My sponsor said he couldn't help me and asked me to find someone else.

After my second sponsor gave up on me, I met a woman who was in FA. I'd reached the point where I was ready to take Step One and admit that I was powerless over food. I remember thinking that I wouldn't be of use to anyone in the world—least of all myself—if I couldn't find a way out of my terrible cycles of eating. I asked the woman to sponsor me and listened to her suggestions. I also began to open up and talk to her.

My FA sponsor had me call her every morning. We talked for fifteen minutes a day, often about God, she tells me now. I have trouble remembering much, but I know I was open to the idea that I needed something revolutionary. I was convinced I couldn't eat in safety. If I went back to fighting the food by myself, I was sunk. I had to tap into something more powerful than me.

My new sponsor whipped my food plan into shape. She guided me to simple foods in measured amounts without any of my usual concoctions. She also started feeding me the FA program. I had just turned twenty, but I already had a long history of destructive eating, and I knew I couldn't stop. My sponsor told me to say a prayer. "Ask for help to stay abstinent and back your prayer up with an action. Pick up the phone and talk with another program member. Your abstinence is a partnership with God, and your prayer and action are the 1 percent you have to do. God will do the rest."

Another program member suggested that I pray whenever a food obsession or craving hit me. "Get on your knees and don't get up until you've asked God to have the craving removed. Then stand up and get on with your day, as if God had removed it," he said.

I jumped into the program, grateful for the suggestions, but I did have one more break of abstinence about one month later. I got into an argument with my sponsor over my food plan. After a phone call to someone whom I knew would agree with me, I had a mental binge of self-righteousness that took me over the cliff again. With one bite of extra food and the binge that followed, every bit of hopelessness and despondency came back. That night, the couple I was living with came home and found me sitting alone in the dark, an empty bowl in my lap.

My nighttime eating proved to me that there is no solution for me in food. I called my sponsor the next morning and told her what I'd done. She said, "Do you want this program? Do you want to get better? Then simply resume doing what you need to do." I followed her guidance, and one day at a time, I have been abstinent ever since.

I was given the gift of abstinence because I was willing to go to any lengths for my recovery. A couple of days after my last binge, I received word that my sister had died in an accident. I was devastated and afraid to go home for the memorial service, but I took my scale for measuring my food and my phone list with the names and phone numbers of members of our fellowship, and I stayed abstinent.

At the time, I was living in a rural area and getting to the grocery store and to local meetings by hitchhiking. Once a week, I carpooled with friends to an FA meeting two hours away. Realizing that I had to make changes in order to increase my chances for recovery, I began looking for ways to move to a city. I hated leaving the country, but I put my recovery first and found a rooming house that was just a twenty-five-minute walk from many FA meetings.

In my new home, I gave up my old patterns of isolation. I went to four meetings a week and connected with people in fellowship at lunches and dinners. I wrapped the program around me. Twenty years of hard experience was enough for me, and I learned to work this program as if my life depended on it. I knew what was waiting for me if I didn't.

In recovery, I began to involve myself with life instead of withdrawing from it. I got a part-time job moving patients around in one of the city hospitals. This was overwhelming because I didn't know how to be a colleague, employee, or friend, and I took every bump in the road as a reason to judge and criticize myself.

My FA friends kept telling me to focus on my actions and stop worrying about my thoughts and feelings. The possibility of a full-time job gave me another opportunity to remember that feelings aren't facts. I was at first frightened to apply for the position, but an FA old-timer reminded me that work is just what all ordinary people do. Her simple guidance helped me feel I wasn't facing the challenge alone when I applied for and got the job.

After two years of recovery, I began to think about returning to school. With the encouragement of a friend in the program, I completed my GED and dared to ask for an application to the local state university. One essay at a time, I answered all the questions, and I was accepted provisionally into a summer program. In the fall, I entered school full-time.

In many ways, I was starting life from scratch, and I felt overwhelmed again, but people in the FA fellowship helped me whenever I felt lost or confused. After I got a little more comfortable with myself, I started dating. Studying, socializing, and doing a part-time work-study job, I started to mature. I learned how to face life and persevere instead of running away.

Five and a half years later, I graduated summa cum laude, with a 3.94 GPA. I got a job in industry, but I didn't enjoy it, so I entered a PhD program instead. My first semester back in school was horrendous. I was doing my own research, teaching two laboratory sections of general biology, and taking three classes. The workload was too much, and I compromised my sleep. I also nurtured my own fear and insecurity and quickly got into a bad state, emotionally and spiritually. I had to learn again, in this new set of circumstances, that my abstinence and serenity are the highest priorities in my life. I cannot make school more important than my recovery.

I've now completed my first two years of graduate school, and life has gotten progressively better. I've confronted some of the anxieties that drove me away from school when I was young. I still work more slowly than other people, and I sometimes have a hard time meeting the deadlines for my assignments, but I've come to more self-acceptance. I don't worry so much about other people's standards of success and failure. I trust that if this academic program does not work out, it will be because I am supposed to be somewhere else.

I am not sure what will come next. Graduate school is good, but I have decided to stop short of a doctorate and leave with a master's degree. I've recently been exploring possibilities in a related but new field, and I am optimistic! I can imagine myself waking up every morning excited to go to work.

Today, I am thirty-three years old and living back in the country, in a place I love. I never had a pound to lose, but I belong in FA, and I have been continuously abstinent since I was twenty. Because my abstinence and recovery are the top priorities in my life, I am free to listen to my heart and not limit myself. I am no longer driven by fear or food. I live with a sense of hope.

Perfection Not Required

◇ ◇ ◇

I THINK I WAS BORN a food addict. Food was on my radar way before I had reason for it to be. As a child, I was treated with love and respect. My family is Jewish, and we celebrated the holidays around our dining room table. We each had our place there—Mom, Dad, my brother, and me. We were a circle. I remember lots of laughter. I also felt a sense of God, though I didn't call it that at the time. At eight or nine, I said to my father, "The world makes sense, Daddy. There's a logic to the universe."

My brother was two and a half years older than I was. He was born missing the lower left chamber of his heart, and by the time I came along, he had already had several open-heart surgeries. I felt bad for my brother. He was physically awkward, and other children made fun of him. I know that I was anxious about him, but I can't draw a straight line between those feelings and my eating.

From an early age, I was just someone who ate addictively—period. I remember first bingeing when I was only two or three years old. Later, as I grew a little older, no one ever taught me how to shoplift, or how to steal money from my mother's purse, or how to lie once I was caught. I wanted sugar, and I did whatever I needed to do to get it. There was a component to my disease of food addiction that was decidedly physical. It had nothing to do with emotions or psychology.

When I was in the sixth grade, our family moved, and my brother's life improved. A couple of years later, my parents learned of an operation that had been successfully used to repair heart defects like his. My brother had a life expectancy of only twenty-five or thirty years, and they hoped for a total cure and a long life for him. To our shock, the operation failed and my brother died. I was devastated. Everything that had made sense to me as a child was smashed. The circle at our dining room table was broken. We returned to our house to sit shiva for the period of mourning after my brother's funeral, and I went into the kitchen. You could say that I didn't come out of the kitchen for the next seven years.

I've learned in FA that food addiction is a progressive illness, and I can see that progression clearly in my own life. I gained 30 pounds the year my brother died. After that, I kept dieting and getting bigger. By age sixteen, I was a full-blown food addict. I had no sense of my irresponsibility and immaturity, no awareness of the burdens I placed on my parents because of my eating. I spent the summer before college in an acting program in England. I left for London with boxes of diet bars and pouches of powder for shakes, but I forgot part of my blender at home. My parents shipped that heavy piece of kitchen equipment across the Atlantic Ocean so their daughter could do her diet, but I lasted only three weeks before I began bingeing again.

The night of my flight home, I spent all my remaining British money on candy—"for my parents and friends," of course. I remember looking up from eating the candy and seeing my plane come in, but I must have passed out, because when I woke up, the plane was gone. I called my parents collect and was furious that they were upset with me. The next day, when I flew back to the U.S., I binged on the plane and then binged again in the airport waiting for my father. On the way home, I had to ask my father to stop the car so I could be sick beside the road.

I managed to lose 30 pounds before college began, and my mother and I spent about $300 on new clothes for me. Once I got to school, however, I ate one bite of food off my diet plan, and a month later I no longer fit into anything. My disease got worse from there. I saw a therapist for eating disorders. I kept food journals. I went regularly to a yoga center, where people ate brown rice and talked about unconditional love. I listened to a guru tell us that we were beautiful inside and out. And I kept bingeing.

Spirituality is wonderful. Eating healthy food is wonderful. Getting therapy for your emotions and working on how you think about yourself are also wonderful, but if you still have a drug in your system— and food is a drug for me—there's no possibility for actual change. Despite the therapy, meditation, yoga, and all of my talk about God, the only God that I had in my life was food. Food was my Higher Power.

When I found my first twelve-step program, for compulsive overeaters, I weighed about 200 pounds. I'm five feet, three inches tall. My hair was teased out and colored pink and yellow. I had terrible hygiene. I rarely washed my clothes because I didn't want them to shrink. All of my blouses were food stained at my chest, where I had a continental shelf. I never understood why people put napkins on their laps. Food never made it to my lap!

In that first food program, we all defined our own abstinence. I had three "moderate" meals each day, including sandwiches for lunch. When moderate turned into mountainous, I began bingeing again on flour and sugar, and I became suicidal. Two hundred pounds of weight on my body didn't bring me to the point where I was ready for FA: Fear did. I was so terrified I would kill myself that I was finally able to really ask for help.

I got a sponsor and ultimately spent seven weeks in a treatment center, where I learned about food addiction. When I came home, I immediately connected with people who were doing the FA program. They were weighing and measuring their food, abstaining from flour and sugar, and learning the Twelve Steps through AWOLs. At that point, I was weighing and measuring my meals, but I was still attached to what I was eating. I used huge amounts of condiments, ate greasy food, and found apples and potatoes the size of small meteors.

During my first AWOL, I met a woman who had lost 100 pounds and was completely neutral regarding food. She was also confident and comfortable with herself. I wanted freedom from food badly, and I asked her to sponsor me. She took a machete to my food plan and then told me I needed to stop doctoring everything I ate with heavy spices and condiments. I got more honest and moderate in my measurements. Eventually, I learned that fancy food made me want to eat more and plain food made me neutral. I learned to keep my meals simple.

My sponsor was strong with me. I was needy and immature, and I wanted her to give me answers. Whenever I was confused, I asked her what I should do. In the beginning, she guided me directly, but we reached a point where she began to push me toward developing a relationship with a Higher Power. "Go to God for help," she'd say. "Ask for an answer and see what you come up with. Then we'll talk about it." With her help, I started doing my own work spiritually. When I faced a situation that confused me, I wanted to run to my sponsor, but then I thought, *No, wait.* I asked God for help with my thinking and later called my sponsor to talk things over. She didn't want me to lean on her. She wanted me to trust God. I did, and I grew up.

It's been almost twenty-five years since I came into FA. When I started, my head was full of negative thinking, especially about myself, and isolation was my way of life. I spent my first six years immersed in recovery. No one ever told me to call other program members three times a day. I wanted to feel better, so I reached out by phone, many times daily. I found that the more I connected with other people in the program, the more quiet time I took, the more literature I read, the more meetings I attended, the more service I did within FA, the better I felt.

I went on in life. I finished college, became a lawyer, married my husband, and finally had children. Instead of FA being something that I did, the program became central to who I am. Fear is at the heart of my addiction. I learned in the program that if I let go of fear, if I trust totally in God, food recedes in importance. If God is my Higher Power, I don't need to turn to food addictively.

In FA, I reached a normal weight, and I've stayed there, which is wonderful, but I've also had some difficult experiences. We all have. Abstinence opens us up to life; it doesn't render us immune to it. I lost my grandmother, whom I loved. I started to grieve about my brother and faced my fear that my sorrow would swallow me up. I accepted that I needed fertility treatments and, after some years of marriage, was able to have two children. When my first child was diagnosed with autism, I fell into fear and sadness for some months, but through it all I kept praying, and I stayed abstinent and free from food obsession. Eventually, I found my way back to faith and hopefulness.

I am sure now that there is a God, and I never have to be afraid again. Whatever life may bring, God will give me the strength I need to face it, so I choose today to embrace everything as a gift. Times of happiness are blessings. Hard situations give me the chance to learn a deeper acceptance and faith. I think of them as blessings in disguise.

The happiness I had as a child was destroyed by my addiction and my brother's death, but today I feel joy again. I am amazed by the freedom I have from food. As long as I accept the reality that I have to do the FA program if I want to stay well, I will never again have to suffer from obesity and food addiction—or from fear.

My path hasn't been completely smooth. During my first year of law school, I fell into a period of anxiety. I stopped talking about my feelings, disconnected from my sponsor, and got overtired. One evening, I broke my abstinence at a dinner party. I learned a lot about humility and complacency then, and I started over. I have been abstinent for the seventeen years since. My sponsor stuck with me, and it's now been over twenty years that we've worked together.

I'm not perfect. I have made mistakes in my marriage, parenting, friendships, and work. I'm still learning how to weigh and measure my life so that I'm not overextended and too tired. Despite my shortcomings, though, I've always wanted to get well. I've been willing to talk about what I've done. I think that's why I'm still abstinent and in FA. It's not the mistakes that are dangerous for my recovery, it's my false pride—the fear that I won't be accepted if I'm honest about who I am, and the lying I do to conceal myself. I pray often for humility and the willingness to be myself.

The FA fellowship is an amazing community. We can be who we truly are in FA. I can express what I am thinking and feeling, no matter how embarrassed I might have felt before. I can come out from hiding and into the sunlight. If I'm willing to reach out and be open in the program, I can find out that I am fine the way I am. I don't need to be insecure or frightened anymore.

I think that self-acceptance, neutrality around food, and living in a healthy way—body, mind, and spirit—

are the fulfillment of the Twelve Steps. I have all of that, though I haven't lived my life perfectly. We have to honestly weigh and measure the food we eat. We have to be willing to change. But nobody has to be perfect to get well.

From Indignity to Grace

✧ ✧ ✧

WHEN I WAS IN COLLEGE, I managed to diet my way down to 150 pounds. To stay there, I decided that I had to burn five hundred calories a day through exercise. In my view, those five hundred calories stood at the dividing line between me as a good person and me as a bad person. If I burned the full five hundred, I was adequate and good. If not, I was bad.

I know now that I was subject to a form of insanity, but at the time, I was a woman with a mission. I dropped all my extracurricular activities, cut down my class load, and went to the gym whenever I could. If, according to the exercise machine monitors, I didn't get to five hundred calories, I went back to the gym for more sessions.

One day, I was working hard on the stair climber when a skinny, blond girl approached me. "You know, a person of your size really shouldn't be exercising like that," she said. I looked at her, speechless. I wanted to curse, but I couldn't. I dropped my head, got off the machine, pulled myself together, and went to the cafeteria for 472 calories worth of Hungarian tetrazzini—for a starter.

Fifteen years ago, when I came into the program, it was late in July and ninety degrees outside. I was miserable. I'm five feet, one inch tall, and at the time, I weighed about 200 pounds. I was wearing a girdle under my jean shorts and sweating profusely. Beyond buxom, I was embarrassed by the bra straps digging into my back and the spillage in my front. My hips measured fifty-two inches, and my thighs rubbed together.

Today, I'm sitting in my living room in a pair of tiny shorts and a tank top. I weigh 105 pounds, and I am comfortable. I've been abstinent and at this weight consistently for the past fourteen years, with the exception of the two times I got pregnant. I gained weight appropriately then, and I was healthy and back in my pre-pregnancy jeans within four months. All of this is a miracle.

I was a normal baby of about 6 pounds, but I weighed 19 pounds within three months of my birth. My baby fat never went away. At eight, I was already heavy, so my mom sent me to a commercial weight loss program. I lost my weight there and received a lifetime membership card, clearly a curse at that age. I kept the pounds off long enough to receive an invitation to serve as a lecturer, which I declined. Five years later, at thirteen, I was 168 pounds—a sideways growth spurt.

I went to a weight loss camp for the first time the following summer and came home weighing 127. When I went back to camp for the fourth time at nineteen, I was

203. Between camp sessions, I'd struggled, trying other commercial programs, diets, compulsive exercise, and any other gimmick I came across in my teen magazines.

My mom made sure I always had a wardrobe. If we found pants that fit, we bought them in five colors. Every season, I took brand-new clothes, or ones I'd hardly worn, to Goodwill or the Salvation Army, because I'd outgrown them faster than I could wear them.

I remember when I was in eighth grade, I was dying to wear a pair of the most popular jeans. I had to lie all the way back on my bed, suck everything in, and poke the tip of a metal hanger into the eye of the zipper to get enough leverage to get the pants closed. Three years before, I'd stuffed myself into a pair that was just as tight. When I was walking up the stairs in my elementary school, they split up my backside. The indignity! I was wearing magenta-colored corduroys with bright, white underpants beneath.

High school came and went. I started college at 175 pounds and reached over 203 by the end of my first year. Had I only been troubled by my weight and body image, I might have found peace eventually, but I had a much larger problem. The disease of food addiction is physical, mental, and spiritual. The physical level was obvious: I couldn't stop eating, and I was fat. The mental and spiritual levels were invisible to me until I'd been in recovery for some time, but even my early life was full of examples of my irrationality and inability to cope.

Low-level depression had been a constant for me. I worried ceaselessly as a child. Because of the drug addiction of a member of our family, our house was filled with tension and fighting. We lived with uncertainty and chaos. At eight years old, I reached a turning point mentally. *Who is in charge?* I asked myself, and I decided that I should be. This became a cornerstone of how I functioned. If there was a problem, I should fix it.

I'd begun therapy when I was young and continued with it off and on for the twelve years prior to joining FA. As I matured, I felt the same drive and compulsion for men that I felt when I was rummaging for food in my cupboards. Once I entered college, I began sleeping with all kinds of men.

I'd felt suicidal for years, and during graduate school, I was put on heavy doses of antidepressant and anti-anxiety medications. I walked around with a big smile on my face, telling everyone I was fine. Typically, I ate and wrote papers late at night. I got up in the morning after three or four hours of sleep, drove to a coffee shop for breakfast, hit the vending machine during the break in my first class, finished class, left to sleep with some-one, went back to school for another class, bought more food, slept with someone else, and went home to write another paper. The medications just made it easier for me to live in my chaos. They kept me calm.

As I headed toward 200 pounds again, I realized that my weight was never going to get where I wanted it to be. I'm a fighter and I keep trying to the bitter end, so whenever I felt hopeless, I looked for ways to accept my weight. I practiced a carefree attitude: Love me or leave me. I labeled myself "gently rounded," "pleasantly plump," or "Rubenesque." I made friends with my belly. I named my breasts. I explained that the source of the problem was my genes or my slow metabolism. I told myself I had nice hair, a great smile, lovely skin. I rationalized. Sure, I wished I could go shopping with my girlfriends and find anything I wanted right off the rack, but at least I had three plus-size stores to patronize, and shopping was easy for me.

I landed a job that began soon after I graduated from college. I was trying to stop myself from going to men as a means of comfort and escape, and I was completely lost. Two or three times a week, I went to a friend's house to cry and tell her how miserable, fat, and alone I felt. My friend was in a twelve-step program for compulsive overeaters, and one Tuesday night, she asked if I'd like to go to a meeting sometime. Without any knowledge of such meetings, I said yes. I then drove around the corner to the nearest convenience store, so I could be well supplied during my ride home. I made three additional stops at fast-food restaurants; paused to throw up, which I'd started doing a couple of weeks before; and then went to the house of a man I hadn't seen in eight months, where I spent the night. I didn't register this as a last binge, but somehow the thought of "meeting" and "food" made me so anxious, I had to eat.

On Thursday, my friend drove us to a tiny meeting, where we happened to learn about FA. As it turned out, the nearest FA meetings were held in the city where I lived. Two days later, my friend, my guardian angel, picked me up at my front door and drove me a block and a half down the street for my first FA meeting. My Higher Power was in my life before I knew it, because I don't think I would have gone to the meeting by myself.

That night, I was introduced to a woman who was available to sponsor. During the meeting, she had stood in the front of the room and shared her story. For me, this was an incredible experience, during which I registered only that she was beautifully thin and that fifteen years before, she had been 90 pounds overweight. I didn't hear anything else in the meeting. I was ready to sign up.

The woman, who offered to sponsor me, gave me no food plan. First, she showed me a list of local meetings and asked me which four I'd be willing to commit to attending. I thought, *This woman is out of her mind. I'm not going to four meetings a week. I am twenty-four, and I have plans, places to go, people to see.* She stood calmly and waited in silence. I murmured, "I don't think I can do that." She waited longer, and then I heard myself saying, "I see that there are four meetings in this neighborhood, so I guess I'll go to those." Only then did she give me a food plan.

My lack of fight was a spiritual experience for me. I balked, but I conceded, an attitude that defined my recovery for my first five years. I took the food plan. I was determined. I had to get abstinent. In another spiritual experience, I was somehow immediately willing to buy a scale and change dinner out with friends to a meal at their house, which I weighed and measured for myself. I went to bed that night feeling like a million dollars. I hadn't achieved great successes and my name wasn't on billboards, but I felt good about me. The next morning, I called my sponsor at 7:00 a.m. to tell her my food plan for the day—and to commit myself to doing whatever I needed to do in order to stick to it.

I began the amazing process of FA recovery as my sponsor guided me toward an abstinent way of life. I committed my food plan to my sponsor, ate what I committed to, and began to use my daily call to her to ask some questions. For the first time, I felt that it was all right for me not to know everything. I didn't have to feel inadequate. She wanted me to ask, and I wanted to listen and learn.

My sponsor did make the suggestion that I not date for a year, which seemed absurd and unfair. I said yes, and then whenever she asked if I'd been dating, I told her no. I conveniently dismissed the one-night stands I'd had earlier in the week because they weren't "dating." I'd just been hanging out and sleeping with someone—just having a good time. Eventually, I'd confess, and she'd encourage me to understand that such encounters were interfering with my recovery.

Four months into my abstinence, I went to England with some girlfriends who were not in our program. By the time I came home four days later, I'd slept with three men. I'd learned to be honest, so I told my sponsor, and she did the kindest thing anyone could ever do for me: She told me she couldn't support such behavior, and she stopped working with me.

When I hung up the phone at the end of the conversation with my sponsor, I immediately called in sick to work. I was on a mission to find a new sponsor. For the rest of the day, I made continuous calls, with only a break for lunch. I was trying to find someone who would give me the amazing program that had allowed me to lose 40 pounds in four months *and* allow me to date.

Seven hours later, I gave up. I said to the final person I spoke with, "Fine! I won't date for one year." We agreed to work together, and I hung up, mentally noting that exactly one year from then, on December 4, 1997, my life would begin again.

Unfortunately, I did not make it to December 4, 1997—at any rate, not abstinently. On October 4 that year, I broke my abstinence. I'd gotten a cold and decided I needed vitamin C. Wistfully remembering the sweet, chewable vitamins I'd had as a child, I found a chewable, orange-flavored version for adults. The first ingredient was sucrose, which is sugar, but in my view at the time, vitamins were vitamins, so I picked up the package.

I ate one vitamin in the drugstore, one at the cash register, another in the parking lot, one in my car, and one when I got home. Four days later, I'd eaten all but a few of the 250 tablets. I chewed the last seven or eight pills after a couple of frustrating phone calls trying to arrange for someone to speak at my FA meeting. I was responsible for finding the speakers, and I felt ashamed that I'd let my group down.

As I swallowed the last vitamins, I thought, *That's better*, and then I was flooded with the awful knowledge that I had broken my abstinence. I saw that I had used food to help me push away my horrible feelings of inadequacy. As soon as I got home from my meeting, I called my sponsor to tell her.

Realizing that I had broken fourteen months of abstinence with chewable vitamin C, I felt furious. Why hadn't I eaten something worthwhile?! I decided to go to the supermarket to buy everything I wanted for a binge.

I had my keys in my hand, and I was just about to walk out of my studio apartment when the telephone rang. I didn't answer it. I grabbed my coat. The phone rang again. I didn't answer it then, either.

One step toward the door, and the phone rang again. Angrily, I threw down my keys. "For God's sake!" I said, and I picked up the phone. A friend in FA answered and talked me off the ledge. She and God kept me from walking out the door to eat flour and sugar in quantities that probably would have prevented me from ever returning to FA. She saved my life.

After talking with my sponsor and thinking about what I'd done, I realized that I had kept people at arm's length during my entire fourteen months in the program. I was still running the show. I still felt responsible for my own recovery. I took credit for the weight I'd lost. I was too great for myself, and I needed a good dose of humility.

I went back to beginning my abstinence again, and in a major turning point for me, I let go of my determination to date. I accepted that it would be best for me to refrain from dating for an indefinite time, to trust that I would be shown when I was ready to start going out again.

One year of abstinence later, when my sponsor suggested that I could start dating, I had another spiritual experience. My commitment had become my own. I didn't want to date, because I was in the process of building a relationship with God through doing and living the Twelve Steps. I could never have developed that relationship if I had been blocked from God by using food or men. I'd long since gotten off the antidepressants and anti-anxiety medication. I was raw. I was naked to my-self as I was, stripped down to the person God meant me to be, and I knew that I shouldn't begin dating until I'd completed all Twelve Steps in my AWOL and had the beginnings of a solid foundation for an abstinent life.

After I completed my AWOL, I spent two years dat-ing periodically, entering healthy, monogamous rela-tionships as a whole person. I had dignity and integrity. Today, I'm married, with two children, and my husband and I just celebrated nine happy years together.

We receive many gifts in abstinence and recovery. My marriage and children are wonderful joys. Another, dif-ferent gift is the ability to face difficulties without turn-ing to food. A few years ago, my chronic back problem turned acute after a truck hit my car from behind and injured me. Months of alternative therapies and two op-erations on my spine failed to end the terrible pain I felt in my back and leg. By the time I was scheduled for the more major intervention of a spinal fusion, I had to have my husband's help to walk to the bathroom at night or, if he was away, I had to crawl.

Ten days after the surgery, my pain was worse than it had ever been. I had a terrible reaction to the medica-tion I was given and was soon hospitalized again, this time for complications that were misdiagnosed. I was unable to digest or eliminate anything I ate, and it took the doctors some time to realize that my colon, stomach, and intestines were paralyzed.

In the first weeks after my third surgery, despondency hit me hard. My back was no better, and I had new pains that were sometimes agonizing. For a while, I thought that I would be crippled for the rest of my life. In the midst of my struggles, I was given a stark view of myself as an addict. I felt ill in every way and had absolutely no sensation of hunger, but I knew that if anyone had put a box of cookies in front of me, I'd have wanted to eat them all. After more than twelve years of recovery, I still had an insane impulse to try to fix my discomfort through food.

I thank my Higher Power every day that I did not eat addictively. God hadn't left me, and as I got well, He worked through people to take care of me. I couldn't go out, so for eight weeks, a group of FA members came to our house every Saturday to bring me the best medicine there was: an FA meeting. My husband had to travel for his work, so others in the fellowship came by to help with the laundry and dishes, to bathe and play with our children, and to take out our trash.

On every level, I was carried through my difficulties. The telephone was vital. Whenever I phoned, I found encouragement. "Take this one day at a time," an FA friend would say, or "Remember that this too shall pass." Above all, people helped me laugh. We've got some hilarious people in our program. They've learned how to be of good cheer and to bring light to hard situations.

My back is fine today, and my digestive system is working perfectly. I am deeply grateful for my health, my family, and my relationship with God. Whether I'm happy or sad, I know I mustn't ever lose sight of the facts that I am a food addict and that God is with me. When I ask God for help, I have peace of mind, and with that peace, I never have a need to take the first addictive bite.

The Twelve Steps

✧ ✧ ✧

Introduction

✧ ✧ ✧

A S THE STORIES in the preceding section make clear, FA helps food addicts see that we have far more than a simple problem with weight. We have to become different people if we want to get abstinent and stay abstinent. Our usual reactions to life—anxiety, resentment, insecurity, depression, and the urge to escape such feelings—drive us to eat addictively.

The Twelve Steps are the means by which we are led to a fundamental change in how we respond to the ups and downs of life. Both actions and principles, the Steps transform us, as long as we remain abstinent and continue to do them thoroughly. They offer us a road to a different way of living and to a spiritual awakening that releases us from any desire to eat addictively, one day at a time.

A structured process for learning and doing the Twelve Steps, AWOL (A Way of Life), stands at the foundation of abstinence and recovery in FA. In AWOL groups or one on one with their sponsors, abstinent FA members focus on each Step in sequence, completing one before beginning another. Because long-term, successful members of FA view AWOL as essential to recovery, they stay continually involved, either as leaders or participants.

The six chapters that follow briefly discuss each of the Twelve Steps in the context of FA and AWOL. They are written from the perspective of members with decades of abstinence and continuous involvement in the AWOL process. Though they are implicitly addressed to beginners in FA, we intend them to be helpful to anyone seeking a better understanding of the Steps and FA recovery. They are offered as additions to *Alcoholics Anonymous*, *Twelve Steps and Twelve Traditions*, and AWOL's *The Little Red Book*.

Please see appendix 3 for a complete list of the Twelve Steps and, for more about AWOL, consult the glossary in appendix 1 and the FA history in appendix 2.

Chapter 7

The Foundation—Steps 1–3

Step One: We admitted that we were powerless over food —that our lives had become unmanageable.

IN FA, MEMBERS DON'T PRESUME to diagnose anyone else as a food addict. *Am I powerless over food? Is my life unmanageable?* Each of us faces these questions alone. No one can answer for anyone else.

Many of us told ourselves that we had a simple problem with weight, but eventually we had to become honest. Rather than simply seeing ourselves as fat, overlooking the desperate, self-destructive nature of our efforts to stay thin, we were forced to confront the patterns of our eating. No matter our size, how much we understood ourselves and our problems, or how hard we tried, there always came a moment when the temptation to eat became irresistible. We started to eat addictively again. We were powerless.

While it was sometimes difficult to admit that food ruled us, the second part of Step One was often even harder. An unmanageable life? Not us! Some of us prized self-sufficiency and worked hard to meet or exceed the highest standards in all areas of our lives. Others of us adopted the opposite approach—rebellious and defiant, we did whatever we wanted to do. If we hadn't accomplished much, we rationalized our lack of success as a matter of choice. Regardless, as *Alcoholics Anonymous* notes, in all of us, "self-will ran riot."

Step One asks us to let go of our pride and look at the evidence. At first, it may take some time to recognize the signs of an unmanageable life, but there are usually many. We faced stacks of unpaid bills. Our bedrooms were piled with unfolded laundry and dirty clothes, or we were neurotically driven to clean and re-clean every room in our house. We spent thousands of dollars on psychiatrists but lied about what we were eating. Our priorities were skewed and extreme. We took care of everyone else at the expense of our own health, or we never noticed their needs. The opinions of others mattered too much or not at all. Some of us could barely get off the couch and out the door, while others almost lived at work and hardly saw our families. We thought about food constantly. Given all this and more, could we call our lives anything other than unmanageable?

With Step One, we are given a big dose of humility. We have more than a food problem, bad as that is. We have a life problem, and the evidence over the years proves that we haven't been able to solve either one.

Step One provides the foundation for our lives in recovery. To remain abstinent and do the remainder of the Steps, we have to be willing to stay honest with food and try some unfamiliar actions and attitudes. Whenever we balk, we go back to Step One. Inevitably, it reminds us that anything is better than the misery of addictive eating. Step One reminds us of a stark choice: We can try changing, or we can return to addictive eating.

Step Two: Came to believe that a Power greater than ourselves could restore us to sanity.

Before we can begin to believe that a Power greater than ourselves can restore us to sanity, we have to ask ourselves whether we are sane. *Alcoholics Anonymous* aptly notes that "sanity" is a strong word, but when we look at our behavior and its effects, we have to admit we can't easily claim that we are in our right minds. Is the life-threatening brutality we inflict on our bodies sane? Do we think we are fat when we are actually far too thin? Have we convinced ourselves that we belong in a size twelve when all we can truly wear is a size twenty-four? If we can no longer fit into our pants, do we believe that the dry cleaner is responsible for shrinking them? How many other people do we know who conceal how much they eat?

Once we admit our insanity, we have to ask if, by our own power, we can restore ourselves to sane thought and behavior. How long have we tried to improve our lives, using how many different methods? No one ever comes into FA with a successful record of personal transformation, though most of us have tried every means available to us. In the face of the extreme nature of our past feelings and our inability to deal with them, we have to admit that we've never been able to render ourselves sane. As matters stand, we see that we can't expect to do it in the future, either—not if we have to do it alone.

Given our helplessness, Step Two then asks us to become willing to believe that some Power—whatever it might be—can aid us by restoring us to sanity. When we don't yet believe, our AWOL leaders and sponsors help make the Step accessible by focusing us on our own experience. They ask us if we were able to maintain a steady discipline of sane eating before FA. Of course, we know that we were not. They then point out that we have successfully stayed abstinent, one day at a time, since beginning the FA program. Each morning we've asked a Higher Power for help to stay abstinent. Each day we've received the help we needed. Is this not enough evidence to make us willing to believe in a Greater Power that can directly help us with our eating and our daily lives?

Further, they ask if we are able to see evidence of a Higher Power in the lives of people we know in FA. Any of us can immediately think of examples that amaze us. We know people who maintain 100-pound weight losses for decades, or who are living happy, productive lives despite a history that includes suicide attempts, severe depression, or several hospitalizations. We see people face cancer, disabilities, and even the death of loved ones while maintaining their abstinence. It is difficult to deny that some Power is helping them.

Given our own experience, no matter how short our time in FA, any of us has the data we need to at least become willing to believe. If we feel rebellious, we recall the misery of our addictive eating. Those memories make us more flexible. We don't want to repeat the past.

Step Three: Made a decision to turn our will and our lives over to the care of God as we understood Him.

Step Three frightens us, but it becomes as gentle as it is meant to be when we slow down and look carefully at each phrase. First, we need to remember that no one is asking us to turn our will and lives over to God. Instead, we are being asked to "make a decision" to turn our will and lives over to the "care" of God. Further, this "God" is not the deity we'd rejected when young or questioned when older. We are free to reach our own understanding of whatever Higher Power there might be.

Making a decision to turn our will over to the care of "God" may still seem threatening at first. What would "God" ask us to do? Quit our job? Leave our marriage? Move to another continent and become a missionary? And how are we to understand "God's" will?

Many of us find it helpful to return to the phrase "Higher Power" at this point. We begin there. Even without knowing "God," we do have some experience to draw upon. After all, we've been able to stop eating addictively when we've asked for help from whatever Higher Power there might be. We also have to admit that we are aware of at least one aspect of that Power's will: Surely we are not to return to addictive eating.

Knowing those facts, we have everything we need. Whenever we are confused, we ask our Higher Power to take care of our will—to guide us to the choice that supports our recovery and to give us the strength and willingness to follow through appropriately. Rather than being an esoteric exercise, this request turns out to involve a lot of common sense. Could it be our Higher Power's will that we spend days making cookies for a big grammar school bake sale, immersing ourselves in the tempting smells of desserts we know we can't safely eat? Obviously not. If we are embarrassed by an error we've made, does our Higher Power want us to lie and blame someone else? Again, certainly not. No one imposes imperatives on us, but we see clearly that if we violate our own values or willfully ignore danger signs regarding food, our discomfort will eventually drive us back to addictive eating.

Once we make a decision to give our will to the care of our Higher Power, we need the reassurance that it is safe to do so. We tried our hardest to run our own lives and the results nearly killed us, so we can surely experiment safely with another approach for just one day. We don't have to do it forever. We can make a decision to try, knowing that we can change our mind later if the new approach doesn't work. Why not try to relax and let go a little, trusting that the Power that keeps us abstinent can take care of us and help us face whatever challenges us in a given day?

The more we try this approach, the more peace we experience in our lives. One day at a time, we begin to ask our Higher Power for help with the problems that have always frightened us: our relationship with troubled teenaged children, layoffs at work, misunderstandings with our spouses or partners, issues with our health.

Morning by morning, we practice trust that we will receive the help we need and that the outcome will be bearable, manageable, and ultimately good. The results of our trust amaze us.

Fortunately, as hard as it first looks, Step Three is possible for all of us. We cannot proceed without it. Because we give our will and our lives to our Higher Power's good care, we can ask for and receive the willingness and strength we need to face our past.

CHAPTER 8

Facing the Past—Steps 4–9

THE NEXT SIX STEPS enable us to look at who we have been and what we have done. We'd never need these Steps if we were comfortable with ourselves. Instead, when we are honest, we have to admit that we feel shame, remorse, and guilt whenever we think of some of our past behavior. We need to stop and take stock of ourselves.

Step Four: Made a searching and fearless moral inventory of ourselves.

Step Four would be difficult for anyone, but it is particularly hard for us food addicts. While we can admit there were problems with our own behavior, it is far easier and more natural for us to blame others for our troubles. If people hadn't treated us as badly as they have and if life hadn't dealt us the blows we've suffered, we wouldn't be the way we are!

In our AWOLs, we are led to focus on ourselves. Leaving aside any analysis of the wrongs of others, we take an inventory of our own shortcomings. When have we been resentful, selfish, dishonest, or unfairly critical? How often have we been driven by anger or fear? What impact has our behavior had on our children, spouses, or partners? There is plenty for us to see.

Alcoholics Anonymous reminds us that no business owner takes an inventory of stock in his or her head. The assessment has to be done in writing. Our sponsors and AWOL leaders give us needed guidance. They remind us that we need to write freely. Our inventories are for our Higher Power and ourselves only, so good grammar, neat handwriting, and correct punctuation are irrelevant. Unless we are injured, they urge us to write by hand. They say this will help us be honest. The words will flow directly from our hearts, and we will have to work more slowly than we would if we were sitting before a computer, editing while writing.

Following our sponsors' suggestions, we pray for help before we begin. We're bolstered by their assurance that our Higher Power will never show us more than we can handle. There are memories that frighten us or evoke intense regret and shame, but if we feel we want to avoid a topic, we especially ask our Higher Power for the willingness to write about it.

We're grateful for concrete advice. Our sponsors remind us to be mindful of our abstinence while we are writing our inventories. It's easy to turn back toward addictive eating when we feel uncomfortable, so they urge us to maintain the simplicity and discipline of our lives and our food plans. They also help us to stay focused. Inevitably, as we write, we fearfully imagine the next

Step, when we'll have to talk about all we've discovered. "The Fifth Step will never be as you expect it to be, so don't think about it now. Stay right where you are on Step Four," they say.

Step Four isn't easy, but it's always possible. We have two choices: examine ourselves and continue in our recovery, or run away again and ultimately return to addictive eating. Whenever we balk, we go back to Step Three, reminding ourselves that we've made a decision to rely on our Higher Power's help whenever we feel resistant or afraid.

Step Five: Admitted to God, ourselves, and to another human being the exact nature of our wrongs.

The Fourth Step confronts us with some unpleasant truths. Naturally, when we first approach this Step, we want to avoid facing anyone who is part of our lives and thus might know us long term. Better to deal with a stranger! If we have to talk with someone, why not go on a retreat and speak with a priest? Failing that, a therapist or life coach seems like a good option—someone we can choose to leave and never see again.

Long experience in FA convinces us that we food addicts are isolators. Whether we look like party people or loners, all of us have tried to keep many aspects of ourselves hidden. This reinforces our addiction. Resentments stand intact. Distorted perceptions of ourselves remain unquestioned.

Because of our tendency to hide, we do not turn to outsiders. Instead, we make all necessary arrangements to share our inventories with our sponsors. They understand food addiction and the Fourth and Fifth Steps as no one else can. In addition, they know us well. More than anyone else, they can help us see the parts of our personalities and the patterns of behavior that drive our addiction. We can't hide from them.

In FA, both the sponsor and the sponsee make the Fifth Step a high priority. There is no substitute for face-to-face interaction. When we live far from our sponsors, we may speak with them daily by phone and yet never see them. In such cases, even if we are separated by hundreds of miles, one of us flies to the other—sometimes as far as from Australia to Massachusetts or California to Tennessee. This requires planning, effort, and perhaps some financial sacrifices, but with help from our Higher Power, we manage. When we want to get well, we find a way.

Our sponsors help us carefully choose the time and the place for our Fifth Step. Sometimes one or both of us has to take time off from work. Because we must freely speak of anything and everything that has most deeply troubled us, our sponsors carefully protect our privacy. They avoid restaurants, parks, beaches, or rooms where our conversation might be overheard by members of either of our families. They also choose times when children won't be returning home from school or neighbors dropping by.

By sharing our inventories with our sponsors, we grow by a quantum leap. We hide nothing, yet, to our amazement, we are met with calm acceptance. As we speak and our sponsors talk about their own experiences, we begin to lose our lifelong feelings of isolation. We see as never before that we are neither terrible nor unique. We are simply human.

After we are done, our sponsors remind us to take an hour of quiet time by ourselves, as recommended by *Alcoholics Anonymous.* They also gently encourage us to set aside any expectations regarding the outcome of the Fifth Step. Some of us experience immediate relief; others may feel raw or vulnerable for a while. Regardless, we are all grateful for the help we've received to look at ourselves.

Most of all, through the acceptance we feel from our sponsors, we gain a new sense of our Higher Power. We understand that this Power surely must accept us as fully as our sponsors do, and thus we become better able to accept ourselves. Only then can we begin to change.

Step Six: Were entirely ready to have God remove all these defects of character.

Step Seven: Humbly asked Him to remove our shortcomings.

When new to FA, many of us have difficulty understanding or remembering Steps Six and Seven, but the need for them becomes obvious as we progress in our recovery. After writing and sharing our inventories, we are painfully aware of the shortcomings that have been revealed to us, yet we repeatedly fall back into old behaviors. Before we can stop ourselves, we berate our children or make unreasonable demands of others we love.

Whenever we are discouraged, our sponsors remind us that we've never had the power to change ourselves. In joining the program, we had to admit that we couldn't control the way we ate. Now we have to accept that we can't alter ourselves—at least not by our unaided will.

Steps Six and Seven carefully set us on a path of conscious change. Brilliantly, the founders of AA saw that before we can go to a Higher Power for help with our defects of character, we have to make sure that we are willing to let them go.

As discussions continue in AWOL, we are surprised to discover our own ambivalence. Certain character defects yield benefits we depend on. Initially, it seems easy to let go of dishonesty, for example. None of us wants to embezzle funds at work or blatantly lie to our children. But when it comes to seemingly innocuous lies that allow us to snag a sick day when we aren't sick or dishonestly apply for unemployment, we may be reluctant to embrace full honesty.

If we don't want to let go of a shortcoming, we pray for willingness. We cannot will ourselves to be willing, but food is the ultimate convincer. Whatever our bluster or denial, we know that we feel terrible about ourselves when we violate our own values and standards. Because such uncomfortable feelings will surely force us back to addictive eating, we accept that our old attitudes and behaviors are no longer an option. We have to be willing to change.

Steps Six and Seven are action Steps. We can't expect to be the passive recipients of a transformation. Each day, in all the little moments of our lives, we seek the power and mindfulness to make choices we aren't used to making. Our prayers are concrete: "Please help me praise my daughter instead of criticizing her" or "Please help me let go of my anxiety and do the best I can with the bills I've been avoiding." Gratefully relying on God's power, we make progress. Perfection is never possible, but when we fall, we fall forward, and inch by inch, we begin to change.

Step Eight: Made a list of all persons we had harmed, and became willing to make amends to them all.

As hard as it is to face our shortcomings, it is sometimes even harder to write a list of the people we have harmed. We shudder at the thought of approaching some who belong on our list. We don't want to, despite the promise that this will free us from our regrets about the past.

Our AWOL leaders remind us to stay on Step Eight. Whether we are willing to approach particular people is irrelevant. Our job is simple: to consider whom we have harmed and how. Since our list is for our eyes only, we put it in a place where no one might accidently find it.

As we pray and begin to write our list, we think most immediately of obvious wrongs: incidents of stealing or of money borrowed and never returned, of unfaithfulness in love relationships, of lies and broken promises, and, often, patterns of rage, criticism, or unfair blame. The Fourth and Fifth Steps also help us see the damage we've done because of our self-centeredness—our withdrawal from those who care about us and our inability to see or respond to their needs.

The objective, balanced perspective of our sponsors is essential as we make our lists. Sometimes we lose sight of our own part in a relationship gone bad, or we take blame when none belongs with us. If we've suffered sexual abuse, violence, or incest, we might need help to see that no one had the right to mistreat us and that we owe no amends to the abuser for the abuse.

Our AWOL leaders and sponsors always encourage us to look carefully at our families and ourselves. We soon see that family members belong on our list. Even if they have wronged us, we keep the focus on ourselves. There are plenty of reasons to regret our own behavior— the lies we told so we could be alone to eat, for example, or the many times we criticized or disengaged. We usually need help to see that we ourselves also belong on our list. We've done the best we could, but we've damaged ourselves terribly with food and with the self-destructive choices we've made in almost every area of our lives.

The list of people we have harmed changes over time. As we grow in our abstinence and recovery, our vision and understanding increase. Progressing from one AWOL to another, we refer to our list each time, adding more names as they come to us and noting when we've completed an amends.

Step Nine: Made direct amends to such people wherever possible, except when to do so would injure them or others.

It often takes time, prayer, and many conversations before we begin to understand Step Nine. In making an amends, we need to do much more than say we are sorry.

An amends represents our best effort to right a wrong. Face to face if possible, we are to fully admit what we have done and then make restitution, either financially or through our changed behavior. The well-being of the person we are approaching is our first priority, and our amends are to be offered without any expectation or demand that we be forgiven.

Throughout the discussions of Steps Eight and Nine, our AWOL leaders warn us against premature attempts to make amends. Sometimes, without realizing our true motives, we selfishly want to relieve our feelings of guilt and remorse as soon as we can. Rushing forward before we clearly grasp Step Nine, we risk causing greater harm and permanent damage.

Before we approach anyone we've wronged, it is imperative that we wait until we have completed discussion of Step Nine in our AWOLs, made a commitment to take that Step, and talked about our plans with our sponsors. Even then, we have to check ourselves first to see if we are ready. We ask ourselves several questions:

Do we truly understand exactly what we have done in terms of our own shortcomings and motives?

Has our behavior changed? If we are continuing to yell at our children many times a day, for example, a verbal apology offers only empty words.

Are we still angry? If so, we probably can't clearly see and acknowledge our own part in a problem. Acting before we're ready, we might justify ourselves. "I wouldn't have yelled at you if you hadn't been so demanding!" we might say, blaming our victim. Ill will can also surface in clumsy apologies for our resentment or jealousy. We cause further harm if the people we're addressing had no idea we were angry.

Are we sure that our amends won't cause further harm? Will it bring up memories a person might find painful or unnecessarily confront someone with matters we should face on our own? In our intimate relationships we have to be especially careful. If we have been unfaithful or abusive, we need ample time, prayer, and discussion with our sponsors before we take any action. We have to be certain that we aren't secretly wishing for some kind of revenge or trying to escape our feelings of guilt. No matter how bad we feel, it is never appropriate to seek out a former lover if reopening communication could negatively affect anyone involved—our current lover, our former lover, or that lover's current partner or children.

Any amends requires preparation. In prayer and quiet time, we first ask our Higher Power if we should proceed. If the timing is right, we think carefully about where and when we should make the amends. As with a Fifth Step, privacy and ample time are imperative. One member regretfully remembers attempting to make an amends to her mother while they were eating lunch in a crowded cafe, just before they went to a movie. The amends was hurried and careless because the member was not yet spiritually ready. A true amends followed many years later, only after she'd more completely let go of her anger and fear.

We may unexpectedly run into someone and know on the spot that we should make our amends immediately, but in general, it is safest to talk beforehand with our sponsors. We need help considering a variety of questions. Should we make an amends by letter or wait many months until we can go back to our old neighborhood in person? If a letter seems better, is the draft we've written clear and free of any trace of bitterness or blame? Do we seem to be on the right footing and ready to proceed?

Our sponsors occasionally counsel that we wait. Sometimes they see anger or confusion in us, or they are aware that our negative behaviors have not yet changed. Other times, they sense our fear and urge us to go to God for help with our anxiety or lingering resentment so we can avoid further delay. Always, they help us keep the well-being of the person we want to approach foremost in our mind. The welfare of that person must guide what, when, how, and whether we are to communicate with him or her.

We all have moments when our pride makes us resist or we feel afraid of the consequences of our amends. Remembering that we have decided to give our will to the care of our Higher Power, we can pray until we are willing to move ahead, regardless of what might happen to us. One member lied on her financial aid application and had to meet with a dean to say so, risking loss of needed support. Many of us have made face-to-face financial amends to the managers of stores from which we've stolen.

Even when it seems impossible, we find a way to do the Ninth Step. If the people we wronged have died, we can make our amends in quiet time and prayer, turning our spirit toward theirs and expressing our regret. We can visit their graves to be with them and can sometimes make logical recompense to someone else. If we neglected our grandparents, and they are no longer alive, we might give our attention instead to an elderly aunt or a neighbor who needs us now. Our changed attitudes and actions become a key part of our amends. We think of what we can do for others instead of worrying about what we can gain for ourselves.

Many of us have difficulty righting some of the greatest wrongs we have committed: the physical and mental abuse we've inflicted on ourselves. Abstinence is the first and most important amend we make to ourselves and others. With abstinence as our foundation, we are slowly able to change our attitudes and choices. Instead of avoiding medical help, we schedule regular appointments and address any problems related to our health, eyesight, and teeth. When we are ready and have time, we listen to our longings rather than denying them, returning to school for a degree or learning to play an instrument if we wish. We consciously turn away from berating ourselves and use our quiet time to ask for a change in how we see and treat ourselves.

Abstinence is and will continue to be our biggest and most important amend to ourselves and to others, as the AA literature reminds us, but abstinence alone is never enough. We have to take concrete action, as well. When we are not yet willing or clear about what we should do, we pray and wait until our Higher Power makes us ready.

CHAPTER 9

A Daily Inventory—Step 10

I N THE FIRST THREE STEPS, we admit our powerlessness and turn to a Higher Power for help. Steps Four through Nine enable us to face the past and address the damage we've done. When we are thorough, we are finally ready and able to live in the present, but only by doing the last three Steps each day can we sustain our recovery.

Step Ten: Continued to take personal inventory and when we were wrong, promptly admitted it.

We may notice an irrational and unconscious expectation in ourselves as we do all the Steps. Though we know theoretically that no human being is perfect, we somehow expect to live a mistake-free existence. Are we saints? Are we angels? How do our haloes look?

No haloes here! In Step Ten, as we look for our own shortcomings, we remember that we're imperfect and try to keep a sense of humor. *Oh, no!* we laugh in our better moments. *Arguing with my five-year-old again?! Really, what's the matter with a yellow skirt and purple shoes if that's what she wants to wear? And can't I let my husband handle his clean socks in peace? Do I have to instruct him regarding his folding technique?* Sometimes we catch ourselves before it's too late. *Whoa there*, we think, *shouldn't I call customer service instead of beating my computer with a baseball bat?*

Step Ten provides needed humility and the ability to stay aware of our defects of character. We will never be perfect, no matter how many AWOLs we complete or how often we pray.

To help us avoid trouble before we are hip deep in it, we learn to stop throughout the day whenever we are uncomfortable.

Asking our Higher Power to help us see ourselves, we often spot shortcomings. Perhaps we lashed out defensively when a colleague offered a constructive suggestion, or, if we tend toward timidity, we might have failed to speak up when we were treated rudely. Over time, if we continue to take no action, we place our abstinence at risk. A dangerous kernel of discomfort takes root in us. As addicts, we can't tolerate such feelings long term without returning to addictive eating. As the saying goes, we are, by our nature, "comfort- and relief-seeking missiles."

The Serenity Prayer helps us think and discern appropriate action. "God, grant me the serenity to accept the things I cannot change, the courage to change the things I can, and the wisdom to know the difference." There is always something we cannot change: a person, place, or situation. Inevitably, too, there is something we *can* alter: our own attitudes and choices. Turning to our Higher Power in prayer and talking with our sponsors and others in our program, we seek to learn what we should do. If we owe an apology, we make it, acknowledging our part in the problem and expressing our intent to do better. If the problem is not ours, we ask God to help us let go and leave it to God's care.

Each night, after we thank our Higher Power for our abstinence, we take an inventory of our day and ourselves. When have we helped others, and when has God aided us? Have we chosen fear instead of faith or anger instead of generosity?

Our old self would have flinched from these daily inventories, but we come to welcome them. Whether we've been abstinent one month or twenty years, we find that we still need to examine ourselves. With time, we're better able to maintain a level-headed sense of perspective and a dash of humor. Sober self-awareness is quite different from self-hate, and haloes are not among our options.

At the end of our inventory, we place the cares of the day in God's hands. If we are willing to let resentments, sharp self-criticism, and anxiety slip to the floor beside us, we can get into bed with a sense of hope and peace.

Chapter 10

Prayer and Meditation—Step 11

Step Eleven: Sought through prayer and meditation to improve our conscious contact with God as we understood Him, praying only for knowledge of His will for us and the power to carry that out.

By the time we reach Step Eleven, we know a little about prayer. We ask our Higher Power each morning for the willingness to stay abstinent that day, and we say thank you at night. Our sponsors have already introduced us to meditation.

Despite such beginnings, however, we don't always feel secure in our connection with a Higher Power. We understand the necessity that we make a decision to turn our will and lives over to the care of God each day, but we may not be exactly sure how to do that. Uncertain about the difference between our will and God's will, we sometimes still feel confusion and anxiety as we approach major, and even minor, decisions.

Further, because of FA and abstinence, our lives increase in complexity and richness, leaving us with an even greater need for a Higher Power. Although we cope more maturely and effectively, Step One is powerfully real to us. Still dogged by many shortcomings, we may not yet be confident in our relationships, and our lives often feel unmanageable.

Step Eleven opens the way for us to enter into a daily relationship with a Power that can give us the guidance and security we need to live comfortably. With the help of our sponsors and AWOL, we begin turning to our Higher Power with anything that troubles or confuses us. Should we take a new job? Is it time to speak to our angry daughter now, or should we give her time to calm down first? Instead of assuming we are facing our problems alone, we try trusting that we'll be given an understanding of what we should do and the strength to do it.

Gradually, we learn to go to our Higher Power with every aspect of our lives. Of course, we avoid frivolous or selfish prayers. We don't ask for fancier cars or more jewelry, but we openly tell God of our deepest wishes and hopes, making sure to end our prayers by acknowledging our acceptance of God's will. Given our history, it is clear that we don't necessarily know what is best for us or others. "Watch out what you pray for," our friends laugh, telling stories of times they prayed for and got their own way, to their later dismay. Ending our prayers with "Thy will be done" or "If it be Thy will" makes sense.

It's often said that prayer is the act of speaking to God and meditation is the act of listening. In FA, though we commonly speak of "quiet time," we mean meditation.

In the beginning, many of us thought that taking a long walk, sitting on an empty beach with a cup of coffee, driving in our car with the radio and CD player off, or other quiet activities would fulfill the need for quiet time. We soon learn, however, that we have to seek a deeper stillness if we want to make ourselves as present as possible to our Higher Power.

Physical relaxation is a spiritual act for a food addict. Most of us describe our past selves as "tense" or "tightly wound." We had trouble trusting people and generally adopted a defensive posture, expecting the worst of the world. Letting go physically thus becomes an act of trust.

Commonly, we make ourselves as comfortable as possible before we start our quiet time. We don't intend to sleep, so we don't lie down, but we find a posture that relieves us of any physical stress or strain. We take off our glasses if we wear them and cover ourselves well if we tend to be cold.

After we shut our eyes, we each find our own way toward quietness. It's helpful to remember our intent: to relax in the presence of our Higher Power, to open ourselves to guidance, to let go of the burden of our own wills and wishes, and to stay still for at least thirty minutes. Some begin by releasing tension from each part of their body; others turn immediately toward their Higher Power. We can start with a prayer or focus on our breathing. A passage from *Twenty-Four Hours a Day*, our daily meditation book, may draw us, or a single word repeated slowly may calm us.

In quiet time, we slow down. The rush of daily activity blocks the small voice we hear inside when we are still. Sometimes we hear words of guidance—*go,* or *stay.* Other times, we're simply aware of a feeling that nudges us strongly in a direction we know is right. *Make amends now,* or *Don't make yet another empty apology; change your behavior instead!*

When we begin the practice of quiet time, almost all of us struggle. Our minds jump like rabbits. Our bodies are tense. Popping open our eyes to check the clock, we wonder repeatedly if our half hour has been completed yet. Fortunately, perseverance pays off. Though it sometimes takes almost the full thirty minutes, we begin to experience a comfortable, comforting peace.

We soon learn to make quiet time a top priority by scheduling a regular time for it, usually in the morning before we begin our day. We start to understand this as a necessity. Life does not go well if we cut ourselves off from the Power that gives us the willingness and strength to abstain. Eventually, we also begin to count on the peace we find in quiet time, looking forward to it with a feeling of need.

No one can ever rightly claim to have a perfect understanding of God's will, but with time, we become more practiced at recognizing it. One primary marker is whether a course of action will support our abstinence. We *know* that our Higher Power doesn't want us to destroy ourselves or harm others by a return to addictive eating. When we feel most conflicted, we can always begin by looking for the action that most strengthens and protects our abstinence.

We notice other signs. When we pray and take the time to listen, we aren't led to choices that put us at odds with our own nature and values. We become aware of hidden motives. One member remembers wistfully envying friends who became doctors. For several years she considered applying to medical school. Only in FA did her Higher Power help her see that she simply wanted the title "doctor." She actually had little aptitude for medicine.

God's way also seems signaled by circumstances that easily fall into place. We can't hear the quiet, inner voice of guidance unless we stay open to all options, even those that initially seem unappealing or unlikely. When we feel like we are beating our heads repeatedly against a single spot on a concrete wall, we often find that we are leading with our own will rather than seeking God's. We've demanded a new job, a baby or a spouse, a different house, a higher salary—on our timetable, in our way. Through the Steps, we begin to understand the need for patience, acceptance, and personal exertion. If we want something, we need to work for it.

FA teaches each of us to listen for the voice of our own Higher Power. Wisely, we are warned of the dangers of arrogantly leaping forward alone. We talk with our sponsors and other experienced members before making major decisions, but through prayer and quiet time, as *Alcoholics Anonymous* promises, we began to "intuitively know how to handle situations that used to baffle us."

No one in FA is, was, or ever will be perfect, but each day, through Step Eleven, we use prayer and meditation in practical and concrete ways to help us live our lives. "God," one member prayed, "show me clearly your will.

How can I help my drug-addicted son?" Another turned to God many times a day as she struggled with her disappointed hopes to become pregnant. "Please, God," she prayed, "if it be your will, may I get pregnant. Please give me a baby or else help me accept that my husband and I can't have another child."

Step Eleven takes time. Sometimes several years pass before we finally calm down and begin to feel the presence of God. Nonetheless, each day, we practice and try again, understanding that we can't gain conscious contact with our Higher Power on our own terms. To develop that contact, we have to accept a way of life based on a disciplined habit of prayer, meditation, and self-reflection. We need to let go of frenetic activity and practice patience, humbly accepting that God's timetable for sending answers and resolving problems probably won't match our own. Above all, we need faith—the expectation that God wants to communicate with us and will give us the answers we seek.

Chapter 11

A Way of Life—Step 12

Step Twelve: Having had a spiritual awakening as the result of these steps, we tried to carry this message to food addicts, and to practice these principles in all our affairs.

S TEP TWELVE ASSUMES that we have had a "spiritual awakening." By the time we reach Step Twelve, we see that this is true. A Higher Power is no longer an abstract concept to us. Instead, we have a working faith. Increasingly, we rely on our Higher Power. We ask for help and practice trusting we'll receive it.

Discussions in AWOL help us see another aspect of our spiritual awakening. In the past, we were always at the center of our own universe. Our feelings and wishes dominated our consciousness and shaped our priorities. We believed ourselves to have been deprived—we never received enough love, attention, money, or opportunities. Even when we seemed most generous, we rarely, if ever, gave with no strings attached. In return for kindness, we expected appreciation and praise.

As we approach Step Twelve, if we've been rigorously abstinent and have honestly done the preceding eleven Steps, we are not the people we were before. To the best of our ability, we avoid lying or exaggeration to boost our image or gain an advantage. When we make commitments, we keep them, and when we are wrong, we admit it. We are less judgmental, more generous, and kinder to our families and friends. These changes in our personality are the result of our efforts to know and do God's will. Once we become aware of them, we know we've had a spiritual awakening.

Step Twelve describes an urge that flows naturally from the Eleventh Step: the wish to pass on the gifts of abstinence and recovery that have been given to us. It is also a call to action, however. *Because* we have been spiritually transformed, we are responsible for carrying FA's message of hope to those who still suffer from food addiction.

Our sponsors see life within FA as an endless opportunity to help someone else, and they urge us to participate. First, they remind us that our primary form of service is to stay abstinent ourselves. This spares our families and everyone around us the destructive effects of our active addiction. They then point out many other ways we can be helpful in FA. We can add to any group's strength by attending regularly and arriving early. We can help set up chairs or offer a friendly word to someone who arrives alone. With more abstinence, we become able to lead meetings, answer the questions of newcomers, sponsor others, and participate in FA work beyond our local level.

In the beginning, even the prospect of the most modest service makes many of us uncomfortable. We are particularly nervous about speaking at meetings and sponsoring, but whenever we want to hide, our sponsors explain why we must offer whatever help we can.

First and foremost, our sponsors say, if we don't reach out to other addicts and talk about our addiction, we'll forget that our disease is incurable. Service helps us remember that we are in remission from food addiction for just one day and only if we continue to live the Twelve Steps.

Second, they remind us that while we need FA to stay abstinent, FA also needs us. The existence of our meetings depends on the service of each member. Someone has to unlock the room, arrange for speakers, greet newcomers, and inform the public of our meeting times and places.

Third, they promise that service will set us free from the miserable self-centeredness that used to force us to turn to food. If we look for ways to help others, our daily troubles and worries recede in importance. We gain a more balanced perspective on our lives and have the deep satisfaction of being useful members of our fellowship.

When we resist, our sponsors tend to bring up humility. Perhaps we don't want to speak at meetings because we are comparing ourselves to others or are afraid we'll be judged. We criticize ourselves for being less articulate or organized. They point out that we may have confused sharing about recovery with a performance. Have we forgotten to ask our Higher Power to use us for good, or have we overlooked the simplicity of our goal? We're trying to help others by talking about our own experience of the progressive illness of food addiction and the source of our recovery. Who knows more about the effects of food addiction on our lives than we do?

When we are afraid to sponsor, our sponsors remind us that we are probably overreaching ourselves. Again they suggest that instead of comparing ourselves to others whom we admire, we practice more humility. Our role is to help our sponsees find their own Higher Power, simply by sharing our personal experience. It isn't our place to tell people that we will "let" them do something or to forbid them to do something else. We don't have to be—and shouldn't attempt to be—social workers, therapists, marriage counselors, dating coaches, or spiritual leaders. As fallible food addicts in recovery, all we can offer are our suggestions and thoughts about how we gained abstinence and maintain it. Sponsees hold the tool of sponsorship in their own hands. If they don't want our suggestions or trust our recovery, honesty requires that they move on to another sponsor of their choice.

As we continue in abstinence, recovery, and service, we discover that our sponsors are right. We *need* to give service. When we feel cravings for the foods we used to eat, or when anxiety about work or family makes us think too much about ourselves or our next meal, reaching out to a newcomer relieves our obsession and worries as nothing else can.

We also come alive to a new sense of responsibility. No longer suffering ourselves, we want to help those who are still struggling with addiction. Our perspective shifts. We look at FA in terms of what we can give, rather than what we can get, and we make the needs of those who are new our first concern. At meetings, rather than socializing with sponsees or friends, we make an effort to turn to newcomers and to those who are sitting alone. We schedule FA meetings at times that support the recovery of newer members, and urge ourselves to telephone or respond to a call from a fellow member, even when we are busy.

Sometimes we have the opportunity to do Twelfth Step work when people who know us ask why we are so much healthier and happier than we used to be. Other times, we ask God for a way to bring up the subject of FA with someone who is suffering. The book *Alcoholics Anonymous* reminds us to avoid promotion. Rather than pushing people to attend a meeting or haranguing them about their eating, we serve them best by remaining abstinent ourselves. When they are ready and reach out to us, we talk about our personal experience with food addiction, give them some literature, and, if possible, invite them to a meeting.

Need and duty first motivate our Twelfth Step involvement, but our experiences are far from grim. More than any other activity in our lives, Twelfth Step work gives us joy and security. We can make gold out of the most painful aspects of our past. We were spared spiritual and physical death when someone in FA reached out to us. Through the Twelfth Step, we can pass on the gift we've received. The satisfaction and privilege of playing a role in another's recovery will never be matched by any worldly honor or reward.

The final part of the Twelfth Step helps us make FA our way of life. We are advised to "practice these principles in all our affairs"—to use the Steps inside and outside of FA to guide and strengthen us in every aspect of our lives.

The practices of honesty, self-reflection, gratitude, and service guide us wherever we are, but we often find it hardest to apply FA principles in our relationships with our families. Our early abstinence may be as difficult for our parents, spouses, and children as it is for us. In many ways, we become strangers to them. They feel pushed aside and are angry and hurt.

Often, we are angry, too. Our addiction numbed us. In abstinence, we wake up. Patterns that had been established for years suddenly feel unacceptable. We may be hurt or enraged by the passivity or remoteness of our partner or spouse. When we seek to reestablish intimacy, we are dismayed to discover ancient resentments that divide us. Our teenage children may rebel against reasonable boundaries, and relatives may criticize our unwillingness to spend hours cooking the family's favorite dishes.

To practice FA's Steps and principles within our families, we have to stop blaming others for the conflicts we experience and look instead at ourselves. What part have we played in creating the difficulties that plague us? Has our spouse or partner withdrawn from us because we have long since emotionally abandoned him or her? Struggling with intimacy ourselves, have we chosen a partner who would never demand it of us? Are we verbally abusive? Do we smother, neglect, or angrily try to control our children?

One long-time FA member vividly remembers the turmoil in her marriage after she came to the program. Her account of how she responded is probably relevant to anyone with family or intimate friends who are having trouble adjusting to a loved one being in the program:

> When I first came into FA, I was totally self-centered. I wasn't thinking about how my husband or children felt. I wasn't thinking of them at all. Everything was about me.
>
> Before I began FA, my husband did anything he could to please me. He drove me wherever I needed to go, waited for me without complaint, and bought the foods I liked to eat. Then, I found the program. Suddenly I was on the telephone talking to FA friends all the time, and he was sitting by himself. I was running out to meetings. He was at home with a house full of kids. When I came back, I was filled with smiles and life. It was almost as if I had another lover. My focus was on recovery and he was cut out. He had no role anymore.
>
> My husband began to get angry. He became so distant that at one point, I felt I'd have to choose between my marriage and this program. I had four kids. I didn't want a divorce! I called someone in the program, crying, and said that I had to leave. She said only one thing: "You can't."
>
> I prayed and cried and then I heard a voice that said, "You have to talk with him." So, for the first time,

I told my husband the truth. I'd always said I was tired. I'd never admitted that I was depressed or afraid, that I couldn't stand my sense of failure and didn't care anymore whether or not I woke up in the morning. Addictive eating did that to me.

My husband listened and then told me he wanted me to go to the program. That was the beginning of everything changing. When I invited him to come to a meeting, he appreciated being included, and he felt better once he saw what was going on.

If we could only think of how our families might be feeling! Now I tell people who are struggling like I was to be sure to be open. We need to tell the truth about why we're going to FA so everyone can understand that we really have to go.

After I'd been abstinent a while, I noticed a difference in our home. I realized that I was the one who had needed to change. Eating addictively, I'd been irritable and angry. When I had a bad day, the kids fought. Then my husband yelled, and pretty soon everyone was tense. I learned that when I got crazy, everyone got crazy. When I got abstinent and sane, sanity permeated our home.

This member's memories match the experiences of many of us. In the beginning, most of us were unaware of our own self-centeredness. With time and abstinence, however, we got better at practicing the twelve-step principles outside and inside our homes. As we became more honest and humble, more respectful and generous, in almost all cases, our family members, colleagues, and friends began to respond in kind.

Chapter 12

There Is Hope

WE HOPE THAT OUR personal stories and our discussion of food addiction and the Twelve Steps have been helpful to you. Above all, we wish to share with you the gift we've received from FA: the understanding that abstinence and long-term recovery are possible.

Knowledge of our illness freed us. When we first met and listened to people speak in FA, we learned that we weren't weak willed. We weren't lazy gluttons. Our shame and self-disgust began to lift as we acknowledged that we might be food addicts. We weren't bad people. We were ill. And we were no longer alone. There was nothing we had eaten and no behavior of ours related to food that shocked anyone in an FA meeting. They understood us completely. They could identify with our experience, and, we soon discovered, we could identify with theirs.

Most important, we began to feel hope. This was not the familiar, fleeting faith of our past—the high expectations we used to have as we approached yet another diet.

Instead, we saw solid proof of the impossible. We met people who were just like us, but who were free from obsession. They were slender, comfortable in their bodies, and happy. They'd found a way of life that gave them peace and stability, sustaining them through every joy and challenge.

If you've never been to FA and our stories have touched you, please consider attending a meeting. Should there be no meeting nearby, you can contact us through our website (www.foodaddicts.ORG). Once we are in touch with you by telephone or email, we can connect you with other FA members who can guide and encourage you. We promise: *No one will ever put you on a scale or embarrass you, whatever your weight. Your privacy will be assured, and you will be charged no fees. FA is free.*

Whether you are able to go to a meeting or not, please remember our stories. Know that you are not alone. There is help. And there is always hope.

Appendices

✧ ✧ ✧

Some Frequently Used Terms

Abstinence. Freedom from addictive eating. FA's abstinence is the equivalent of AA's sobriety. Based on a specific, individual food plan worked out with an FA sponsor, it consists of weighed and measured meals exclusive of foods made with flour or sugar and any eating between mealtimes. The FA definition of abstinence—and abstinent FA members—existed long before the formal establishment of FA as a distinctive program and organization. For a fuller discussion of abstinence, please see chapter 2 and the history of FA in appendix 2.

Alcoholics Anonymous. Affectionately referred to as the "Big Book" by members of AA and FA, *Alcoholics Anonymous* was the first written source for recovery in AA. It played a key role in the development of FA and has helped shape individual recovery within the program ever since.

AWOL. AWOL (A Way of Life) is the foundation of abstinence and recovery in FA. Developed by a treatment center in Canada, AWOL is a structured process for the study of the Twelve Steps. In AWOL groups or, less frequently, one on one with their sponsors, abstinent FA members focus on each Step in sequence, completing one before beginning the next. AWOL groups function independently from FA as a whole. They are not governed by any individual or organization, and no FA member is required to join one.

Big Book. Refers to *Alcoholics Anonymous*, the primary source for recovery in AA and FA.

FA. Refers to Food Addicts in Recovery Anonymous.

Food Addiction and Food Addicts. Addiction has been described as a progressive illness in which an individual develops a physical, mental, and emotional dependence on a substance or behavior—in the case of food addiction, a dependence on unlimited quantities of food or foods made with flour or sugar. Overeating, undereating, bulimia through purging or overexercising, tasting and chewing without swallowing, and obsession with weight or food are some of the symptoms of food addiction. The manifestations of the illness are not necessarily physically apparent. Some food addicts are overweight, some are severely underweight, and some are able to maintain a normal size.

Higher Power. As food addicts, FA members turn to a Power greater than themselves for the strength to remain abstinent. Each person finds and develops his or her own relationship with this Power. Some call it God. Others do not. FA is a spiritual, not a religious, program.

Meetings, Committed Meetings. The leaders and those who speak at FA meetings must have at least ninety days of continuous abstinence. Speakers are encouraged to talk specifically about their experience of food addiction and FA recovery. Leadership is rotated. Because food addiction is rooted in the sufferer's tendency to isolate, FA meetings are always held in person—not on the Internet or via the telephone. FA members who have attained long-term abstinence always stress the importance of making recovery their top priority. They attend the same meetings each week, referring to them as their "committed meetings."

The Program. Used as a synonym for FA and for the practices and attitudes that support FA recovery.

Quiet Time. A daily period of prayer, meditation, and contact with one's own Higher Power.

Sponsor and Sponsee. Sponsors are experienced, abstinent FA members who introduce newcomers to FA and guide them in their recovery. The helpful, one-on-one relationship with a sponsor continues as less experienced members ("sponsees") progress in their recovery and become sponsors themselves. Each member chooses his or her own sponsor, guided by the commonly heard suggestion "Find a sponsor who has what you want and ask how it was achieved."

The Tools. The tools are actions that help FA members obtain and sustain abstinence. They include the use of a sponsor, regular participation in FA meetings, frequent contact with other FA members by phone, and the reading of FA and some AA literature.

The Twelve Steps. The Twelve Steps originated in Alcoholics Anonymous. (See appendix 3.) Food addicts who learn and live the Steps experience a change of personality and a spiritual awakening. If practiced daily, the Twelve Steps can ultimately remove the desire to eat addictively, one day at a time.

The Twelve Traditions. The Twelve Traditions also originated in Alcoholics Anonymous. (See appendix 4.) The Traditions guide relationships between FA meetings and the individuals they are meant to serve, between various FA groups, and between FA and the world outside FA.

A Brief History of Food Addicts in Recovery Anonymous (FA)

IN THE EARLY 1980s, the organization that became Food Addicts in Recovery Anonymous began to take shape within an existing twelve-step program intended for compulsive overeaters. The shift began when two members of that program began leading AWOL groups. AWOL (A Way of Life) offers a systematic means for doing the Twelve Steps in sequence. The abstinence, recovery, and insights that participants gained from AWOL ultimately led to the founding of FA.

AWOL originally emerged from a treatment center for alcoholics in Canada. Staff members there saw clients become sober under their care, then helplessly watched them relapse as soon as they left the center. Realizing that only the Twelve Steps could bring about the personality change and spiritual awakening necessary for an addict's sustained recovery, the center created AWOL as a series of closed meetings in which alcoholics were led through the Steps in a careful, uninterrupted sequence.

The original AWOL in Canada required participants to formally commit to their recovery as a condition for their ongoing participation. Before they could begin work on the Steps, the alcoholics had to make several promises, which were called "commitments." First and foremost, they agreed to remain sober throughout the AWOL. Any return to drinking would indicate a need for the participant to begin again on the First Step—the admission and acceptance of powerlessness over alcohol. In order to do the Steps in an uninterrupted sequence, participants also promised not to miss two meetings in a row. Those creating the AWOL further asked that participants abstain from the use of recreational drugs or mood-altering medications. They defined the goal simply: a personality change and a spiritual awakening that would enable participants to turn to a Higher Power for help with every aspect of their lives and emotions.

In 1977, two women in Chelsea, Massachusetts, opened an AWOL for others who were also members of the program for compulsive overeaters. They used all but one of the commitments set by the Canadian treatment center. The group was closed to new members after a brief introductory period. Participants agreed to abstain from alcohol, drugs, or mood-altering medications and promised not to miss two consecutive meetings. Abstinence, the equivalent of AA's sobriety, was defined as three weighed and measured meals a day, excluding any flour, sugar, or eating between mealtimes. Because neither leader had ever seen anyone attain long-term recovery, however, they decided against making uninterrupted abstinence a requirement for participation.

As the two early members led the first AWOL group, they came to a new and transformative understanding of their illness. They realized that they were not confronting an "eating disorder" or a compulsion but rather an addiction that affected the body, mind, and spirit. They saw abstinent members of the group swept back into destructive eating after only one taste of a food containing flour or sugar. Physical changes such as weight gains were only one symptom of relapse. The return to eating also led to a breakdown of the personality, manifested by extreme mood swings, resentment, rage, depression, anxiety, obsession with food and weight, lying, and, ultimately, an inability to sustain abstinence or meet personal responsibilities.

At the conclusion of the first AWOL, the two leaders looked around the room and saw a small handful of others who had remained abstinent with them throughout. They then understood with excitement that after years of struggle and dieting, they had found a solution for their problem. Uninterrupted, one-day-at-a-time recovery from food addiction was possible for those who did the Twelve Steps abstinently through AWOL.

When the two women opened their second AWOL, they established a pattern that remains in effect to this day. In a written introduction to the commitments, they wisely noted that AWOL was organizationally separate from the twelve-step program to which they belonged. Meetings in the twelve-step program were open to everyone at all times, and leadership was regularly rotated. In contrast, AWOLs were closed meetings with unchanging leaders who set the requirements—the commitments—for participation. By emphasizing the separation between the two, the women ensured the ongoing integrity of the twelve-step meetings and gave AWOL co-leaders the freedom to use whatever AWOL commitments they believed would be most effective.

As increasing numbers of members successfully studied and did the Steps in AWOL, they brought their recovery back to their own meetings. Rather than seeing meetings as support groups for people struggling with compulsive overeating, these members viewed them as opportunities for members to learn about and affirm the principles vital for recovery from a fatal illness: food addiction. This shift in vision led to a change in the form of meetings.

In what was a radical move at the time, meetings began to require that members have ninety days of abstinence before they addressed the meeting as a whole. Chairs were laid out in rows rather than in circles, and speakers were asked to address the group from the front of the room. This deemphasized the dynamics of the group and emphasized instead the learning made possible by the sharing of the speakers. It also helped speakers avoid their inevitable impulse to isolate or hide.

Attitudes toward other program practices changed, as well. Because members in recovery saw addiction as a devastating and ultimately fatal illness of the body, mind, and spirit, they emphasized the actions supporting recovery with a new seriousness. Those new to FA were encouraged to establish a disciplined schedule of meetings each week and to choose a sponsor—an abstinent, experienced FA member whom they could call each day. Sponsors helped their sponsees to stay in close contact with other FA members and to turn to a Higher Power for help with their abstinence and lives.

In 1996, a group in Chelsea formally adopted definitions of *food addiction* and *abstinence*. The words captured the essence of the new approach, and the passage was incorporated into the format that was read aloud at each meeting:

> Food addiction is a disease of the mind, body, and spirit for which there is no cure, but it can be arrested a day at a time by our adapting to a disciplined way of eating and the twelve-step program of FA. When we abuse food by using it as a drug, our lives become unmanageable.
>
> Food addicts have an allergy to flour, sugar, and quantities that sets up an uncontrollable craving. The problem can be arrested a day at a time by the action of our weighing and measuring our food and abstaining completely from all flour and sugar.
>
> FA defines abstinence as weighed-and-measured meals with nothing in between, no flour, no sugar, and the avoidance of any individual binge foods.

As other groups in the Boston area began to adopt the definitions of food addiction and abstinence, as well as related meeting practices, the new program spread beyond Massachusetts. Individuals from other states contacted Massachusetts members, seeking someone who could sponsor them. When Boston-area members moved or traveled, they took the program with them, establishing meetings in California, Michigan, Florida, and Texas.

By 1998, it was clear that a new program had emerged based on a unified definition of abstinence and the use of AWOL groups for the study of the Twelve Steps. On March 28 of that year, several members held a meeting in Chelsea to explore the possibility of forming a separate organization. The organization's first formal gathering—an intergroup meeting—was held on May 31, 1998, unifying eighteen meetings with 177 members. Because a fellowship called Food Addicts Anonymous already existed, members selected Food Addicts in Recovery Anonymous, or FA, as their group's name.

Since its founding in 1998, FA has continued to grow, spreading farther across the United States and into Canada, England, Australia, New Zealand, and Germany. FA remains distinguished by its single definition of abstinence, its decision to hold only in-person meetings, the expectation that members won't speak in front of a meeting until they have at least ninety days of abstinence, and the belief that sustained recovery is impossible without the Twelve Steps.

AWOLs remain foundational in FA recovery, but, as ever, AWOL groups function independently from FA as a whole. No organizational body or individual governs or influences the development of AWOLs, and no FA member is required to join one. Since the commitments taken by participants are set by each pair of AWOL co-leaders, AWOLs now vary widely. They are complemented by the efforts of some FA sponsors who use the AWOL process to guide their sponsees through the Twelve Steps individually.

Today, there are more than four thousand FA members throughout the world. In Sweden, Turkey, South Africa, Israel, and other areas where an FA fellowship does not yet exist, individuals have found recovery through close contact with more experienced FA members living elsewhere.

FA members everywhere remain united by the fundamentals of the FA program and the Twelve Steps. We have admitted our powerlessness over food, have accepted the boundaries and necessities of abstinence, and have turned to a Higher Power to help and guide us.

Whatever our differences or the geographical distances that separate us, we believe we can and must reach out together to help *anyone* who needs and wants FA. This is the responsibility and privilege of our abstinence.

The Twelve Steps

1. We admitted we were powerless over food—that our lives had become unmanageable.

2. Came to believe that a Power greater than ourselves could restore us to sanity.

3. Made a decision to turn our will and our lives over to the care of God *as we understood Him.*

4. Made a searching and fearless moral inventory of ourselves.

5. Admitted to God, to ourselves, and to another human being the exact nature of our wrongs.

6. Were entirely ready to have God remove all these defects of character.

7. Humbly asked Him to remove our shortcomings.

8. Made a list of all persons we had harmed, and became willing to make amends to them all.

9. Made direct amends to such people wherever possible, except when to do so would injure them or others.

10. Continued to take personal inventory, and when we were wrong, promptly admitted it.

11. Sought through prayer and meditation to improve our conscious contact with God *as we understood Him*, praying only for knowledge of His will for us and the power to carry that out.

12. Having had a spiritual awakening as the result of these steps, we tried to carry this message to food addicts, and to practice these principles in all our affairs.

The Twelve Traditions

1. Our common welfare should come first; personal recovery depends on FA unity.

2. For our group purpose there is but one ultimate authority—a loving God as He may express Himself in our group conscience. Our leaders are but trusted servants; they do not govern.

3. The only requirement for FA membership is a desire to stop eating addictively.

4. Each group should be autonomous except in matters affecting other groups or FA as a whole.

5. Each group has but one primary purpose—to carry its message to the food addict who still suffers.

6. An FA group ought never endorse, finance, or lend the FA name to any related facility or outside enterprise, lest problems of money, property, and prestige divert us from our primary purpose.

7. Every FA group ought to be fully self-supporting, declining outside contributions.

8. Food Addicts in Recovery Anonymous should remain forever nonprofessional, but our service centers may employ special workers.

9. FA, as such, ought never be organized; but we may create service boards or committees directly responsible to those they serve.

10. Food Addicts in Recovery Anonymous has no opinion on outside issues; hence the FA name ought never be drawn into public controversy.

11. Our public relations policy is based on attraction rather than promotion; we need always maintain personal anonymity at the level of press, radio, and films.

12. Anonymity is the spiritual foundation of all our Traditions, ever reminding us to place principles before personalities.